WOMAN and HOME

GREAT BRITISH COOKERY

WOMAN and HOME

GREAT BRITISH COOKERY

LUCY KNOX

HAMLYN

First published in Great Britain 1994 by
Hamlyn an imprint of Reed Consumer Books Limited
Michelin House, 81 Fulham Road, London SW3 6RB
and Auckland, Melbourne, Singapore and Toronto
Text and photographs copyright © 1994
Woman and Home
Design copyright © 1994
Reed International Books Limited

ISBN 0 600 58364 3

A CIP catalogue record for this book is
available at the British Library

Printed in Spain

ACKNOWLEDGEMENTS

Art Director Jacqui Small
Design Manager Bryan Dunn
Designer Bobby Birchall, Town Group Consultancy
Executive Editor Susan Haynes
Editor Elsa Petersen-Schepelern
Jacket Photography Tim Imrie
Jacket Stylist Carolyn Russell

WOMAN AND HOME
Orlando Murrin Editor
Sue Dobson

RECIPE DEVELOPMENT
Lucy Knox Cookery Editor
Sarah Lowman Deputy Cookery Editor
Wendy Salmon Cookery Assistant

Linda Tubby, Linda Collister, Mary Gwynn,
Penny Baker, Elizabeth Winslade
John Webber of Kinnaird
Rosemary White, Norah Brown

PHOTOGRAPHERS
Melvin Grey, Theo Bergström, Steve Baxter
Jerry Tubby, Andrew Williams, Tim Imrie
Bill Richmond, Dave Jordan,
Anthony Gould-Davies

STYLISTS
Carolyn Russell, Sue Russell,
Kay McGlone, Susie Gettings

AUTHOR'S ACKNOWLEDGEMENT
I must say a huge thank you to my mother Gina,
for teaching me to cook, to my father Peter, for his
encouragement, and to Keith Richmond for all the
hours spent trying the recipes with me. And, finally,
to my Test Kitchen Team without whom this
would not have been possible.

CONTENTS

Introduction

In *Great British Cookery* we take you on a culinary journey around the country, stopping off to enjoy some of the best recipes in the land.

We start in the North with family favourites like roast beef and Melbury Yorkshire pudding, steak and kidney pie and marmalade roly poly; together with a truly traditional northern tea of fat rascals, York biscuits, pikelets and fruit scones.

From the Heart of England there are delicious recipes using apples, plums and pears – such as country apple cake and perry and ginger trifle – and Stilton, the King of English Cheeses.

And from London and the South East, the fertile Garden of England, delicious desserts from the freshest summer berries, like summer fruit meringue basket, classic strawberry ice-cream and summer pudding.

The flat, arable farmlands of East Anglia are the bread basket of Britain and the source of several excellent game recipes such as cider-cooked pigeon, hot game pie and boned Norfolk turkey.

Warmed by the Gulf Stream, the West Country enjoys the mildest climate in the British Isles. Try the Somerset roast pork in apples and cider, the Cornish pasties and the Devon clotted vanilla ice-cream,

Creamy Scots porridge, baked kippers and ham and haddie for breakfast would warm up any winter's day, while for afternoon tea north of Hadrian's Wall there are pancakes, toddy cake, Dundee cake and black bun.

The Welsh are famous for their lamb, laverbread and leeks. Our splendid roast lamb is ideal for Sunday lunch, laverbread quiche for supper on Saturday and the Caerphilly and leek bundles an excellent starter for special occasions.

For centuries Irish cooking has been based on good wholesome staples like meat, bread and potatoes. We have Irish stew, glazed roast goose, beef in Guinness and Irish colcannon.

All these classic dishes demonstrate the enduring qualities of *Great British Cookery*. All have been double tested by the expert team in the Woman and Home Test Kitchen. We hope you enjoy them.

CHAPTER ONE

The North

Cooking in the North of England has traditionally been rooted in a desire to serve economical, delicious dishes for working men and women living a hard life in an often-cold climate. The aim was to keep a large family well fed for as little as possible.

Nothing is wasted in Northern cooking, and many of the meals which we associate with the urban heartlands of the industrial North – like Merseyside, Manchester, Bradford, Leeds, Sheffield and Newcastle – were designed as a substantial repast for men and women working in factories or on farms.

Although the popular image is still of 'Coronation Street' and William Blake's 'dark satanic mills', these modern cities are surrounded by mile upon mile of unspoilt, rolling countryside.

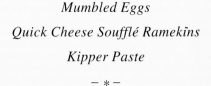

This is where top quality beef and lamb is bred, as well as the milk to make the cheeses – like Lancashire, Wensleydale and Cotherstone – for which the North is justly famous.

The long stretches of rugged coastline have long played a vital role in the local economy. Some of the best kippers in Britain are smoked in the North East and Northerners cheerfully claim the fish and chips served here (in yesterday's newspaper for the authentic taste) are the best in the world.

Mumbled Eggs
Quick Cheese Soufflé Ramekins
Kipper Paste

— * —

Roast Beef
Game Chips
Melbury Yorkshire Pudding
Cumberland Sauce

— * —

Lancashire Hot Pot
Tripe and Onions
Shepherd's Pie or Cottage Pie
Steak and Kidney Pie
Cumberland Sausage and Lentil Stew

— * —

Broad Beans with Ham
Roast Potatoes
Pan Haggerty
Mange Tout
and Green Bean Sauté

— * —

Rhubarb Ginger Mousse
Lemon Sauce Pudding
Marmalade Roly Poly
Cumberland Apple Pudding

— * —

Pikelets
Lardy Cake
Rich Fruit Cake
Teacakes
Fruit Teacakes
Ginger Parkin
Fruit Scones
York Biscuits
Fat Rascals

MUMBLED EGGS

SERVES 2 TO 3

85 g (3 oz) unsalted butter
115 ml (4 fl oz) double cream
6 eggs, size 3, beaten
Salt and pepper
Wholemeal toast, buttered

Put half the butter and half the cream in a pan and melt over a low heat. Bring to the boil. Add the eggs and seasoning and cook gently, stirring constantly, until set. Stir in the remaining butter and cream. Pile on to hot buttered toast.

As a variation, add a little chopped fresh tarragon and chives, or serve with a little chopped smoked salmon.

QUICK CHEESE SOUFFLÉ RAMEKINS

SERVES 6

60 g (2 oz) fresh breadcrumbs
140 ml (¼ pt) single cream
70 ml (2½ fl oz) milk
110 g (4 oz) Cheshire cheese, grated
Salt, pepper, mace and cayenne pepper,
all to taste
1 tablespoon Worcestershire sauce
3 eggs, size 3, separated
6 ramekins, buttered

Mix the breadcrumbs with the cream and milk. Leave to stand for about 10 minutes. Set the oven at Gas Mark 7, 425°F, 220°C. Mix the grated cheese, seasonings, Worcestershire sauce and egg yolks into the breadcrumb mixture. Taste, and adjust the seasoning. Whisk the egg whites stiffly and carefully fold in. Spoon into the ramekins. Bake for about 12 to 15 minutes until puffed and golden. Serve immediately.

KIPPER PASTE

SERVES 4

Traditionally, bloaters – smoked herrings
– were used to make this fish paste,
however kippers are now more
readily available.

4 kippers
2 teaspoons lemon juice
85 g (3 oz) unsalted butter
1 teaspoon anchovy sauce
Freshly ground black pepper
To complete:
110 g (4 oz) clarified butter
4 small ramekins

Simmer the kippers in boiling water for
about 10 minutes. Remove from the
water and remove the skin and large
bones. Break the fish into flakes and
place in a blender or food processor
with the remaining ingredients and
process until well mixed.

To complete, divide the paste
between the ramekins and pour a little
clarified butter over the top of each.
Chill until ready to serve or for up to
2 days. Serve the kipper paste with hot
buttered toast, or in sandwiches with
watercress or cucumber.

PREVIOUS PAGE LEFT *A farm near*
Richmond in Yorkshire.
PREVIOUS PAGE RIGHT *Fruit Scones*
(recipe page 23)
LEFT *Rich Northern pastures are ideal*
for dairy herds.

RIB OF BEEF WITH CARAMELISED SHALLOTS

SERVES 8 TO 10

Traditional Roast Beef is hard to beat, especially when accompanied by Yorkshire Pudding.

A 3.6 kg (8 lb) rib of beef, chined
Salt and freshly ground black pepper
2 tablespoons English mustard
1 tablespoon olive oil
280 ml (½ pt) Madeira
For the caramelised shallots:
16 shallots, peeled
3 large sprigs of thyme
2 cloves garlic, crushed

4 tablespoons groundnut oil
60 g (2 oz) unsalted butter
30 g (1 oz) caster sugar
For the gravy:
(makes 280 ml/½ pt)
140 ml (¼ pt) red wine
570 ml (1 pt) good-quality beef stock
Salt and freshly ground black pepper
Flat-leaf parsley, to garnish

Set the oven at Gas Mark 8, 450°F, 230°C. Trim any excess fat from the meat and season well with black pepper and a little of the mustard. Place the rib of beef in a roasting tin, with the fat side uppermost, and roast for 30 minutes. Reduce the oven temperature to Gas Mark 4, 350°F, 180°C.

Mix together the oil and mustard and spread over the meat. Return to the oven and continue to roast for a further 2 hours for rare meat, 2½ hours for medium rare, or 3 hours for medium- to well-done meat. Baste frequently. After an hour, drain off any excess fat and pour over the Madeira.

Lay the shallots on top of a large piece of double-layer foil. Add the thyme and garlic, and sprinkle over the oil. Seal the edges of the foil to make a parcel, securing the edges well. Bake in the oven for 1 hour.

To make the gravy, pour the wine and beef stock into a heavy-based pan and bring to the boil. Continue boiling until it has reduced by half - this will take 5 to 8 minutes.

Remove the meat from the oven and transfer to a warmed plate. Cover and leave for 20 minutes before carving. Skim off the fat from the juices in the roasting tin, add the reduced wine and stock. Stir the gravy well over a low heat on top of the stove, scraping up all the meat juices. Season with salt and pepper, to taste. Bring to the boil and simmer until thickened and reduced by half.

To caramelise the shallots, melt the butter in a heavy-based pan and stir in the sugar. Add the shallots, cook until golden, and serve with the beef, garnished with flat-leaf parsley, accompanied by Game Chips (see below) and piping hot gravy.

GAME CHIPS

SERVES 8

1.1 kg (2½ lb) large potatoes of
similar size, peeled
Oil for deep-fat frying

Salt
Freshly chopped parsley,
to garnish

Cut the potatoes into thin slivers using either a mandolin or food processor. Soak in cold water to remove the excess starch, drain and dry them thoroughly between layers of absorbent kitchen paper.

Heat the oil to 350°F, 180°C. When hot, add the slivers of potato, a few at a time, making sure they are kept moving so that they don't stick together. Cook for 2 to 3 minutes or until golden brown and crisp. Drain well on absorbent kitchen paper. Transfer to an ovenproof dish and keep warm in a low oven. Sprinkle with salt and freshly chopped parsley before serving.

MELBURY YORKSHIRE PUDDING

SERVES 4 TO 6

2 tablespoons beer
140 ml (¼ pt) milk
110 g (4 oz) flour
½ teaspoon salt
2 eggs, size 3, beaten
4 tablespoons dripping, lard or oil
85 g (3 oz) Melbury or Cheddar cheese,
frozen and grated
A roasting tin

Mix the beer with the milk. Make the mixture up to 280 ml (½ pt) with water.

Sift flour and salt into a bowl, make a well in the centre and add the beaten eggs and liquid. Gradually work in the flour from the sides to make a smooth batter. Leave to stand for an hour.

Set the oven at Gas Mark 8, 450°F, 230°C. Heat the fat in the roasting tin until almost smoking. Pour in half the batter. Sprinkle the grated cheese over the top, and cover with the remaining batter. Bake for 35 to 40 minutes until it is puffed up and golden.

CUMBERLAND SAUCE

Serve hot or cold with ham or game.

2 oranges
1 lemon
230 g (8 oz) good-quality redcurrant jelly
6 tablespoons port
1 teaspoon ready-made English mustard
Salt, pepper and grated nutmeg, to taste
1 tablespoon red wine vinegar

Thinly pare the rind from the oranges and lemon and slice into needle-thin shreds. Put into a small bowl and cover with boiling water. Leave to soak for about 1 minute, then drain. Squeeze the fruit and put juices into a small pan with all the remaining ingredients. Warm gently, stirring frequently, until the jelly melts, and the sauce is smooth. Add the rinds and simmer until the sauce thickens slightly. Leave to cool, then chill until ready to serve.

LANCASHIRE HOTPOT

SERVES 6

This popular and flavoursome dish is an excellent way to cook lamb chops.

15 g (½ oz) dripping or white fat
1.1 kg (2½ lb) middle neck of lamb chops
230 to 280 g (8 to 10 oz) lambs' kidneys,
cored and quartered
0.9 kg (2 lb) potatoes, peeled and sliced
280 g (10 oz) onions, thinly sliced
Salt and freshly ground black pepper
430 to 570 ml (¾ to 1 pt) good lamb stock
A little melted dripping or white fat
A 3.45 litre (6 pt) deep ovenproof dish

Set the oven at Gas Mark 4, 350°F, 180°C. Heat the fat in a frying pan and quickly but thoroughly brown the chops and kidneys in batches. In an ovenproof casserole, layer the meat with sliced potatoes and onions, starting and finishing with potatoes. Season each layer well. Pour over the stock and brush the top layer of potatoes with melted dripping. Cover the dish and cook in the oven for 2 hours. Remove the lid and turn the oven up to Gas Mark 7, 425°F, 220°C for 30 minutes more to brown the top.

OPPOSITE *An English country cottage.*
PREVIOUS PAGE *Typically English – Roast Beef with Caramelised Shallots and Game Chips.*

TRIPE AND ONIONS

SERVES 4

Butchers' stalls in the North have all types of offal, but tripe should be available in most places.

340 g (12 oz) pre-cooked tripe
340 g (12 oz) onions, sliced into rings
430 ml (¾ pt) milk
Salt and pepper
40 g (1½ oz) butter
40 g (1½ oz) flour
A little chopped parsley, for sprinkling

Wash and dry the tripe, then cut it into pieces about 7.5 cm (3 in) square. Put the tripe and onions, milk, 430 ml (¾ pt) water and seasoning into an enamel or stainless-steel pan (this keeps the tripe's colour) and bring to the boil.

Then melt the butter in a saucepan, stir in the flour and whisk in the tripe liquid. Stirring continuously, bring the sauce to the boil and simmer for about 1 to 2 minutes. Add the tripe and onions and serve when heated through. Sprinkle with chopped parsley and serve with mashed potatoes.

SHEPHERD'S PIE OR COTTAGE PIE

SERVES 4 TO 6

Choose trimmed cooked lamb to make a traditional shepherd's pie, or lean cooked beef to make a cottage pie.

455 g (1 lb) cooked lamb or beef
1 tablespoon oil
1 medium onion, finely chopped
1 medium carrot, finely diced
110 g (4 oz) mushrooms, sliced
1 tablespoon flour
280 ml (½ pt) good lamb or beef stock or gravy
1 tablespoon chopped parsley
1 tablespoon Worcestershire sauce
1 tablespoon tomato ketchup
Salt
Freshly ground black pepper
1.1 kg (2½ lb) potatoes, peeled
170 ml (6 fl oz) milk, heated
60 g (2 oz) butter

Finely dice or coarsely mince or process the meat. Heat the oil in a heavy saucepan. Add the onion, cover and cook gently until very soft, stirring frequently. Stir in the carrot and mushrooms and cook over a medium heat for a couple of minutes. Stir in the flour. Cook for a minute or two then stir in the stock, parsley, Worcestershire sauce and tomato ketchup. Bring to the boil, stirring constantly. Stir in the meat and season to taste. Spoon into a heatproof baking dish. Set the oven at Gas Mark 4, 350°F, 180°C.

Boil the potatoes until tender. Drain well, then dry the potatoes in the pan over a low heat for a couple of minutes. Mash the potatoes, then beat in the hot milk, butter and plenty of seasoning. Pile the potatoes on top of the meat mixture. Bake for 35 to 40 minutes until bubbling.

TO FREEZE: open-freeze until firm, wrap in cling film and foil, and freeze for up to 1 month.

TO USE FROM FROZEN: thaw overnight before baking as above.

STEAK AND KIDNEY PIE

SERVES 6

A typical English dish famous throughout the world. The filling can be cooked the day before if you wish; the pastry should cover a cold filling prior to cooking.

For the rich beef stock:	5 lambs' kidneys, skinned and cored
1 large beef bone, chopped into pieces	40 g (1½ oz) plain flour
1 onion, chopped	Salt and freshly ground black pepper
1 carrot, chopped	1 tablespoon sunflower oil
4 black peppercorns	The rind of ½ a small orange
Salt	115 ml (4 fl oz) ruby port
1 stick celery	230 g (8 oz) can oysters in
For the filling:	salt water (optional)
1 large onion, finely chopped	**For the pastry lid:**
60 g (2 oz) unsalted butter	680 g (1½ lb) frozen puff pastry, thawed
0.9 kg (2 lb) lean rump steak	Beaten egg to glaze
in one thick piece	A 1.45 litre (2½ pt) oval pie dish

To make the rich beef stock, set the oven at Gas Mark 7, 425°F, 220°C. Roast all the ingredients for the stock, except the celery, for 1 hour or until well browned (do not allow to burn). Tip into a pan with 570 ml (1 pt) of water. Add 280 ml (½ pt) water to the roasting tin and place over a medium heat. Scrape the bits from the tin to dissolve in the water. Add to the pan. Bring slowly to the boil, simmer for 1 hour until reduced by a third, and remove any scum from the surface. Reduce the heat, strain and put to one side. Taste and adjust the seasoning. When cold, remove the fat from the surface. Cover the stock and store in the fridge until required – up to 2 days.

To make the filling, fry the onion gently in 30 g (1 oz) butter until softened and transparent. Using a slotted spoon, remove from the pan and set aside. Remove the pan from the heat. Trim any fat off the steak and cut the meat into 4 cm (1½ in) cubes. Halve the kidneys, then cut each half into three.

Set the oven at Gas Mark 2, 300°F, 150°C. Sift the flour into a bowl and season well with plenty of salt and freshly ground black pepper. Toss the pieces of steak in the seasoned flour. Remove the steak and add the kidney to the flour. Add the remaining butter to the pan and heat until it has melted. Seal the steak pieces over a high heat in small batches, remove from the pan using a slotted spoon and set aside. Remove the kidney from the flour and quickly toss in the hot pan.

Transfer the fried onion, steak and kidney to the pie dish. Tuck the orange rind down into the meat pieces and sprinkle 1 teaspoon of the flour over the meat. Heat the stock and pour 60 ml (2 fl oz) over the meat. Add the port. Cover the pie dish with tightly fitting foil and cook for 1½ hours. Leave to cool without removing the foil.

Remove the foil and orange rind, add the oysters if using, adjust the seasoning and add a little more beef stock if desired. Set the oven at Gas Mark 8, 450°F, 230°C.

To make the lid, roll out the pastry on a lightly floured work surface to a 6 mm (¼ in) thickness. Cut a strip about 2 cm (¾ in) wide for the rim of the pie dish and a lid 1 cm (½ in) wider than the pie dish. Brush the rim with water and apply the strip of pastry. Place the lid on a tray and brush with beaten egg. Use any pastry trimmings to garnish with pastry leaves (see photograph), but make the pastry rose when the lid is on the pie. Chill the lid for 10 minutes.

Brush the pastry on the pie dish rim with beaten egg and attach the lid. Add the pastry rose and glaze with beaten egg. Take care not to glaze the sides of the pastry leaves or this will prevent the pastry from puffing up. Using the knife, gently knock back the edges, then score into the rim with a fork to make a pattern.

Bake for 10 to 15 minutes until the pastry is golden brown, then reduce the oven to Gas Mark 6, 400°F, 200°C and continue cooking for a further 15 minutes. Cover the pastry with foil if it starts to brown too quickly.

Serve hot with creamy potato, parsnip purée and caramelised baby carrots.

CUMBERLAND SAUSAGE AND LENTIL STEW

SERVES 8

Cumberland sausage is a tasty, spicy English sausage made from coarsely chopped pork and black pepper. This meaty stew tastes best served with hot jacket potatoes to soak up all the delicious juices.

1.8 kg (4 lb) uncooked ham on the
bone or knuckle
340 g (12 oz) lentils
1 to 2 tablespoons vegetable oil
455 g (1 lb) onions, chopped
2 cloves garlic, crushed
2 bay leaves
½ teaspoon coriander seeds, ground
Pinch of ground cloves
1 large green pepper, deseeded and
cut into strips
680 g (1½ lb) Cumberland sausage,
cut into 2.5 cm (1 in) pieces
Salt and freshly ground black pepper
2 tablespoons freshly chopped parsley,
to garnish

Place the ham in a bowl, cover with cold water and soak overnight.

The next day, simmer the ham in a large pan of boiling water for 1 hour; a preserving pan is ideal. Drain the ham and leave to cool before removing the meat from the bone and cutting it into 2.5 cm (1 in) cubes. Cover the lentils with cold water, then drain.

Heat the oil in a large, heavy-based frying pan and fry the onions and garlic for 5 minutes or until softened but not coloured. Remove from the pan with a slotted spoon. Set aside. Add the bay leaves, the lentils, coriander, ground cloves and enough water to cover. Stir well and bring to the boil Reduce the heat and simmer for 1 hour.

Add the strips of green pepper, Cumberland sausage, ham pieces and 430 ml (15 fl oz) water. Stir well and simmer for a further hour.

Season to taste, and serve, garnished with freshly chopped parsley.

BROAD BEANS WITH HAM

SERVES 4 TO 6

0.9 kg (2 lb) young broad beans
1 gammon steak
4 tablespoons red wine
1 tablespoon soft, light brown sugar
4 cloves
60 g (2 oz) butter, melted
Salt and pepper
3 tablespoons chopped parsley

Shell the broad beans. Put the gammon steak in a pan with the wine, sugar, cloves and 140 ml (¼ pt) water. Bring to the boil and simmer until the gammon is tender. Drain and cut into thin strips.

Meanwhile cook the broad beans in boiling salted water. Drain them well and mix with the gammon. Mix the melted butter with the seasoning and parsley and pour over the beans.

ROAST POTATOES

The vegetable that has stood the test of time. These should be crisp and brown outside – light and floury in the centre.

Set the oven at Gas Mark 5, 375°F, 190°C. Put 2 tablespoons of white fat or clean dripping in a roasting tin and place in the heated oven.

Parboil evenly-sized potatoes for about 5 minutes, then drain.

While the potatoes are still hot, hold each one in a tea-towel and scrape the surface with a fork – this helps them become crisp. Put the potatoes into the roasting tin, baste them thoroughly and roast for about 1 hour at the top of the oven until crisp and brown.

Potatoes can also be roasted around a joint of meat. They may not brown quite so well, because the temperature for roasting meat is often lower.

ABOVE *Pan Haggerty (top right) and Mange Tout and Green Bean Sauté.*

PAN HAGGERTY

SERVES 6

Lancashire cheese melts well during cooking, and so is ideal to use in this classic vegetable dish. As a variation, sprinkle the top with breadcrumbs before browning under the grill.

680 g (1½ lb) potatoes
230 g (8 oz) onions
15 g (½ oz) butter
1 tablespoon oil
170 g (6 oz) mature Lancashire or similar
Cheddar-style cheese, grated

Peel the potatoes and onions and cut into thin slices. Heat the butter and oil in the frying pan. When foaming, add a layer of potatoes, then a layer of onion and grated cheese. Season well. Continue layering, seasoning each layer and finishing with a layer of cheese. Cover the pan with a lid or baking tray and cook gently for about 45 minutes or until the vegetables are cooked. Remove the lid, sprinkle the top with breadcrumbs (if using), and brown under a hot grill. Serve immediately.

MANGE TOUT AND GREEN BEAN SAUTÉ

SERVES 8

Balsamic vinegar is made from the juice of Trebbiano grapes and fermented in wood over several years. To give a piquant flavour, stir it into dishes at the end of the cooking time.

455 g (1 lb) mange tout, topped and tailed
230 g (8 oz) French beans, topped and tailed
1 to 2 tablespoons olive oil
60 g (2 oz) pine nuts, toasted
Salt and freshly ground black pepper
1 tablespoon Balsamic vinegar

Cut the mange tout and beans diagonally into 2.5 cm (1 in) lengths. Blanch the mange tout in a large pan of boiling, salted water for 1 minute, then drain and refresh under cold water, and reserve. Blanch the beans in the large pan of boiling, salted water for 3 minutes. Drain and refresh under cold water, and reserve.

Heat the oil in a heavy-based pan. Toss the mange tout and beans in the hot oil for about 1 minute until hot, remove from the heat, stir in the pine nuts, seasoning and vinegar, and serve immediately.

RHUBARB GINGERY MOUSSE

SERVES 4 TO 6

Forced rhubarb is big business in the North. Stem ginger, with its warm, yet citrus-clean taste, complements rhubarb beautifully in this delicious dessert.

455 g (1 lb) rhubarb, wiped, trimmed and
cut into 1 cm (½ in) pieces
15 g (½ oz) stem ginger, finely chopped
2 tablespoons ginger syrup
(from a jar of ginger)
1 teaspoon gelatine
140 ml (¼ pt) double cream

140 ml (¼ pt) yogurt
60 g (2 oz) caster sugar,
or to taste
To decorate:
140 ml (¼ pt) double cream, whipped
30 g (1 oz) crystallised ginger
A 1.15 litre (2 pt) glass dish

Stew the rhubarb with the ginger and syrup over a gentle heat, stirring frequently until the mixture becomes a purée. Leave to cool.

Sprinkle the gelatine over 1 tablespoon of water in a small, heatproof bowl; leave for 5 minutes to sponge. Place the bowl in a pan of hot water until the gelatine dissolves. Cool until lukewarm, then stir into the purée.

Whisk the cream until it just holds a soft peak, and gently fold it into the purée mixture with the yogurt. Add caster sugar to taste.

Pour the mixture into the dish, then cover and chill overnight or until set. Decorate with swirls of whipped cream and crystallised ginger. Serve chilled.

LEMON SAUCE PUDDING

SERVES 4 TO 6

During cooking, the mixture will separate, leaving a rich, gooey, lemon sauce beneath a light and fluffy topping.

85 g (3 oz) butter
170 g (6 oz) caster sugar
The grated rind and juice of 2 medium
lemons
3 eggs, size 3, separated
110 g (4 oz) plain flour
¼ teaspoon baking powder
280 ml (½ pt) milk and water mixed
A 2 to 2.3 litre (3½ to 4 pt) ovenproof dish,
buttered

Set the oven at Gas Mark 4, 350°F, 180°C. Beat the butter, sugar and the lemon rind until light and fluffy. Add the egg yolks, beating well, and then gradually stir in the sifted flour and baking powder alternately with the lemon juice. Gradually beat in the milk and water (at this stage, the mixture will look curdled). Whisk the egg whites stiffly and fold in quickly.

Pour the mixture into the prepared dish. Stand the dish in a bain-marie – a roasting tin filled 1 cm (½ in) deep with hot water.

Bake for 50 to 60 minutes until puffy and golden. The lemon sauce will form below the sponge top.

MARMALADE ROLY POLY

SERVES 6

Use homemade marmalade to make this hearty pudding even more delicious.

230 g (8 oz) self-raising flour
1½ teaspoons ground ginger
1 tablespoon caster sugar
110 g (4 oz) shredded suet
(vegetable or beef)
5 tablespoons thick-cut marmalade
A little milk
Caster sugar for sprinkling
A 23 by 33 cm (9 by 13 in)
piece of foil, greased

Put a pan, half-filled with water, with a steamer above it, on to boil. The water must be boiling before the pudding is put on to cook.

Sieve the flour, ginger and sugar into a bowl and stir in the suet. Add enough cold water to bind into a soft but not sticky dough. Knead very lightly until smooth. Turn on to a lightly floured work surface and roll into a rectangle 20.5 by 30.5 cm (8 by 12 in). Spread the dough evenly with the marmalade, leaving a 1 cm (½ in) border all round. Brush the edges with milk and roll up evenly starting from one short side. Transfer the roll to the greased foil and wrap the roll up loosely to allow for expansion. Seal the ends and edges well. Put the roll in the steamer, cover with a lid and steam for 1½ to 2 hours. Remove from the foil, sprinkle with caster sugar and serve with custard or marmalade sauce.

OPPOSITE TOP *Rich farmland.*
OPPOSITE BOTTOM *Rhubarb Gingery Mousse; rhubarb is an important crop in the North of England.*
RIGHT *Lemon Sauce Pudding (top), Cumberland Apple Pudding (centre), and Marmalade Roly Poly.*

CUMBERLAND APPLE PUDDING

SERVES 6

170 g (6 oz) Bramley cooking
apples, wiped
170 g (6 oz) fresh white breadcrumbs
110 g (4 oz) caster sugar
110 g (4 oz) shredded suet
(vegetable or beef)
½ teaspoon baking powder
¼ teaspoon ground mixed spice
1 teaspoon ground ginger
The grated rind of 1 lemon
2 eggs, size 3, beaten
60 ml (2 fl oz) milk
5 tablespoons golden syrup
A 1.15 litre (2 pt) pudding basin, greased

Quarter and core the apples, but do not peel. Grate them coarsely, then mix with all the dry ingredients and the lemon rind. Beat the eggs with the milk and 1 tablespoon of the syrup, then work into the dry mixture to make a soft consistency.

Spoon the remaining syrup into the base of the pudding basin, then top with the pudding mixture. Cover securely with greased greaseproof paper and foil, then steam for 2 hours, topping up the pan with more boiling water from time to time to make sure it doesn't boil dry. Turn the pudding out on to a serving dish, and serve hot with custard, yogurt or cream.

PIKELETS

MAKES ABOUT 28

A Northern version of crumpets that once provided a delicious, cheap and satisfying dish when served during the winter months.

340 g (12 oz) strong white
plain flour
½ teaspoon salt
1 sachet easy-blend yeast
140 ml (¼ pt) milk, or milk and water
mixed, warmed to blood heat
1 teaspoon bicarbonate of soda
A little oil, for greasing
A griddle or heavy-based
frying pan

Sift the flour, salt and yeast into a warmed mixing bowl. Add 340 ml (12 fl oz) of warm water and beat well to form a smooth, stiff batter. Continue to beat for a further 5 minutes, then cover the bowl with oiled cling film and leave in a warm place for 1 hour.

Mix the warm milk together with the bicarbonate of soda and beat into the yeast mixture to form a smooth, runny batter. Cover again and leave in a warm place for about 30 minutes until the mixture becomes frothy.

In the meantime, lightly grease the frying pan or griddle, and heat. Pour the batter on to the griddle in 7.5 cm (3 in) long lines and cook for about 6 to 7 minutes until set and bubbles have risen to the surface and burst. Turn them over and cook for a further 1 to 2 minutes until golden.

Wrap the pikelets in a clean tea-towel while cooking the rest of the batter. Serve them straight from the griddle, or toasted and spread with lashings of butter.

LARDY CAKE

MAKES ONE 18 CM (7 IN) SQUARE CAKE

A deliciously moist teatime cake that's a firm favourite with all the family.

455 g (1 lb) strong plain flour
A pinch of salt
30 g (1 oz) caster sugar
1 sachet easy-blend yeast
1 egg yolk, size 3
230 to 280 ml (8 fl oz to ½ pt) milk,
warmed to blood heat
230 g (8 oz) lard
170 g (6 oz) golden granulated sugar
½ teaspoon mixed spice
85 g (3 oz) sultanas, washed and dried
85 g (3 oz) currants, washed and dried
For the glaze:
60 g (2 oz) golden granulated sugar
A 18 cm (7 in) deep, square tin,
greased and base-lined

Sift the flour into a warmed mixing bowl with the salt and sugar. Stir in the yeast, egg yolk and milk, and mix to make a soft but not sticky dough. Turn out on to a lightly floured work surface and knead for about 10 minutes until it becomes smooth and elastic. Place the dough in an oiled bowl, cover with oiled cling film and leave in a warm place until doubled in size – about 1 to 1½ hours.

Knock back the risen dough. Then, on a lightly floured work surface, roll it out to a rectangle 30.5 by 18 cm (12 by 7 in). Spread two-thirds of the dough with a third of the lard, sprinkle over a third of the sugar, followed by a third of the mixed spice and fruit. Fold the plain third over the filling, then fold the remaining third in to make three layers. Give the folded dough a quarter turn to the right, then roll it out again to the original size.

Repeat the process twice more, each time using a third of the lard, sugar, mixed spice and fruit. Finally, turn and roll the dough to a 18 cm (7 in) square to fit the tin. Cover the tin with oiled cling film and leave to prove in a warm place until doubled in size – about 1 hour.

Meanwhile, set the oven at Gas Mark 7, 425°F, 220°C. Just before baking the cake, criss-cross the surface with a sharp knife. Bake for 15 minutes, then cover with a sheet of greaseproof paper to prevent over-browning. Reduce the temperature to Gas Mark 5, 375°F, 190°C and bake for a further 45 minutes to 1 hour.

Meanwhile, to make the glaze, pour the sugar into a pan with 70 ml (2½ fl oz) of cold water. Heat gently until the sugar has dissolved, bring to the boil and continue boiling for 1 minute. Remove from the heat.

Turn the cake out on to a wire rack, remove the greaseproof paper and brush with the hot glaze. Cut into thick slices and serve warm.

TO FREEZE: open-freeze the unglazed cake until firm. Wrap in greaseproof paper and foil, and freeze for up to 2 months.

TO USE FROM FROZEN: thaw on a wire rack at room temperature for 3 to 4 hours, then warm in a low oven before serving.

RICH FRUIT CAKE

MAKES ONE 23 CM (9 IN)
ROUND CAKE

*Moist and packed with dried fruit – serve
it in the traditional Northern way, with
Wensleydale cheese.*

625 g (1 lb 6 oz) sultanas
310 g (11 oz) currants
255 g (9 oz) glacé cherries
140 g (5 oz) finely chopped mixed peel
140 g (5 oz) whole blanched almonds
230 g (8 oz) unsalted butter
230 g (8 oz) soft, light brown sugar
5 eggs, size 3
310 g (11 oz) plain flour
2 teaspoons ground mixed spice
1½ tablespoons black treacle
5 tablespoons brandy

Set the oven at Gas Mark 2, 300°F,
150°C. Thoroughly wash the dried fruit
and leave to drain on absorbent kitchen
paper. Roughly chop the almonds.

Cream the butter until soft, then add
the sugar and beat until light and fluffy.
Beat the eggs together, then gradually
add to the creamed mixture, beating
well after each addition. Sift the flour
and mixed spice and, using a metal
spoon, fold into the mixture. Add the
remaining ingredients, mix well and
spoon into the prepared cake tin.
Smooth the surface. Make a hollow in
the centre of the mixture so that the
cake will rise evenly during baking.

Wrap the tin in a double layer of
brown wrapping paper and tie with
string. Cook for 3½ to 4 hours. Cover
the top of the cake with greaseproof
paper after about 1½ hours to avoid
over-browning. It is cooked when a
skewer inserted into the centre comes
out clean. Leave to cool in the tin.

Remove the lining paper and wrap
the cake in fresh greaseproof paper,
then in foil, and store in a cool, dry
place. The cake will stay fresh for up to
3 months.

LEFT *Rich Fruit Cake, served in the
traditional way, with a slice of good
Wensleydale cheese.*

TEACAKES

MAKES 12

Yorkshire teacakes were traditionally plain, although the fruited varieties are now more common.

340 g (12 oz) strong plain white flour
110 g (4 oz) plain wholemeal flour
½ teaspoon salt
60 g (2 oz) unsalted butter
60 g (2 oz) soft, light brown sugar
1 sachet easy-blend yeast
1 egg, size 3, beaten
230 ml (8 fl oz) milk, warmed to blood heat

Sift the flours and salt together and return any bran left in the sieve to the bowl. Rub in the butter until the mixture resembles fine breadcrumbs. Stir in the sugar and yeast. Add the egg and milk, and mix to a soft but not sticky dough. Turn the dough out on to a lightly floured work surface and knead for 10 minutes until smooth and elastic. Place in a lightly oiled bowl and cover with oiled cling film. Leave to prove in a warm place until the dough is doubled in size - about 1 hour.

Remove the dough from the bowl and knead it lightly. Divide the dough into 12 evenly-sized pieces and shape into buns. Place on greased baking trays and cover loosely with a piece of oiled cling film. Leave in a warm place until doubled in size about 30 minutes.

Set the oven at Gas Mark 5, 375°F, 190°C. and bake for 20 to 25 minutes until browned. The cakes should sound hollow when tapped underneath. Serve warm from the oven, or split and toast them and serve with butter.

TO FREEZE: open-freeze the cakes until firm, then pack them in a rigid plastic container for up to 2 months.

TO USE FROM FROZEN: thaw on a wire rack at room temperature for about 2 hours.

FRUIT TEACAKES

MAKES 12

Follow the above recipe for Teacakes, but sift 1 teaspoon of mixed spice into the flours. Stir in 110 g (4 oz) sultanas with the sugar. Freeze as above.

GINGER PARKIN

MAKES ONE 20.5 CM (8 IN)
SQUARE CAKE

Parkin is an old Yorkshire oatmeal cake containing treacle. Traditionally eaten in November, it is best made several days before eating, otherwise it tends to be too moist and difficult to cut.

230 g (8 oz) plain flour
1 teaspoon ground ginger
A pinch of salt
1½ teaspoons bicarbonate of soda
340 g (12 oz) medium oatmeal
110 g (4 oz) unsalted butter
110 g (4 oz) soft, light brown sugar
230 g (8 oz) black treacle
30 g (1 oz) stem ginger, finely chopped
2 eggs, size 3, beaten
140 ml (¼ pt) milk

Set the oven at Gas Mark 4, 350°F, 180°C. Sift the flour with the ginger, salt and bicarbonate of soda, then stir in the oatmeal.

Gently heat the butter, sugar and treacle, stirring frequently until the butter has melted. Leave to cool, then stir into the dry ingredients with the stem ginger, eggs and milk. Mix well and pour the mixture into the prepared tin and bake for about 45 minutes to 1 hour or until firm.

Cool in the tin for 5 minutes then turn out on to a wire rack and leave to cool completely. Store, wrapped in greaseproof paper, for several days before serving. Serve sliced and buttered.

TO FREEZE: open-freeze the cake until firm. Wrap in greaseproof paper and foil and freeze for up to 2 months.

TO USE FROM FROZEN: thaw on a wire rack at room temperature for 3 to 4 hours.

Opposite top *From front: Fruit Scones,*
Ginger Parkin, Fat Rascals, Lardy Cake,
and Rich Fruit Cake.
Right *English dairy herds produce milk*
rich in butterfat, and good English butter is
excellent for baking.

FRUIT SCONES

MAKES ABOUT 6

Melt-in-the-mouth scones – ideal to serve
as a substantial snack or for afternoon tea.

455 g (1 lb) self-raising flour
1 teaspoon mixed spice
110 g (4 oz) unsalted butter
60 g (2 oz) golden granulated sugar
85 g (3 oz) sultanas
2 eggs, size 3, beaten
About 140 ml (¼ pt) milk
Beaten egg, to glaze
A 10 cm (4 in) round cutter

Set the oven at Gas Mark 8, 450°F,
230°C. Sift the flour and spice into a
bowl and rub in the butter so that the
mixture resembles fine breadcrumbs.
Mix in the sugar and sultanas. Stir in the
eggs and enough milk to make a fairly
soft but not sticky dough.

Roll out the dough on a lightly
floured work surface and cut out the
scones, re-rolling the trimmings as
necessary. Place on a greased baking
tray and brush with a little beaten egg.
Bake for 12 minutes or until firm and
golden. Transfer to a wire rack and
leave to cool. Serve the scones warm,
halved and buttered with jam and
lightly whipped cream.

TO FREEZE: open-freeze the scones
until firm, then pack them in a rigid
plastic container for up to 2 months.

TO USE FROM FROZEN: thaw the
scones at room temperature on a wire
rack for about 2 hours.

YORK BISCUITS

MAKES ABOUT 28

These biscuits were usually offered to the
parson when he visited his parishioners for
Sunday tea.

85 g (3 oz) unsalted butter
85 g (3 oz) caster sugar
230 g (8 oz) self-raising flour
60 ml (2 fl oz) milk
A 5 cm (2 in) round cutter

Set the oven at Gas Mark 3, 325°F,
170°C. Cream the butter and sugar
together until pale and light. Fold the
flour into the butter mixture, then add
the milk and mix to a dough that's stiff,
but not sticky. Knead the dough well,
then roll out on a lightly floured work
surface to about 3 mm (⅛ in) thick and
cut out 28 biscuits.

Place on greased baking trays and
bake in the oven for about 30 minutes
until pale golden in colour. Leave the
biscuits to cool on the baking trays for
2 minutes to firm up, then transfer to
wire racks to finish cooling.

Store in an airtight container for up
to 2 days before serving.

TO FREEZE: open-freeze the biscuits
until firm, then pack them in a rigid
plastic container for up to 2 months.

TO USE FROM FROZEN: thaw at room
temperature on a wire rack for 2 hours.

FAT RASCALS

MAKES 10

Also known as Turf Cakes, Fat Rascals
were cooked on a griddle over an open
turf or peat fire.

455 g (1 lb) self-raising flour
A pinch of salt
230 g (8 oz) unsalted butter
110 g (4 oz) soft, light brown sugar
110 g (4 oz) currants, washed and dried
140 ml (¼ pt) milk and water, mixed
Golden caster sugar, for sprinkling
A 9 cm (3½ in) round cutter

Set the oven at Gas Mark 4, 350°F,
180°C. Sift the flour and salt into a large
bowl and then rub in the butter until the
mixture resembles fine breadcrumbs.
Stir in the sugar and currants, and add
enough milk and water to make a soft
but not sticky dough. Roll the dough out
on a lightly floured work surface to a
1 cm (½ in) thickness and then cut out
10 rounds. Place on a greased baking
tray and sprinkle with a little caster
sugar. Bake for about 30 to 35 minutes
until golden.

Leave them to cool on the baking
tray for 2 minutes, then transfer to a
wire rack to finish cooling. Store them
in an airtight container for up to 2 days
before serving.

TO FREEZE: open-freeze the cakes
until firm, then pack them in a rigid
container for up to 2 months.

TO USE FROM FROZEN: thaw at room
temperature on a wire rack for 2 hours.

The Midlands

The Midlands, from the beautiful fruit-laden orchards of the Vale of Evesham in the south, to the lush dairy pastures of Cheshire in the north, has some of the richest agricultural land in the country.

Here in the Heart of England they produce prime British beef; famous pies; cakes, ales and cheeses; hops, apples, pears and plums; and some of the purest mineral water in the world.

Herefords, with their characteristic red coats and white faces, are a cross between the British Red Longhorn and cattle introduced from the Low Countries in the 17th Century, and they thrive on the abundant grass. Large tracts of Derbyshire and Northamptonshire are devoted to rearing sheep. The rolling, wooded countryside of the Midlands provides perfect cover for pheasants, rabbits and hares – and the town of Melton Mowbray, in the heart of fox-hunting country, is justly proud of its pork pies.

Stilton, the King of Cheeses, is a registered trademark and may only be made from British milk in the three counties of Derbyshire, Leicestershire and Nottinghamshire. Other famous cheeses include Shropshire, Sage Derby and Red Leicester, which was originally produced by adding carrot or beetroot juice to the milk left over from making Stilton. Cheshire, which is the oldest cheese in the British Isles, was mentioned in the Domesday Book.

Stilton and Celery Soup
Stilton, Apple and Onion Flan
Potted Cheese
Stilton, Cranberry, Apple and Port Filo Pie
— * —
Cider Braised Lamb with Mixed Rice
Pork with Cider and Horseradish
Duck and Cranberry Casserole
Oxtail Stew
Beef Cobbler
Melton Mowbray Pork Pie
Spinach and Chicken Pie
Latticed Bacon and Egg Pie
— * —
Cheesy Topped Vegetable and Bean Hot Pot
Rabbit with Red Wine
Country Vegetable Casserole
— * —
Perry and Ginger Trifle
Traditional Bramble Pie
Gooseberry Crumble Pie
Gooseberry Ice Cream
Shrewsbury Biscuits
Almond Bakewell Tart
— * —
Fruit and Cider Cake
Country Apple Cake
— * —
Iced Berry Mousse
Gooseberry Chutney
— * —
Hot Cider Punch

STILTON AND CELERY SOUP

Although this great British cheese is delicious all year round, it has always been associated with Christmas. The flavours of Stilton and celery marry perfectly to make this creamy, rich, winter soup.

30 g (1 oz) unsalted butter	3 tablespoons of white wine
1 onion, chopped	140 g (5 oz) Blue Stilton, crumbled
1 head of celery, chopped	140 ml (¼ pt) double cream
30 g (1 oz) plain flour	Salt and freshly ground white pepper
850 ml (1½ pt) chicken stock	Flat-leaf parsley, to garnish

Melt the butter in a heavy-based pan and add the onion and celery. Cook for about 5 minutes or until softened but not coloured. Stir in the plain flour and cook for 1 minute. Remove the pan from the heat and gradually stir in the chicken stock and white wine. Return to the heat and bring to the boil stirring constantly. Reduce the heat and simmer gently for 20 to 30 minutes.

Pour the mixture into a liquidiser or food processor and purée until smooth. Return to a rinsed out pan, add the crumbled Stilton and heat, stirring constantly, until melted. *Add the cream, season to taste and serve piping hot with with good crusty bread.

TO FREEZE: *do not add the cream. Leave the soup to cool, then pour it into a rigid plastic container. Freeze for up to 1 month.

TO USE FROM FROZEN: thaw overnight in the fridge. Reheat, add the cream and season to taste.

STILTON, APPLE AND ONION FLAN

For the pastry:
170 g (6 oz) plain flour
A pinch of salt
85 g (3 oz) unsalted butter
For the filling:
60 g (2 oz) unsalted butter
170 g (6 oz) onions, thinly sliced
110 g (4 oz) Bramley cooking apples, peeled and cored
170 g (6 oz) Stilton, crumbled
2 eggs, size 3, beaten
140 ml (¼ pt) milk
Salt and freshly ground black pepper
A 11.5 by 35.5 cm (4½ by 14 in) fluted tranche tin

Set the oven at Gas Mark 6, 400°F, 200°C and place a baking tray in the oven to heat.

To make the pastry, sift the flour and salt together in a bowl. Rub in the butter until the mixture resembles fine breadcrumbs. Add enough cold water to make a soft but not sticky dough. Wrap and chill for 10 minutes.

Roll out the pastry on a lightly floured surface into a rectangle and use to line the tranche tin. Lightly prick the pastry case with a fork and chill for a further 10 minutes.

Line the pastry with greaseproof paper and fill with baking beans. Stand the tin on the hot baking tray and bake 'blind' for 10 minutes. Remove the beans and greaseproof paper and bake for a further 10 minutes.

To make the filling, melt the butter in a frying pan, add the onions and cook until soft but not coloured. Cool.

Place the onion in the base of the flan case, grate the apples on top and sprinkle with crumbled Stilton. Whisk together the eggs, milk and seasoning and pour over the onion, apple and Stilton. Bake for 25 to 30 minutes until puffed and golden. Serve hot or cold.

TO FREEZE: leave to cool, remove from the tin, open-freeze until firm, then wrap in cling film.

TO USE FROM FROZEN: thaw on a wire rack for 3 hours. Warm through in a low oven before using.

LEFT *Stilton and Celery Soup.*
ABOVE *Stilton, Cranberry, Apple and Port Filo Pie.*
PREVIOUS PAGE LEFT *Hereford produces wonderful apples, as well as splendid beef cattle.*
PREVIOUS PAGE RIGHT *Melton Mowbray Pork Pie.*

STILTON, CRANBERRY, APPLE AND PORT FILO PIE

SERVES 6 TO 8

A spectacular pie. It is ideal for vegetarians, and meat eaters will love it too.

230 g (8 oz) fresh or frozen
cranberries, thawed if frozen
140 ml (¼ pt) port
85 g (3 oz) caster sugar (or to taste)
455 g (1 lb) crisp dessert apples
340 g (12 oz) Stilton, derinded and
coarsely grated

½ teaspoon freshly chopped thyme
Salt and freshly ground black pepper
½ teaspoon freshly grated nutmeg
7 large leaves filo pastry
85 g (3 oz) butter, melted
A 21 cm (8¼ in) round, loose-based
spring-release tin

Place the cranberries, port and sugar in a small pan, mix well and bring slowly to the boil. Reduce the heat and simmer gently for 10 minutes until the berries soften. Drain any excess port liquor. Leave to cool slightly.

Set the oven at Gas Mark 4, 350°F, 180°C. Place a baking tray in the oven to heat.

Peel the apples and chop them into small cubes. Mix in the Stilton cheese, thyme, seasoning and nutmeg, then stir in the cranberries.

To assemble the pie, take two pieces of filo, brush with melted butter and line the tin, leaving the edges overhanging the top. Keep the remaining pastry covered with damp kitchen paper or a tea towel.

Fill the pastry with half the Stilton mixture. Cut a piece of filo in half, brush with melted butter and lay both pieces on top of the Stilton mixture. Spoon the remaining cheese mixture on top. Cut another piece of filo pastry in half, then brush with melted butter and lay it on top. Fold over the edges form the sides. Arrange the remaining filo pastry on top of the pie, and brush with any remaining butter.

Place the tin on the preheated baking tray and bake for 25 minutes until the top of the pastry is golden. Release the spring and remove the pie from the tin. Return to the oven for a further 10 minutes to brown the sides of the pie. Leave to stand for 5 minutes after cooking. Serve warm.

The pie can be prepared and chilled up to 2 hours before cooking.

POTTED CHEESE

SERVES 6

A great way of using up leftover cheese.

110 g (4 oz) unsalted butter
230 g (8 oz) Cheshire or Cheddar cheese,
grated, or Stilton, crumbled
3 to 4 tablespoons cream
A little sherry or port to taste
A pinch of cayenne pepper
1 teaspoon Worcestershire sauce
Salt and pepper
85 g (3 oz) butter, clarified (optional)
6 ramekins

Soften the butter, then mix in all the other ingredients except the clarified butter and work to a paste. Taste, and adjust seasoning if necessary. Spoon mixture into ramekins or a serving dish and press down. Top with a layer of clarified butter if wished, or cover with cling film. Chill until firm.

CIDER BRAISED LAMB WITH MIXED RICE

SERVES 6 TO 8

An ideal supper dish served with fresh green vegetables.

A 1.8 to 2.3 kg (4 to 5 lb) leg of lamb
2 to 3 cloves garlic, cut into slivers
3 tablespoons olive oil
A sprig of rosemary
Salt and freshly ground black pepper
340 g (12 oz) mixed grain rice
60 g (2 oz) seedless raisins
430 ml (¾ pt) dry cider
A 410 g (14½ oz) can chopped tomatoes
The juice of ½ a lemon

Set the oven at Gas Mark 3, 325°F, 170°C. Trim any excess fat from the lamb. Make small slits in the meat and insert slivers of garlic into each slit.

Heat the oil in a heavy-based flame proof casserole and brown the lamb well on all sides to seal. Add the sprig of rosemary and seasoning, cover and cook in the oven for 1½ hours. Remove from the oven.

Turn the oven up to Gas Mark 4, 350°F, 180°C. Add the rice to the lamb and stir in the raisins, cider, tomatoes and lemon juice. Season well, then cook, uncovered, for a further 1 to 1¼ hours, stirring occasionally, until the rice is tender and all the liquid has been absorbed. Serve the lamb sliced with the rice and fresh green vegetables.

PORK WITH CIDER AND HORSERADISH

Try a medium dry cider from a single variety of apples such as Breakwell's Seedling to make this delicious and simple supper dish.

680 g (1½ lb) pork fillet, trimmed of any fat
1 to 2 tablespoons olive oil
30 g (1 oz) unsalted butter
2 Granny Smith apples, peeled, cored and sliced
1 large onion, finely sliced
2 tablespoons caster sugar
280 ml (½ pt) medium dry cider
1 tablespoon creamed horseradish
Salt and freshly ground black pepper

Using a very sharp knife, slice the pork fillet diagonally into slices about 1 cm (½ in) wide.

Heat the oil in a heavy-based frying pan. Add the pork slices in batches and brown well on both sides. Remove from the pan using a slotted spoon, and drain on absorbent kitchen paper. Set the meat aside.

Add the butter to the frying pan and heat until foaming, add the apples slices, onion and sugar. Cook for about 5 to 8 minutes, stirring occasionally, until the apples and onions are golden brown. Remove from the pan with a slotted spoon and reserve.

Pour the cider into the frying pan, bring to the boil and simmer until it has been reduced by half (this should take about 5 minutes). Stir the creamed horseradish into the sauce.

Return the pork, onions, apples and seasoning to the pan, cover and cook for a further 5 to 10 minutes, or until the pork is tender.

Serve immediately with boiled or steamed rice and a selection of seasonal green vegetables.

LEFT *Cider Braised Lamb served with mixed rice.*

THE MIDLANDS

29

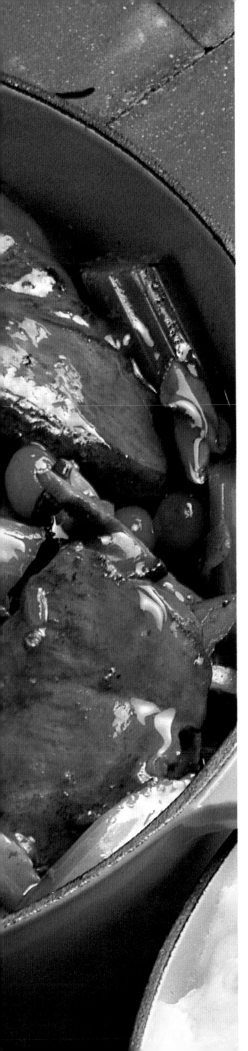

DUCK AND CRANBERRY CASSEROLE

SERVES 4

The sharp taste of cranberries is the perfect accompaniment to the richness of duck.

4 duck breasts
For the marinade:
1 onion, quartered
1 carrot, quartered
1 clove garlic, sliced
2 bay leaves
½ teaspoon black peppercorns, crushed
140 ml (¼ pt) cranberry juice
For the casserole:
2 tablespoons olive oil

1 onion, chopped
1 to 2 cloves garlic, or to taste, crushed
230 g (8 oz) shiitake or oyster
mushrooms, quartered
4 sticks celery, washed and sliced
230 g (8 oz) fresh or frozen cranberries
280 ml (½ pt) good-quality duck
or chicken stock
Salt and freshly ground black pepper
A heavy-based flameproof casserole

Place the duck breasts with all the ingredients for the marinade in a shallow dish. Cover and chill overnight, turning the breasts occasionally.

The next day, remove the duck from the marinade. Strain the marinade and reserve the liquid. Set the oven at Gas Mark 3, 325°F, 170°C.

Heat the oil in a flameproof casserole and fry the duck pieces in batches until golden on all sides. Drain on absorbent kitchen paper and set aside. Fry the onion and garlic in the oil for 5 minutes until softened but not coloured. Then add the mushrooms and celery and cook for a further 5 minutes. Return the duck breasts to the casserole and add all the remaining ingredients with the reserved marinade. Stir the casserole well, cover and bake in the oven for 1 to 1½ hours.

To serve, arrange the duck pieces and vegetables in a serving dish. Keep warm in a low oven. Pour the liquid into a pan and boil rapidly for 10 to 15 minutes or until reduced and thickened. Taste for seasoning, then pour over the duck. Serve the casserole at once with creamy mashed potatoes and a selection of vegetables.

LEFT *Duck and Cranberry Casserole.*

OXTAIL STEW

SERVES 6

30 g (1 oz) lard
1.6 kg (3 ½ lb) oxtail, cut into segments
85 g (3 oz) bacon, cubed
2 medium onions, sliced
1 bunch fresh thyme, crumbled
1 teaspoon finely chopped parsley
1 bay leaf, crushed
½ teaspoon whole allspice, crushed
Pinch of celery seed
570 ml (1 pt) good quality beef stock
280 g (10 oz) turnips
455 g (1 lb) baby carrots
Salt and freshly ground black pepper
15 g (½ oz) butter, softened
15 g (½ oz) flour
A large, heavy-based flameproof casserole

Set the oven at Gas Mark 2, 300°F, 150°C. Heat the lard in the casserole on top of the stove until hot and cook the oxtail pieces in batches until well browned and sealed on all sides. Remove from the pan and set aside.

Add bacon and onions. Cook until the onions are soft but not coloured. Return the oxtail to the casserole and stir in thyme, parsley and bay leaf. Stir in allspice and celery seeds, and half-cover the oxtail with stock. Bring the casserole to the boil, cover and place in the oven for 2 hours. Add quartered turnips and carrots. Season, cover and simmer on a low heat for 1 to 1½ hours more, or until tender. Cool and chill.

The next day, remove the solidified fat from the casserole. Mix the butter with the flour to make a *beurre manié*. Warm the casserole through gently, then strain off the juices into a pan. Keep the oxtail warm in a low oven. Bring the juice to the boil, then whisk in the *beurre manié* in small lumps until the sauce is thick and glossy. Pour over the oxtail, stir well and simmer for 10 to 15 minutes. Season to taste, and serve hot with mashed potatoes.

To FREEZE: freeze before adding the *beurre-manié*. Cool, pour into a rigid plastic container, cover and freeze for up to 1 month.

To USE FROM FROZEN: thaw in the fridge. Boil for 15 minutes before adding the *beurre manié*.

BEEF COBBLER

SERVES 6 TO 8

For the casserole:
0.9 kg (2 lb) stewing steak, trimmed and
cut into 5 cm (2 in) pieces
570 ml (1 pt) Guinness
4 large onions, thinly sliced
4 tablespoons vegetable oil
1 bay leaf
1 teaspoon mixed spice
1 tablespoon flour
Salt and freshly ground
black pepper

For the cobbler:
340 g (12 oz) self-raising flour
½ teaspoon salt
85 g (3 oz) butter
3 tablespoons freshly chopped mixed herbs
3 tablespoons creamed horseradish
1 egg, size 3
115 ml (4 fl oz) milk
Beaten egg to glaze
A 5 cm (2 in) plain round cutter
A large, heavy-based flameproof casserole

Put the beef into a glass or china bowl with the Guinness, onions, 1 tablespoon of the oil, the bay leaf and mixed spice. Mix the ingredients together well, then cover and leave to marinate in a cool place for 1 to 2 hours. Strain the marinade through a sieve and reserve. Carefully separate the raw beef from the sliced onions.

Set the oven at Gas Mark 4, 350°F, 180°C. Heat the remaining vegetable oil in a flameproof casserole and brown the beef in batches until sealed and well browned on all sides. Set aside. Add the onions to the oil and cook until softened but not browned. Stir in the flour, remove the pan from the heat and gradually stir in the marinade. Bring the sauce to the boil, stirring constantly, then add the bay leaf and the beef and its juices with the seasoning. Cover and place in the preheated oven for 1¼ hours. Remove the beef casserole from the oven.

Increase the oven to Gas Mark 8, 450°F, 230°C. Sieve the flour and salt together into a large bowl. Rub in the butter until the mixture resembles fine breadcrumbs. Stir in the chopped herbs. Mix the creamed horseradish with the egg and gradually stir into the cobbler mixture, adding just enough milk to make a fairly stiff dough.

Turn out the dough on to a lightly floured surface and roll out to 2 cm (¾ in) thick. Cut into rounds with a plain cutter, re-rolling the trimmings as necessary. Set closely together in a ring on top of the casserole and brush with beaten egg. Put back in the oven, uncovered, and cook for 12 to 15 minutes until the casserole is bubbling and the scones are firm and golden.

To FREEZE: freeze before adding the cobbler, then freeze as for Oxtail (left).
To USE FROM FROZEN: thaw in the fridge, add the cobbler and cook as above.

MELTON MOWBRAY PORK PIE

SERVES 8 TO 10

*The highly seasoned jellied stock is extremely important to the final success of this pie,
so don't skimp on this vital part of the method.*

For the jellied stock:
2 small pork bones, chopped
1 small veal bone, chopped
1 pig's trotter
2 large onions, chopped
1 tablespoon salt
1 teaspoon freshly ground white pepper
4 sage leaves
1 bunch parsley
1 bunch thyme
2 bay leaves

For the filling:
0.9 kg (2 lb) shoulder of pork, free
from skin and gristle
1 teaspoon ground mace

2 teaspoons salt
1 teaspoon finely ground
white pepper
1 teaspoon fresh sage, chopped
1 teaspoon parsley, chopped
40 g (1½ oz) unsalted butter

For the pastry:
85 g (3 oz) butter
85 g (3 oz) lard
115 ml (4 fl oz) milk
570 g (1¼ lb) plain flour
1½ teaspoons salt
Beaten egg, to glaze
A 15 by 7.5 cm (6 by 3 in) deep,
loose-based cake tin, greased

OPPOSITE *Beef Cobbler, with its topping
of herby, spicy brown scones.*
ABOVE *Melton Mowbray Pork Pie.*

To make the jellied stock, place all the ingredients in a large pan and cover with 850 ml (1½ pt) of cold water. Bring slowly to the boil, then reduce the heat and simmer for 2 hours or until the liquid has reduced to about 280 ml (½ pt). Remove any scum from the surface of the stock, strain and adjust the seasoning if necessary. Cool and skim off all the fat – you will find the stock will turn to jelly as it cools. Cover and store in the refrigerator for up to 2 days.

To make the filling, dice the pork into 6 mm (¼ in) pieces and place in a bowl. Mix in the mace, salt, pepper, sage, parsley and 3 tablespoons of cold water. Cover the bowl with cling film.

To make the pastry, place the butter and lard in a pan with the milk and 100 ml (3½ fl oz) of cold water and bring to the boil. Sift the flour and salt into a large bowl, make a well in the flour and pour in the hot liquid. Mix with a wooden spoon, then knead with your hands until smooth, and turn out on to a clean work surface. Wrap one third of the pastry in cling film and reserve.

Roll out the other two-thirds of the pastry into a round, large enough to line the tin. Fold the pastry into 4 and lift the pastry into the tin. Gently ease the pastry over the base and up the sides of the tin, and trim to leave a 1 cm (½ in) overlap. Wrap the remaining pastry in cling film.

Set the oven at Gas Mark 6, 400°F, 200°C. Pack the prepared meat tightly into the pastry case and dot the butter for the filling over the surface of the meat. Tuck the overlap of pastry over the meat and brush the pastry with beaten egg. Roll out the remaining pastry to a circle 20.5 cm (8 in) in diameter for the lid. Using a sharp knife, make a few small holes in the lid to allow the steam to escape. Place the lid on top of the pie, trim, seal the edges with thumb and fingers and glaze with beaten egg. Make a pastry tassel for the centre (see photograph) and glaze with beaten egg.

Place the pie on a baking tray and bake for 15 minutes. Cover the tassel with foil if it starts to brown too quickly, and continue to cook for a further 30 minutes. Reduce the heat to Gas Mark 4, 350°F, 180°C and bake for a further 45 minutes. Carefully remove the sides of the tin.

Glaze the lid again and the sides, then return to the oven for 30 minutes. Glaze the sides again after 15 minutes for a really rich, golden colour.

Remove from the oven and allow to cool for 2 hours. Gently melt the jellied stock and pour into the holes using a funnel. Leave to cool completely. Chill the pie for at least 6 hours, and then serve with baby potatoes and a green salad.

SPINACH AND CHICKEN PIE WITH POTATO PASTRY

SERVES 4

Golden Wonder, Maris Piper, Desirée or King Edward are all floury varieties of potato, suitable for making this pastry.

For the filling:
The juice of 1 lemon
1 teaspoon freshly ground black pepper
2 cloves garlic, crushed to a paste
3 tablespoons olive oil
3 boneless chicken breasts, free from skin,
weighing about 0.9 kg (2 lb)
0.9 kg (2 lb) fresh spinach, or
455 g (1 lb) frozen leaf spinach, thawed
Salt and freshly ground black pepper

For the pastry:
455 g (1 lb) potatoes
340 g (12 oz) plain flour
1½ teaspoons baking powder
A pinch of salt
85 g (3 oz) unsalted butter
1 teaspoon whole fennel seeds
1 egg, size 3, beaten
30 ml (1 fl oz) warm milk
Beaten egg, to glaze

To make the filling, put the lemon juice, pepper, garlic and oil into a bowl. Slice each chicken breast into 3 horizontally, while making sure they retain their shape, then marinate in the lemon juice mixture for 2 hours, turning occasionally.

Blanch the spinach by plunging into salted boiling water for 1 minute, then refresh it in cold water. Drain and squeeze completely dry in a clean tea towel. If using frozen spinach, simply squeeze dry as before. Season with salt and pepper.

To make the pastry, wash the potatoes and cook for 15 to 20 minutes in plenty of salted, boiling water. When tender and just cooked, remove the skins and push the potatoes through a sieve. Sift the flour into a bowl with the baking powder and salt. Rub the butter into the flour with the tips of the fingers until the mixture resembles fine breadcrumbs. Add the fennel seeds, then mix in the sieved potato thoroughly. Add the beaten egg and enough milk to form a smooth dough.

Set the oven at Gas Mark 6, 400°F, 200°C. Wrap 170 g 6 oz) of the pastry in cling film and reserve. Roll out the remainder of the pastry on a lightly floured work surface to a 28 cm (11 in) square. Carefully transfer the pastry square to a greased baking tray and layer chicken slices and spinach on top. Brush the edges of the square with beaten egg and bring the 4 edges together to form a neat parcel. Pinch together and garnish the joins with pastry leaves, made from the reserved pastry. Glaze with beaten egg and cook for 45 minutes. Cover with foil if the pastry starts to brown too quickly, especially over the pastry leaves.

Remove from the oven, cut into slices and serve hot with a selection of fresh vegetables.

BELOW *Spinach and Chicken Pie with Potato Pastry.*
OPPOSITE *Latticed Bacon and Egg Pie.*

LATTICED BACON AND EGG PIE

SERVES 6

For the pastry:
110 g (4 oz) plain white flour
110 g (4 oz) plain wholemeal flour
110 g (4 oz) unsalted butter
60 g (2 oz) mature Cheddar cheese, finely grated
Beaten egg, to glaze
For the filling:
230 g (8 oz) traditionally smoked lean bacon, rind and fat removed
12 quails' eggs
140 g (5 oz) ricotta cheese
100 g (3½ oz) cream cheese
2 eggs, size 3, beaten
30 ml (1 fl oz) double cream
3 tablespoons chives, snipped
½ teaspoon freshly ground black pepper
4 tablespoons pine nuts
A 19 cm (7½ in) loose-based flan ring, 5 cm (2 in) deep, greased

To make the pastry, sift the flours into a mixing bowl, adding any bran left in the sieve to the bowl. Cut the butter into small pieces with a knife, then rub into the flour with the tips of the fingers until the mixture resembles fine breadcrumbs. Add the grated cheese and, using a round-bladed knife, mix in enough cold water to make a firm but not sticky dough. Roll out the pastry on a lightly floured work surface and use to line the flan ring. Reserve the trimmings for the lattice topping. Prick the base with a fork and chill for 15 minutes.

Set the oven at Gas Mark 6, 400°F, 200°C. To make the filling, grill the bacon and leave to cool, then slice into 6 mm (¼ in) strips. Cook the quails' eggs for 3 minutes in boiling water, then plunge them into cold water immediately. When cool, shell the eggs.

Place the ricotta and cream cheese in a bowl, gradually add the beaten eggs, then the cream, chives and pepper and beat well. Fold in the bacon and 1 tablespoon pine nuts. There is no need to add salt. Cover and chill.

Line the pastry case with greaseproof paper, then fill with baking beans and bake 'blind' for 10 minutes. Remove beans and greaseproof paper, cover the edges and cook for 5 minutes more. Lower the oven to Gas Mark 4, 350°F, 180°C.

Arrange the quails' eggs in the pastry case. Add the ricotta mixture and scatter over the remaining pine nuts.

Roll out the reserved pastry and cut into strips 1 cm (½ in) wide. Arrange the strips on top of the filling to form a lattice, then seal at the edges with beaten egg and glaze the lattice. Bake for 45 minutes or until the pie is golden and the centre cooked and slightly risen. Cover the pie with foil if the top starts to brown too quickly.

Serve the pie either hot or cold with baked potatoes and a green salad.

CHEESY TOPPED VEGETABLE AND BEAN HOT POT

SERVES 6

2 tablespoons olive oil
1 large onion, finely chopped
2 cloves garlic, or to taste, crushed
230 g (8 oz) turnip, peeled and diced
110 g (4 oz) swede, peeled and diced
110 g (4 oz) carrot, peeled and diced
A 793 g (1 lb 12 oz) can chopped tomatoes
A 400 g (14¼ oz) can borlotti
beans, drained
140 ml (¼ pt) vegetable stock
1 tablespoon Worcestershire sauce
110 g (4 oz) courgettes, wiped and sliced
1 tablespoon freshly chopped marjoram

1 tablespoon freshly chopped oregano,
or 1 teaspoon dried oregano
Freshly ground black pepper
For the topping:
0.9 kg (2 lb) potatoes, peeled
40 g (1½ oz) butter
60 g (2 oz) plain flour
570 ml (1 pt) milk
Salt and freshly ground black pepper
1 teaspoon made mustard, or to taste
60 g (2 oz) Cheddar cheese, grated
60 g (2 oz) Parmesan cheese, finely grated
A 3.45 litre (6 pt) casserole

Heat the oil in a heavy-based frying pan. Add onion and garlic and cook gently for 5 minutes or until soft but not coloured. Add the turnip, swede and carrot to the pan. Cook gently for 5 to 10 minutes, stirring frequently. Add the tomatoes with their juice, the drained beans, stock and Worcestershire sauce. Bring slowly to the boil, stirring from time to time. Cover and simmer for 10 minutes. Stir in the sliced courgettes, chopped herbs and seasoning, and cook for a further 10 minutes. Taste and adjust the seasoning as necessary. Pour the mixture into the casserole dish.

To make the topping, cook the potatoes in boiling water for about 15 minutes or until tender. Drain well, rinse with cold water and slice when cool enough to handle.

Set the oven at Gas Mark 7, 425°F, 220°C. Arrange the sliced potatoes on top of the vegetable mixture. Melt the butter over a gentle heat, stir in the flour and cook gently for 1 minute. Slowly add the milk, stirring constantly, and bring to the boil. Add plenty of salt and pepper, followed by the mustard to taste. Continue cooking gently for about 2 to 3 minutes, stirring all the time. Remove the pan from the heat and stir in the Cheddar cheese. Taste and adjust the seasoning. Pour the sauce over the potatoes, sprinkle with Parmesan cheese and bake for about 30 minutes or until bubbly and golden. Serve hot with a green salad.

TO FREEZE: open-freeze before baking, then cover with cling film and foil.
TO USE FROM FROZEN: thaw overnight in the fridge before baking.

RABBIT WITH RED WINE

SERVES 4

Rabbit portions are now widely available.

200 ml (7 fl oz) red wine
1 tablespoon sugar
16 large dried prunes
8 rabbit portions
Salt and freshly ground
black pepper
1 tablespoons vegetable oil
1 sprig fresh thyme
2 onions, finely chopped
2 cloves garlic, crushed
2 tablespoons Armagnac
140 ml (¼ pt) double cream or
crème fraîche
A heavy-based, flameproof casserole

In a heavy-based pan, mix together the red wine and sugar, and bring slowly to the boil. Simmer gently until the sugar has dissolved, stirring occasionally.

Add the large dried prunes and continue cooking the mixture for about 10 minutes more. Remove the pan from the heat, cover and leave to stand for 10 minutes. Strain. Reserve liquid and return the prunes to the pan.

Rinse the rabbit in plenty of cold water and pat dry with absorbent kitchen paper. Season with salt and freshly ground black pepper.

Heat the oil in the casserole and fry the rabbit in batches until golden on all sides. Remove from the casserole. Crumble the thyme into the casserole and add the onion and garlic. Continue cooking for 5 minutes or until softened but not coloured. Add the rabbit and cook for a further 5 minutes, stirring frequently. Pour in the Armagnac and carefully ignite, shaking the pan gently until the flames subside. Stir in the wine reserved from the prunes and bring to the boil. Cover and simmer for 30 minutes or until the rabbit is tender.

Remove the rabbit portions from the casserole, add the cream and boil for a further 5 minutes. Return the rabbit to the casserole with the prunes and then continue cooking gently for about 3 to 5 minutes, stirring frequently. Serve immediately with celeriac purée and a selection of steamed vegetables.

COUNTRY VEGETABLE CASSEROLE

SERVES 6

Vegetarians will enjoy this filling and flavoursome casserole. Serve it with white rice or couscous.

ABOVE *Country Vegetable Casserole, cooked in flavourful traditional cider.*
OPPOSITE *Rabbit with Red Wine.*

3 to 4 tablespoons sunflower oil
170 g (6 oz) baby onions, peeled
2 to 4 cloves garlic, or to taste, crushed
110 g (4 oz) swede, peeled and diced
into 2.5 cm (1 in) cubes
110 g (4 oz) baby carrots
340 g (12 oz) baby turnips, peeled and,
if necessary, halved
A 410 g (14½ oz) can chopped tomatoes

110 g (4 oz) pearl barley
A bouquet garni
Salt and freshly ground black pepper
570 ml (1 pt) traditional dry cider
230 g (8 oz) field mushrooms,
thickly sliced
The juice of ½ a lemon
Chopped fresh parsley, to garnish

Set the oven at Gas Mark 5, 375°F, 190°C. Heat 2 tablespoons of the oil in a large, heavy-based casserole dish and fry the onions and garlic for 2 to 3 minutes, stirring occasionally. Add the swede, carrots and turnips and cook for a further 5 minutes. Stir in the tomatoes, pearl barley, bouquet garni, seasoning and cider. Bring to the boil, then reduce the heat. Cover and cook for 1 hour, stirring frequently.

About 5 minutes before the casserole is ready, heat the remaining oil in a pan, add the mushrooms and fry gently for 2 to 3 minutes. Test the casserole vegetables and, if tender, stir in the mushrooms with their cooking juices. Mix in the lemon juice and adjust the seasoning to taste. Remove the bouquet garni, sprinkle over the freshly chopped parsley and serve at once.

PERRY AND GINGER TRIFLE

Perry is made exclusively from traditional perry pears. Allow the flavours of this wonderfully rich trifle to develop overnight before serving. Try to make the Swiss roll 2 to 3 days before making the trifle, as this will allow the sponge to become firmer.

For the cake mixture:
2 teaspoons ground ginger
85 g (3 oz) flour
3 eggs, size 3, beaten
85 g (3 oz) caster sugar
For the filling:
340 g (12 oz) Conference pears
The juice of 1 lemon
30 g (1 oz) unsalted butter
3 to 4 tablespoons medium dry perry
For the custard:
280 ml (½ pt) milk
140 ml (¼ pt) single cream
A vanilla pod

4 eggs, size 3, beaten
15 g (½ oz) caster sugar
1 teaspoon cornflour
For the syllabub:
60 ml (2 fl oz) medium dry perry
30 ml (1 fl oz) brandy
½ teaspoon freshly grated nutmeg
40 g (1½ oz) icing sugar
200 ml (7 fl oz) double cream
To decorate:
30 g (1 oz) stem ginger, cut into
fine julienne strips
A 20.5 by 30.5 cm (8 by 12 in) Swiss roll
tin, greased and lined with greaseproof

Set the oven at Gas Mark 6, 400°F, 200°C. To make the cake mixture, sift the ginger and flour together into a bowl. Place the eggs and sugar in a separate, large bowl set over a pan of simmering water. Whisk until very pale and thick enough to leave a ribbon-like trail when the whisk is lifted for 8 seconds. Remove the bowl from the heat and continue whisking until the bowl is cool. Using a large, metal spoon, fold the flour into the egg mixture. Spoon into the prepared Swiss roll tin, level the surface and bake for 10 to 12 minutes, until pale and golden. Sprinkle a sheet of greaseproof paper just longer than the Swiss roll tin, with caster sugar. Turn the sponge out on to the greaseproof paper, trim and roll up from the short edge. Put aside and leave to cool.

Meanwhile, to make the filling, peel, core and roughly chop the pears. Place them in a pan and sprinkle with lemon juice and 2 tablespoons of water; discard the peel and core. Cover and simmer for 15 minutes until the fruit is very soft. Beat the fruit into a purée. Beat in the butter and leave to cool.

Unroll the sponge, spread the fruit filling over the inside of the sponge cake and re-roll. Thickly slice the filled Swiss roll and arrange in the base of an attractive glass serving bowl. Sprinkle over the medium dry perry.

To make the custard, heat the milk, cream and vanilla pod until scalding hot. Remove from the heat, cover and leave to infuse for about 15 to 20 minutes, remove the pod. Lightly beat the eggs with sugar and cornflour. Pour the warm milk mixture on to the egg mixture, whisking constantly. Return the mixture to the rinsed-out pan and stir constantly over a gentle heat for about 10 to 15 minutes, until it is thickened and smooth. Strain. Leave to cool, then chill. Spoon the custard over the sponge in the serving bowl. Cover and chill overnight.

To make the syllabub, mix all the ingredients, except the cream, and leave to infuse for 30 minutes to allow the flavours to develop. Pour the cream into a chilled bowl and gradually whisk in the perry mixture. Whisk well until pale and very thick. Using 2 dessertspoons, spoon the syllabub on to the top of the trifle forming petal shapes (see photograph on left). Decorate the centre with the julienne of ginger. Cover and chill for at least 2 hours before serving.

LEFT *Perry and Ginger Trifle – perry is both a variety of pear, and the liqueur made from them.*

TRADITIONAL BRAMBLE PIE

SERVES 8

Try this scrumptious version of an established family favourite.

For the pastry:
230 g (8 oz) plain flour
1 teaspoon ground cinnamon
110 g (4 oz) unsalted butter
1 teaspoon golden caster sugar
For the filling:
0.9 kg (2 lb) Bramley cooking apples
2 tablespoons cornflour
230 g (8 oz) blackberries
140 g (5 oz) golden granulated sugar
To complete:
Beaten egg white
Golden granulated sugar, for sprinkling
A 1.15 litre (2 pt) deep pie dish

To make the pastry, sift flour and cinnamon into a mixing bowl. Rub in the butter with your fingertips until the mixture resembles fine crumbs. Mix in the sugar. Add cold water to make a soft but not sticky dough. Wrap and chill 15 minutes.

Meanwhile, to make the filling, peel, core and quarter the apples. Toss the apple slices in the cornflour. Layer the apples and blackberries in the pie dish, sprinkling with the sugar, and finishing with a layer of apples.

Set the oven at Gas Mark 6, 400°F, 200°C. Roll out the pastry on a lightly floured surface to a shape 4 cm (1½ in) larger than the top of the dish. Cut a strip from the edge of the pastry and carefully lay it along the rim of the dish. Lift the remaining pastry on the rolling pin and check the size – it should fit the dish without stretching, and overlap the rim by 6 mm (¼ in).

Moisten the pastry rim with water and place the pastry lid over it, pressing the edges together. To trim the edges, hold up the dish with one hand and, holding a knife at an angle, cut off the excess pastry. Knock up the edges by pressing a finger along the pastry and making small horizontal cuts into the edge, all around the rim, with the back of a knife. (This will prevent the pastry shrinking back into the pie after baking.) Flute the edge at 6 mm (¼ in) intervals, keeping the knife upright and the pastry close to the edge of the dish. Re-roll any pastry trimmings to make leaves to decorate the top. Brush the top with beaten egg white and sprinkle over the sugar.

Bake the pie for 20 minutes, then reduce the heat to Gas Mark 4, 350°F, 180°C, and bake for a further 30 minutes or until the apples are tender. Test by piercing them through the pastry with a thin skewer.

Serve hot or cold with home-made custard or cream.
TO FREEZE: open-freeze uncooked pie; wrap in cling film.
TO USE FROM FROZEN: cook from frozen at the temperature above for a further 10 minutes.

GOOSEBERRY CRUMBLE PIE

SERVES 6 TO 8

Avoid using gooseberries that are squashy or have blemished skins.

For the pastry:
85 g (3 oz) wholemeal flour
85 g (3 oz) plain flour
85 g (3 oz) unsalted butter
30 g (1 oz) soft, light brown sugar
1 egg yolk, size 3
For the filling:
680 g (1½ lb) gooseberries
60 g (2 oz) unsalted butter
170 g (6 oz) soft, light brown sugar
A 2.5 cm (1 in) piece of fresh root ginger, peeled and grated
For the topping:
230 g (8 oz) plain flour
140 g (5 oz) unsalted butter
110 g (4 oz) demerara sugar
1 teaspoon ground ginger
A 20.5 cm (8 in) deep, round, loose-based cake tin,
greased and base-lined with foil

To make the pastry, sift the flours into a bowl, returning bran left in the sieve to the bowl. Rub in the butter with the tips of your fingers until the mixture resembles fine breadcrumbs, then stir in the sugar. Mix in the egg yolk and enough cold water to make a soft but not sticky dough. Wrap the dough in cling film and chill for 15 minutes.

Set the oven at Gas Mark 6, 400°F, 200°C. Line the base of the cake tin with the pastry, and chill for 10 minutes. Line the pastry with a sheet of greaseproof paper, fill with baking beans and bake 'blind' for 15 minutes. Remove beans and greaseproof paper and return to the oven for 5 minutes more.

Reduce the oven temperature to Gas Mark 4, 350°F, 180°C. To make the filling, top and tail the gooseberries. Melt the butter in a large, heavy-based pan, stir in the sugar, and when dissolved, add the gooseberries and ginger. Cover the pan and cook gently for about 5 minutes, or until the skins begin to change colour. Remove the pan from the heat and allow to cool. Drain well, removing any excess liquid from the gooseberries. Add extra sugar to the mixture, if required, and spoon the fruit into the pastry case.

To make the topping, sift the flour into a bowl. Rub in the butter with your fingertips until the mixture resembles fine breadcrumbs, then add the sugar and ginger. Sprinkle in about 2 tablespoons cold water and lightly mix with a fork until small lumps are formed. Spoon over the gooseberry mixture and bake for 25 to 30 minutes. Remove from the oven and cool in the tin. Serve with home-made custard.

TO FREEZE: freeze as in the previous recipe.
TO USE FROM FROZEN: as in the previous recipe.

FAR LEFT *Traditional Bramble Pie.*
LEFT *Gooseberry Crumble Pie.*

ALMOND BAKEWELL TART

SERVES 8 TO 10

*This was first made in the 1800s, when a
cook made this dish by mistake in the town
of Bakewell – it has been a family
favourite ever since.*

340 g (12 oz) shortcrust pastry, made
with 230 g (8 oz) plain flour
For the filling:
200 g (7 oz) butter
85 g (3 oz) soft, light brown sugar
3 eggs, size 3, beaten
140 g (5 oz) ground almonds
140 g (5 oz) self-raising flour, sifted
1 to 2 tablespoons milk
280 g (10 oz) strawberry jam
30 g (1 oz) flaked almonds
A 23 cm (9 in) loose-based, fluted flan tin

Set the oven at Gas Mark 6, 400°F,
200°C. Roll out the shortcrust pastry to
line the flan tin and lightly prick the
base. Chill for 10 minutes. Line with
greaseproof paper, fill with baking
beans and bake 'blind' for 10 minutes.
Remove the baking beans and paper
and bake for a further 10 minutes.
Reduce the oven temperature to Gas
Mark 4, 350°F, 180°C.

Cream the butter and sugar together
until light and fluffy. Gradually beat in
the eggs, gently fold in the ground
almonds and flour followed by the
milk. Spread the jam over the base of
the pastry case. Spoon the cake batter
on top and level the surface. Sprinkle
over the flaked almonds and bake for
35 to 40 minutes or until the tart is firm
to the touch.

Cool in the tin for 10 minutes before
carefully removing. Serve either warm or
cold with lightly whipped cream.

TO FREEZE: cover the cooked tart,
in cling film and freeze for up to
2 months.

TO USE FROM FROZEN: thaw at room
temperature for 4 hours.

GOOSEBERRY ICE CREAM

SERVES 6

*A smooth, fruity ice with plenty of flavour.
Serve with fruit pies or crumbles or with a
fruit purée sauce.*

680 g (1½ lb) gooseberries, washed
170 g (6 oz) golden granulated sugar
2 egg whites, size 3
140 ml (¼ pt) double cream

Top and tail the gooseberries. Place in a
pan with two tablespoons water. Cover
and cook the fruit over a medium heat
until tender. Purée in a processor or
blender, then sieve to remove the pips.

Dissolve the sugar in 140 ml (¼ pt)
water over a low heat. Bring to the boil
and cook until syrupy. Whisk the egg
whites until stiff, then pour the hot
sugar syrup over, whisking continuously. Continue whisking until the
mixture is very thick and meringue-
like. Cool. Lightly whip the cream and
fold into the meringue with the fruit
purée. Freeze until slushy, then whisk
thoroughly, and return to the freezer.

Thirty minutes before serving the
ice-cream, transfer it to the fridge to
soften enough for serving.

You could also add 3 or 4 freshly
picked elderflower heads to the boiling
syrup to give an even more interesting
flavour. Strain before use.

SHREWSBURY BISCUITS

MAKES 18 TO 20

*These lightly spiced, melt-in-the-mouth
biscuits are ideal to serve at any
time of day.*

50 g (2 oz) butter
50 g (2 oz) sugar
1 egg, size 3
50 g (2 oz) currants
175 g (6 oz) plain flour
½ teaspoon mixed spice
Caster sugar, to decorate

Set the oven at Gas Mark 5, 375°F,
190°C. Grease 2 large baking sheets.

Cream the butter and sugar until
pale and fluffy. Add the egg and beat in
well. Fold in the currants, flour and
mixed spice and knead lightly into a
smooth ball.

Roll out on a floured surface to
about 5 mm (¼ in) thickness. Cut into
rounds with a 6 cm (2½ in) fluted cutter
and put on the baking trays. Bake in the
oven for 15 minutes – after 5 minutes
take out and sprinkle with caster sugar,
then continue to cook until firm and
very light brown in colour.

TO FREEZE: open-freeze until firm in a
rigid plastic container.

TO USE FROM FROZEN: thaw on a
wire rack uncovered for 2 to 3 hours.

FRUIT AND CIDER CAKE

MAKES ONE 20.5 CM (8 IN) ROUND CAKE

You can really taste the cider in this moist, easy-to-make cake.

110 g (4 oz) seedless raisins
110 g (4 oz) sultanas
110 g (4 oz) dried dates, roughly chopped
110 g (4 oz) ready-to-eat prunes,
roughly chopped
280 ml (½ pt) sweet cider
455 g (1 lb) self-raising flour
1 teaspoon ground mixed spice

230 g (8 oz) unsalted butter
170 g (6 oz) soft, light brown sugar
110 g (4 oz) walnuts, roughly chopped
4 eggs, size 3, lightly beaten
A 20.5 cm (8 in) round cake tin,
greased and base-lined. Wrap a sheet
of brown paper around the outside of
the tin and tie securely with string.

Place all the dried fruit in a large bowl, then pour over the cider so that all the fruit is completely submerged, and cover with cling film. Leave to soak overnight, stirring occasionally.

The next day, set the oven at Gas Mark 4, 350°F, 180°C.

Sift the flour and mixed spice into a bowl. Rub in the butter until the mixture resembles fine breadcrumbs. Stir in the sugar, walnuts and the beaten egg. Finally, beat in the soaked fruit and cider mixture. Spoon the mixture into the prepared tin and level the surface, making a slight hollow in the centre. Cover the top with a sheet of brown paper and bake for 1 hour 50 minutes, or until a skewer inserted into the cake comes out clean. Cool the cake in the tin for 30 minutes, and then transfer to a wire rack to cool completely.

Wrap in clean greaseproof paper and foil, and store the cake for several days before cutting. The wrapped cake will keep for 2 to 3 weeks.

TO FREEZE: wrap in greaseproof paper and foil, and freeze for up to 3 months.
TO USE FROM FROZEN: thaw at room temperature for 5 to 6 hours.

COUNTRY APPLE CAKE

MAKES ONE 20.5 CM (8 IN)
SQUARE CAKE

680 g (1½ lb) crisp green apples, peeled,
cored and roughly chopped
230 g (8 oz) caster sugar
1½ teaspoons ground cinnamon
1 teaspoon freshly grated nutmeg
395 g (14 oz) self-raising wholemeal flour
1 tablespoon baking powder
230 g (8 oz) unsalted butter, melted
and cooled
4 eggs, size 3, beaten
140 ml (¼ pt) sweet cider
For the topping:
60 g (2 oz) unsalted butter
85 g (3 oz) soft light brown sugar
A 20.5 cm (8 in) deep, square tin,
greased and base-lined

Set the oven at Gas Mark 4, 350°F, 180°C. Mix the apples with 30 g (1 oz) caster sugar and ½ teaspoon each of cinnamon and nutmeg. Sift the flour and baking powder into a bowl, returning any bran left in the sieve. Stir in the remaining caster sugar. Make a hollow in the centre and gradually pour in the melted butter, eggs and cider. Beat well to make a smooth, thick batter.

Spread one third of the batter into the base of the prepared tin. Spoon over half of the apple mixture, pressing the apple chunks into the cake batter. Add half the remaining batter, then the rest of the apples. Finally top with the remaining batter, levelling the surface.

To make the topping, beat the butter with the sugar until pale and light. Add the remaining nutmeg and cinnamon. Spread the mixture over the batter. Bake for 1 hour 45 minutes, or until a skewer inserted into the cake comes out clean. If the top begins to brown before the cake is cooked, cover with a sheet of greaseproof paper. Cool in the tin before turning out. Wrap in clean greaseproof paper and foil and store for several days before cutting. The wrapped cake will keep 2 to 3 weeks.

TO FREEZE: as described above left for Fruit and Cider Cake.
TO USE FROM FROZEN: thaw at room temperature for 5 to 6 hours.

ICED BERRY MOUSSE

SERVES 6 TO 8

*Use any selection of red berries to make
this colourful dessert.*

For the mousse:
230 g (8 oz) mixed red berries, such as
raspberries, redcurrants and loganberries
85 g (3 oz) icing sugar, sifted
The juice of 1 lemon
1¼ teaspoons powdered gelatine
140 ml (¼ pt) double cream
1 egg white, size 3
Two 12.5 cm by 5 cm (5 by 2 in) deep
ring moulds, lightly oiled
For the spun sugar:
110 g (4 oz) caster sugar
To decorate:
110 g (4 oz) raspberries
Mint leaves

To make the mousse, purée the berries in
a liquidiser or food processor, then sieve
and mix in 30 g (1 oz) of the icing sugar.

Place the lemon juice in a small,
heatproof bowl, then sprinkle over the
gelatine and leave to sponge for
5 minutes. Meanwhile, whip the cream
until floppy.

Dissolve the gelatine. Whisk the egg
white until stiff but not dry. Gradually
whisk in the remaining icing sugar.
Continue whisking until stiff and
glossy. Stir the dissolved gelatine into
the fruit purée and mix well. Fold the
cream into the fruit mixture, followed
by the meringue. Pour into the moulds
and freeze for 2 to 4 hours or until set.

Remove from freezer and unmould
on to plates. Return to the freezer until
needed. To use from frozen, transfer to
the fridge for 30 minutes before serving.

To make the spun sugar, place the
sugar and 2 tablespoons of cold water in
a heavy-based pan. Slowly dissolve the
sugar without stirring, then turn up the
heat and boil until it just begins to turn
golden around the edges. Remove from
the heat and, working quickly with a
fork, draw the sugar from the pan on to
an oiled rolling pin. Form into a ball and
use to decorate the mousse.

Decorate with the raspberries and
mint leaves, and top with the spun sugar
just before serving.

GOOSEBERRY CHUTNEY

MAKES ABOUT 1.7KG (3¾ LB) OR
1.45 LITRES (2½ PTS)

*Use one green chilli for a mild flavour, or
two for more 'heat'.*

1.35 kg (3 lb) fresh or frozen gooseberries,
topped and tailed, washed and dried
230 g (8 oz) onions, finely chopped
230 g (8 oz) sultanas
1 tablespoon salt
2 teaspoons ground mixed spice
2 teaspoons chopped fresh root ginger
1 to 2 fresh green chillies, or to taste,
deseeded and chopped
340 g (12 oz) golden granulated sugar
570 ml (1 pt) white wine vinegar
Sterilised jars and covers

Place the gooseberries in a preserving
pan with the onions and 570 ml (1 pt)
water. Bring slowly to the boil, reduce
the heat and simmer, uncovered, for 30
to 40 minutes until the fruit and onions
are soft, stirring occasionally. Add all
the remaining ingredients and mix
well. Cook, stirring gently over a low
heat, until the sugar dissolves. Simmer,
stirring occasionally, for a further 1 to
1½ hours, until the chutney is thick. Pot,
seal and label.

HOT CIDER PUNCH

SERVES 20

Not for the faint-hearted!

8 whole allspice
4 cinnamon sticks
12 cloves
2.3 litres (4 pts) dry cider
280 ml (½ pt) white rum
140 ml (¼ pt) orange juice
2 tablespoons honey or to taste

Crush the allspice, 2 cinnamon sticks
and the cloves, and wrap in a muslin
bag. Pour the cider, rum, orange juice
and honey into a large, heavy-based
pan and heat through until hot, but do
not boil. Warm a large serving bowl,
break the remaining cinnamon sticks
and place in the bowl, and pour over the
hot cider. Serve immediately.

CHAPTER THREE

London
and the South East

E ver since Roman times London, with its deep-water port, access to the sea and proximity to the Continent, has been the country's pre-eminent trading post. It may have been a very long time since anything was actually grown or reared within the city limits, but markets like Billingsgate, Smithfield, Spitalfields and Covent Garden have ensured that Londoners who lived miles from the nearest plough, cow, fishing net or orchard were and are able to eat the freshest and finest food Britain has to offer.

Herds of dairy cattle pepper the landscapes of Hampshire, Berkshire, Sussex and the Isle of Wight, where the lush pasture gives rich fodder. The Suffolk Sheep, a hornless creature with bare, black face and a long body, dominates the fields of the South East. There are plenty of pig farms throughout the region. And poultry – whether the capons and chickens reared in Surrey for the royal table at Hampton Court or the large, white, plump Aylesbury duck which originally came from Buckinghamshire – is important too.

The warm, moist climate and rich soil make the Kent Weald exceptionally fertile. Fruit and vegetables have thrived here in the Garden of England since the 16th Century. This is 'Darling Buds Of May' country, and apples, pears and plums together with strawberries, raspberries, gooseberries, black and redcurrants, all grow in abundance.

Potted Shrimps
Harvest Soup with Watercress
and Peas
Spinach, Watercress and
Bacon Salad
– ✳ –
Bacon and Spinach Flan
– ✳ –
Chicken Breasts with Raisins
Elizabethan Lamb and
Beef Casserole
Beef Casserole with Red Wine
Pheasant with Chestnuts and
Mushrooms
Potted Beef
Beef Hotpot and Spiced
Dumplings
Duck and Olive Casserole
Honeyed Lamb
– ✳ –
Cabbage with Caraway
Steamed Cauliflower
and Broccoli
– ✳ –
Fresh Fruit Terrine
Fresh Berry Trifle
Summer Pudding
Summer Fruit Meringue Basket
Classic Strawberry Ice-cream
Orange Boodle
Sussex Pond Pudding
Victoria Plum Lattice Tart
Pears in Puff Pastry with
Caramel Sauce
– ✳ –
Chelsea Buns
Kentish Huffkins
– ✳ –
Cherry Jam
Traditional Marmalade

ABOVE *Potted Shrimps served with hot toast and garnished with lemon.*
PREVIOUS PAGE LEFT *Strawberries and cream are almost synonymous with Wimbledon. These strawberries and other summer berries grow very well in the rich soils of the South East.*
PREVIOUS PAGE RIGHT *More fresh ripe berries, this time in a Summer Fruit Meringue Basket.*

POTTED SHRIMPS

SERVES 6

Shellfish are plentiful round the south coast. Serve this dish as a light lunch or simple starter.

340 g (12 oz) peeled shrimps or prawns
170 g (6 oz) unsalted butter
1 teaspoon cayenne pepper
Salt and pepper
6 small pots or ramekins

To clarify the butter, melt, then bring it to the boil. Simmer for 2 minutes, skim and pour through muslin or a coffee filter paper to remove the sediment. Wash the shrimps, then put them in a bowl with half the butter. Stir in the mace, cayenne pepper and seasoning. Mix well. Spoon into 6 small pots or ramekins, pressing the shrimps down firmly. Pour over the remaining clarified butter. Cool. Chill overnight. Serve with hot toast and salad.

HARVEST SOUP WITH WATERCRESS AND PEAS

SERVES 4

Serve hot or cold with wholemeal bread.

2 rashers of rindless smoked bacon, chopped
1 onion, chopped
340 g (12 oz) frozen or fresh peas
(no need to thaw frozen peas)
A bunch of watercress
570 ml (1 pt) good-quality chicken stock
Salt and freshly ground black pepper

Place the bacon and onion in a heavy-based pan and dry fry for 2 to 3 minutes. Add the peas, watercress and chicken stock. Bring the mixture to the boil, reduce the heat and stir. Simmer for 8 to 10 minutes. Pour the mixture into a liquidiser or food processor and process until smooth. Season to taste and serve.
TO FREEZE: freeze in a rigid plastic container for up to 1 month.
TO USE FROM FROZEN: thaw in the refrigerator before reheating. Add extra liquid if necessary.

SPINACH, WATERCRESS AND BACON SALAD

SERVES 10 TO 12

Fry the croûtons in advance and store in an airtight container. The salad leaves and dressing can be prepared the day before and stored in the fridge.

6 slices white bread
6 tablespoons olive oil
230 g (8 oz) streaky bacon, cubed
455 g (1 lb) young spinach,
washed and chopped
1 large bunch watercress,
washed and trimmed
1 large bunch flat-leaf parsley,
washed and trimmed
For the dressing:
6 tablespoons olive oil
2 tablespoons sherry vinegar
1 tablespoon lemon juice
Salt and freshly ground black pepper

Remove the crusts from the bread and cut into small cubes. Heat the oil in a frying pan and fry the croûtons until golden. Drain on absorbent kitchen paper. Cook the cubed bacon in a non-stick saucepan until very crisp, then drain on absorbent kitchen paper and leave to cool.

Mix the spinach, watercress and flat-leaf parsley in a salad bowl, and scatter the croûtons and bacon on top.

To make the dressing, place all the ingredients in a screw-topped jar and shake vigorously until well emulsified. Pour the dressing over the salad just before serving.

BACON AND SPINACH FLAN

SERVES 6

This recipe works best with fresh, tender young spinach, as it needs little preparation and cooking.

For the pastry:
170 g (6 oz) plain flour
A pinch of salt
1 teaspoon finely grated nutmeg
85 g (3 oz) unsalted butter
For the filling:
230 g (8 oz) smoked back bacon,
roughly chopped
110 g (4 oz) onions, finely chopped
40 g (1½ oz) leaf spinach, shredded
3 eggs, size 3, beaten
140 ml (¼ pt) double cream
Salt and freshly ground black pepper
A 23 cm (9 in) round, loose-based,
fluted tin

Set the oven at Gas Mark 6, 300°F, 200°C. Place a baking tray in the oven to heat.

To make the pastry, sift the flour, salt and nutmeg into a bowl. Rub in the butter until the mixture resembles fine breadcrumbs. Mix in enough cold water to make a soft but not sticky dough. Wrap and chill for 10 minutes.

To make the filling, place the bacon and onion in a heavy-based frying pan and cook for 5 to 7 minutes so the onion is softened but not coloured.

Roll out the pastry on a lightly floured surface and use to line the flan tin. Lightly prick the pastry case and chill for a further 10 minutes.

Line the pastry with greaseproof paper and fill with baking beans. Stand the tin on the hot baking tray and bake 'blind' for 10 minutes. Remove the baking beans and greaseproof paper and bake for a further 5 minutes.

Arrange the spinach in the base of the pastry case and top with the bacon and onion mixture. Whisk together the eggs, cream and seasoning and pour over the top. Bake in the oven for 25 to 30 minutes until puffed and golden. Serve hot or cold.

CHICKEN BREASTS WITH RAISINS

SERVES 6

An excellent, simple-to-prepare casserole that is ideal to serve at a buffet party.

6 chicken breasts or joints, skinned
60 g (2 oz) seasoned flour
30 g (1 oz) unsalted butter
1 tablespoon olive oil
1 large onion, finely chopped
1 clove garlic, crushed
570 ml (1 pt) good-quality chicken stock
The juice of 1 lemon
½ teaspoon ground cumin
Salt and freshly ground black pepper
110 g (4 oz) raisins
140 ml (¼ pt) double cream
60 g (2 oz) flaked almonds, toasted

Set the oven at Gas Mark 6, 400°F, 200°C. Toss the chicken portions in the seasoned flour. Gently melt the butter in a large, heavy-based pan, add the olive oil and fry the onion and garlic until softened but not coloured.

Add the chicken to the pan and seal on both sides. Continue to cook until the chicken has turned golden brown. Remove the chicken from the pan and place in a flameproof casserole dish.

Deglaze the pan with the stock, lemon juice, cumin and seasoning. Pour this mixture over the chicken and add the raisins. Cover with a tight-fitting lid and cook for 45 minutes or until the chicken is cooked all the way through and the juices run clear when a skewer is inserted into the thickest part. Stir in the cream and heat gently to ensure that the sauce does not boil.

Garnish with the toasted flaked almonds and serve with a selection of steamed vegetables.

ELIZABETHAN LAMB AND BEEF CASSEROLE

SERVES 6

The addition of fresh and dried fruit gives this delicately spiced casserole a delicious sweet and sour flavour – a tradition that goes back to Elizabethan and medieval times.

4 tablespoons sunflower oil
455 g (1 lb) lean lamb, cut into
5 cm (2 in) cubes
455 g (1 lb) lean beef, cut into
5 cm (2 in) cubes
30 g (1 oz) seasoned flour
2 medium onions, finely chopped
2 cloves garlic, crushed
The grated rind and juice of 1 orange
The grated rind of 1 lemon
230 g (8 oz) no-need-to-soak apricots

110 g (4 oz) seedless raisins
60 g (2 oz) no-need-to-soak prunes
110 g (4 oz) Cox's, or other crisp dessert
apple, peeled and sliced
60 g (2 oz) walnut halves
1 cinnamon stick
½ teaspoon ground ginger
½ teaspoon ground mace
Salt and freshly ground black pepper
1 teaspoon dried marjoram
430 ml (¾ pt) red wine

Heat the oil, a little at a time, in a large, heavy-based pan or flameproof casserole. Toss the cubed lamb and beef in the seasoned flour (reserve the unused flour) and quickly brown and seal in the hot oil in batches. Remove the meat from the pan.

Add the onions and garlic to the pan and cook gently until softened but not coloured, stirring occasionally. Stir in any remaining seasoned flour. Return the meat to the casserole with the remaining ingredients and stir well. Bring to the boil, then cover and simmer gently for 2 to 2½ hours or until the meat is very tender. Adjust the seasoning as necessary.

This casserole will improve if it is either frozen (see freezing instructions below) or left in the fridge for 1 or 2 days before serving.

*TO FREEZE CASSEROLES: (unless stated otherwise in the recipe), cool quickly, then pack into a rigid plastic container – make sure that the meat is covered by liquid, otherwise it will dry out – or use an oven-to-freezer casserole dish. Freeze for up to 2 months.

TO USE FROM FROZEN: thaw overnight in the fridge. Stir in about 140 ml (¼ pt) of water then reheat in an ovenproof dish at Gas Mark 4, 350°F, 180°C, for about 1 hour or until the casserole has boiled through thoroughly.

BEEF CASSEROLE WITH RED WINE

SERVES 6

This delicious main course is impressive enough to serve for a winter dinner party.

170 g (6 oz) unsmoked rindless
streaky bacon
3 tablespoons sunflower oil
0.9 kg (2 lb) top rump of beef,
cut into 5 cm (2 in) cubes
30 g (1 oz) flour
430 ml (¾ pt) red wine
280 ml (½ pt) beef stock
1 bay leaf
1 teaspoon dried mixed herbs
2 tablespoons freshly chopped parsley
Salt and freshly ground black pepper
18 baby onions, peeled
170 g (6 oz) mushrooms, sliced
Sprigs of fresh parsley, to garnish

Set the oven at Gas Mark 2, 300°F, 150°C. Place the bacon in a non-stick frying pan and cook until crisp. Heat the oil in a large, heavy-based, flameproof casserole. Toss the cubes of beef in the flour and cook in batches in the oil until brown all over.

Return the beef to the casserole with the red wine and beef stock, and bring to the boil stirring continuously. Add the cooked bacon to the casserole and stir it in thoroughly. Season, by adding the bay leaf, mixed herbs, chopped parsley, salt and freshly ground black pepper. Cover with a tight-fitting lid and cook in the oven for about 1½ hours.

Add the peeled baby onions and continue cooking for 45 minutes. Finally, add the sliced mushrooms and cook for a further 15 minutes. Before serving, skim off any excess fat and garnish with fresh parsley.

TO FREEZE, see left*.

LEFT *Elizabethan Lamb and Beef Casserole.*
OPPOSITE *Duck and Olive Casserole, Pheasant with Chestnuts and Mushrooms, Beef Casserole, Beef Hotpot and Spiced Dumplings.*

PHEASANT WITH CHESTNUTS AND MUSHROOMS

SERVES 8

Braising is one of the best ways to cook pheasant, as it keeps the flesh succulent and moist.

2 pheasants, about 1.1 kg (2½ lb) each,
jointed into 2 breasts and 2 leg portions
30 g (1 oz) flour
4 tablespoons sunflower oil
1 large onion, chopped
2 cloves garlic, crushed
2 sticks celery, washed and sliced
570 ml (1 pt) good-quality
chicken stock

The grated rind and juice of 2 oranges
2 tablespoons freshly chopped thyme
1 tablespoon cornflour
2 tablespoons port
Salt and freshly ground black pepper
230 g (8 oz) roasted and peeled chestnuts
170 g (6 oz) chestnut mushrooms,
thickly sliced
Sprigs of thyme, to garnish

Set the oven at Gas Mark 3, 325°F, 170°C. Toss the pheasant portions in the flour to cover. Heat 3 tablespoons of the oil in a large, heavy-based, flameproof casserole. Brown the pheasant on all sides, then remove and reserve.

Add the remaining oil to the casserole and cook the onion, garlic and celery until softened, but not coloured. Return the pheasant to the casserole with the stock, orange rind, juice and thyme. Bring to the boil, cover and cook in the oven for about 1½ hours or until the meat is tender.

Remove the pheasant portions from the casserole and keep warm.

Mix the cornflour with the port and add to the casserole. Bring to the boil, then simmer until thickened, stirring continuously. Season to taste, stir in the chestnuts and mushrooms and return to the boil. Add the pheasant portions and return to the oven for 20 minutes. Serve with creamy mashed potatoes.

POTTED BEEF

SERVES 4

This is a traditional way of using meat left over from the Sunday roast.

230 g (8 oz) cooked lean beef
(use roast beef or cold salt beef)
110 g (4 oz) rindless bacon rashers, diced
70 g (2½ oz) unsalted butter, melted
2 teaspoons Worcestershire sauce
Salt, pepper, nutmeg and mace, to taste
To complete:
60 g (2 oz) unsalted butter
A medium-sized earthenware dish or
4 individual ramekins

Roughly chop up the beef. Fry or grill the bacon until crispy. Finely mince or process the beef with the bacon. Beat in the melted butter, the Worcestershire sauce and seasonings to taste. Pack the mixture into the earthenware dish or the individual ramekins and smooth over the surface.

To complete, melt the remaining butter and pour on top of the beef. Chill overnight or for up to 4 days. Serve with hot toast.

51

BEEF HOTPOT AND SPICED DUMPLINGS

SERVES 6

Beef and root vegetables are cooked slowly in a rich stock – then topped with fluffy spiced dumplings. A real winter warmer!

2 to 3 tablespoons sunflower oil
0.9 kg (2 lb) stewing steak, cubed
8 baby onions, halved
1 tablespoon seasoned flour
230 g (8 oz) potatoes, peeled and cubed
230 g (8 oz) parsnips, peeled and chopped
230 g (8 oz) carrots, peeled and chopped
A 425 g (15 oz) can consommé

280 ml (½ pt) good quality beef stock
A bouquet garni
For the dumplings:
140 g (5 oz) plain flour
70 g (2½ oz) beef suet
1 tablespoon dried parsley
1 teaspoon dry mustard powder
Salt and freshly ground black pepper

Set the oven at Gas Mark 3, 325°F, 170°C. Heat the oil in a heavy-based flameproof casserole dish on top of the stove. Toss the cubed steak in the seasoned flour (reserve any unused flour). Quickly seal the meat in the hot oil, in batches. Remove from the pan. Add the baby onions to the oil and fry for 5 minutes until softened but not coloured.

Add the other vegetables and cook for a further 5 minutes (check whether you need more oil). Add any of the unused seasoned flour and continue cooking for about 2 minutes, stirring frequently.

Return the meat to the casserole with the consommé, stock and bouquet garni. Bring to the boil, then cover and cook in the oven for 1½ hours or until the meat is really tender.

To make the dumplings, mix all the ingredients in a bowl and add enough cold water (about 6 tablespoons) to make a soft but not sticky dough. Roll into walnut-sized balls. The dumplings may be made up to 1 hour in advance, or frozen if required.

Season the casserole to taste, add the spiced dumplings and return to the oven for a further 10 to 15 minutes or until the dumplings are cooked.

TO FREEZE THE DUMPLINGS: freeze uncooked for up to 1 month.
TO FREEZE THE STEW: quickly cool and place in a rigid plastic container. It may be kept in the freezer for up to 1 month.
TO USE FROM FROZEN: thaw the casserole and dumplings in the fridge overnight. Reheat at Gas Mark 5, 375°F, 190°C for 45 minutes to 1 hour or until piping hot all the way through, adding 140 ml (¼ pt) stock or water if necessary. Add the dumplings and return to the oven for a further 15 minutes.

DUCK AND OLIVE CASSEROLE

SERVES 6

If you prefer a thin gravy, add only 30 g (1 oz) flour to the pan.

6 duck portions
30 to 60 g (1 to 2 oz) flour
1 large onion, sliced
1 clove garlic, or to taste, crushed
60 g (2 oz) unsmoked rindless back bacon, diced
3 sticks celery, washed and sliced
140 g (5 oz) good-quality green olives, pitted
310 ml (11 fl oz) white wine
310 ml (11 fl oz) good-quality duck or chicken stock
2 bay leaves
1 tablespoon fresh marjoram leaves
Salt and freshly ground black pepper
Marjoram leaves, to garnish

Set the oven at Gas Mark 4, 350°F, 180°C. Remove the skin and fat from the duck, reserving the fat. Toss the duck portions in the flour. Heat the reserved fat in a heavy-based, flameproof casserole and cook the onion, garlic and diced bacon until golden brown. Using a slotted spoon, remove from the fat and reserve. Drain off all but 2 tablespoons of the fat.

Fry the duck portions in the fat until golden brown on all sides, and add any remaining flour, if wished. Return the onion and garlic mixture to the casserole with the celery. Add the olives, wine, stock, bay leaves, marjoram leaves, salt and freshly ground black pepper, then bring to the boil, stirring constantly. Cover tightly and cook in the oven for 1 hour or until the duck is tender.

Garnish with the marjoram leaves and serve with boiled potatoes and green vegetables.

TO FREEZE: see page 50*.

HONEYED LAMB

SERVES 12

Ask your butcher to tunnel-bone the leg of lamb for you. The leg is then stuffed and tied as a boneless roast to make carving easier.

A 2.3 kg (5 lb) leg of lamb, tunnel boned
Salt and freshly ground black pepper
For the stuffing:
1 to 2 tablespoons olive oil
1 onion, chopped
2 cloves garlic, crushed
A 2.5 cm (1 in) piece of root ginger, peeled
and chopped
110 g (4 oz) fresh white breadcrumbs

1 tablespoon freshly chopped rosemary
2 tablespoons freshly chopped parsley
1 egg, size 3
2 tablespoons red wine
To complete:
2 sprigs fresh rosemary
4 cloves garlic
170 g (6 oz) thick honey, melted
Lamb's lettuce, to garnish

Set the oven at Gas Mark 6, 400°F, 200°C. Rub the lamb all over with salt and freshly ground black pepper.

Heat the oil and fry the onion and garlic until softened but not coloured. Remove the pan from the heat, stir in the remaining ingredients for the stuffing and season well. Stuff the lamb and tie securely with string at regular intervals.

To complete, place the rosemary and garlic in the roasting tin, then add the lamb. Coat the lamb with the melted honey and pour 140 ml (¼ pt) of cold water around the joint. Roast for 30 minutes, basting frequently, then reduce the heat to Gas Mark 3, 325°F, 170°C, and, basting occasionally, cook for a further 1½ to 1¾ hours – depending on how well you like your meat cooked and the size of the joint. Remove the meat from the roasting tin and leave to cool. Chill overnight.

About 1 to 2 hours before serving, slice the lamb, arrange on a serving platter and chill until required. Garnish with a little Lamb's lettuce just before serving.

CABBAGE WITH CARAWAY

SERVES 6

Caraway seeds add a wonderful flavour to this great English vegetable.

0.9 kg (2 lb) Savoy cabbage
2 tablespoons oil
40 g (1½ oz) butter
1 clove garlic, crushed
1 tablespoon caraway seeds
Salt and pepper

Shred the cabbage. Heat the oil and the butter in a large pan, add the garlic and cook for 1 minute. Add the cabbage and cook gently, covered, for 15 minutes, stirring occasionally. Stir in the caraway seeds and cook for 5 minutes. Season to taste, and serve immediately.

STEAMED CAULIFLOWER AND BROCCOLI

SERVES 8

Quick and simple to cook, cauliflower and broccoli make an ideal accompaniment to any roast meat dish.

0.9 kg (2 lb) cauliflower florets
0.9 kg (2 lb) broccoli florets
Salt and freshly ground black pepper

Steam the cauliflower and broccoli together in a steamer set over a pan of simmering water for 5 to 10 minutes. Season well, and serve immediately.

FRESH FRUIT TERRINE

SERVES 6 TO 8

Ideal for summer entertaining.

680 g (1½ lb) mixed summer berries, such
as raspberries, strawberries, tayberries,
wild strawberries, blueberries and
blackcurrants
850 ml (1½ pt) cranberry juice
Three 11 g (0.4 oz) sachets gelatine
60 g (2 oz) caster sugar
115 ml (4 fl oz) crème de cassis
2 tablespoons ruby port
Fresh strawberries and mint, to decorate
A 1.15 litre (2 pt) terrine, oiled
and lined with greaseproof paper,
or a jelly mould, oiled

Rinse and hull the fruit as necessary.
Quarter the strawberries, but leave the
other berries whole. Arrange the fruit
carefully and attractively in the terrine
or mould.

Pour 140 ml (¼ pt) of the cranberry
juice into a small heatproof bowl,
sprinkle the gelatine over and leave it to
sponge for 5 minutes. Meanwhile, gently heat the remaining cranberry juice
with the sugar until dissolved. Cool,
and stir in the crème de cassis and port.

Dissolve the gelatine by standing
the bowl in a saucepan of hot water, and
then strain it into the crème de cassis
mixture. Chill the mixture until it starts
to thicken, then gently pour over the
fruit. Chill for 4 hours or until set – or
chill overnight if possible.

To serve, turn the terrine out on to a
chilled serving plate, and decorate with
strawberries and mint. Serve with
Greek yogurt or fromage frais.

PREVIOUS PAGE *Fresh Berry Trifle,
Fresh Fruit Terrine and a bowl of luscious
fresh berries.*
TOP RIGHT *Summer Pudding.*
OPPOSITE *Summer Fruit Meringue
Basket – a spectacular finalé to a summer
lunch or dinner party.*

FRESH BERRY TRIFLE

SERVES 10

An ever-popular classic.

For the cake base:
85 g (3 oz) plain flour, sifted
30 g (1 oz) ground almonds
3 eggs, size 3, beaten
85 g (3 oz) caster sugar
4 tablespoons extra-fruit, reduced-sugar,
raspberry jam
3 to 4 tablespoons Kirsch
For the syllabub:
850 ml (1½ pt) double cream

85 ml (3 fl oz) Kirsch
140 g (5 oz) icing sugar
The grated rind of 1 lemon
For the topping:
425 g (15 oz) blackberries, raspberries
and loganberries
1 tablespoon caster sugar, or to taste
(optional)
A 20.5 by 30.5 cm (8 by 12 in) Swiss roll
tin, greased and lined with greaseproof

Set the oven at Gas Mark 6, 400°F, 200°C. To make the cake base, mix the flour and
almonds together in a bowl. Whisk the eggs and sugar together in a large, heatproof
bowl set over a pan of gently simmering water until very pale and thick enough to
leave a ribbon-like trail for 8 seconds when the whisk is lifted. Remove the bowl
from the pan of water and continue whisking until the bowl is cool.

Carefully fold the flour mixture into the egg mixture using a large metal spoon.
Spoon into the prepared tin, level the surface and bake for 10 to 12 minutes until pale
and golden. Cut a piece of greaseproof paper just a little longer than the Swiss roll
tin and sprinkle with caster sugar. Turn out the sponge on to the greaseproof paper
and trim the edges. Roll the Swiss roll up from the short edge and leave to cool.

Meanwhile, gently warm the jam. Unroll the sponge, discard the greaseproof
paper, spread with the warmed jam and re-roll. Cut the Swiss roll into thick slices
and arrange in the base of an attractive glass serving bowl. Sprinkle over the Kirsch.

To make the syllabub, place the cream in a chilled bowl with the Kirsch, icing
sugar and lemon rind, and whisk well until the mixture is light and thick. Carefully
spoon over the sponge. Cover and chill for 2 hours.

To make the topping, carefully mix together the fruit and sugar (if using) and
spoon on top of the syllabub. Serve within the hour.

The Swiss roll should be made 2 to 3 days before making the trifle to allow the
sponge to become firmer. Store, filled with the jam and covered with cling film, in
an airtight container for up to 3 days. Alternatively, place the Swiss roll in a plastic
bag and freeze for up to 1 month.

SUMMER PUDDING

Try this version of a renowned and delicious British summer dessert.

230 g (8 oz) strawberries, hulled and
halved
230 g (8 oz) raspberries
110 g (4 oz) redcurrants, strung
110 g (4 oz) blackcurrants, strung
110 g (4 oz) red cherries, washed, stoned
and halved

110 g (4 oz) caster sugar
About 12 slices of fresh, thinly sliced,
white bread
A selection of fresh summer berries,
to decorate
A 1.45 litre (2½ pt) pudding basin

Place the fruit in a heavy-based, non-aluminium saucepan with the sugar and 60 ml
(2 fl oz) of cold water. Cook over a gentle heat for 5 to 6 minutes, stirring occasionally, or until the sugar has dissolved and the juices from the fruit begin to run. Strain
well and reserve the juice. Leave to cool.

Reserve 3 or 4 slices of bread. Remove the crusts from the remaining slices, then
cut in half lengthways. Using one of the whole slices, dip the bread into the reserved
juice and place it, juice side down, in the bottom of the pudding basin.

Dip the halves of bread into the juice and use to line the sides of the basin, over-
lapping them slightly so there are no gaps. Spoon the fruit into the basin. Cover the
top with the remaining whole slices of bread, ensuring that there are no gaps, and
cutting the bread to shape if necessary.

Cover with cling film, and top with a plate that fits just inside the rim of the
basin. Put a weight on top of the plate, and chill for at least 8 hours, or overnight.

To serve, remove the weight, plate and cling film, and gently ease the sides of the
pudding away from the edges of the basin with a palette knife. Turn the pudding out
on to a chilled serving plate, decorate with a selection of summer berries and serve
with lightly whipped cream.

TO FREEZE: place in a plastic bag. Seal and freeze for up to 1 month.

TO USE FROM FROZEN: remove from the plastic bag and thaw for 3 hours before
turning out.

SUMMER FRUIT MERINGUE BASKET

*Crisp, white meringue and succulent
summer fruits combine to make a delicious
dessert.*

5 egg whites, size 3
280 g (10 oz) caster sugar
For the filling:
140 g (5 oz) blackcurrants, strung
140 g (5 oz) redcurrants, strung
140 g (5 oz) raspberries
140 g (5 oz) blueberries
15 g (½ oz) caster sugar
2 tablespoons Kirsch
570 ml (1 pt) double cream,
well chilled
A baking tray lined with baking parchment
A large nylon piping bag fitted with
a star tube

Set the oven at Gas Mark ¼, 225°F,
110°C. Mark a circle measuring approx-
imately 22 cm (8¾ in) in diameter in the
centre of the baking parchment.

Whisk the egg whites until stiff but
not dry. Gradually whisk in the sugar
until the mixture is stiff and glossy.
Spoon the meringue into the piping bag
and pipe out the base of the basket on
the prepared baking tray to within
2.5 cm (1 in) of the edge of the circle
marked on the parchment. Use the
remaining meringue to pipe 6 S-shaped
scrolls around the edge to form a 'nest',
(see photograph on left).

Bake for 3½ to 4 hours until the
meringue is pale and crisp. Turn the
oven off and leave the meringue to cool.
When cold, remove from the oven and
carefully remove the baking parchment.

To make the filling, place the fruit in
a large bowl. Sprinkle with the caster
sugar and Kirsch and stir very gently.

Whip the cream in a chilled bowl
until thick. Spoon two-thirds into the
meringue basket and place half the fruit
mixture on top. Spoon the remaining
cream on top, then add the remaining
fruit. Serve within 3 hours.

The meringue can be made in
advance and then stored in an air-tight
container for up to 3 days.

CLASSIC STRAWBERRY ICE-CREAM

SERVES 8

Take advantage of a glut of strawberries to make this rich ice-cream to serve throughout the year.

**455 g (1 lb) strawberries, hulled
and chopped
170 g (6 oz) icing sugar, sifted
The juice of ½ lemon
570 ml (1 pt) double cream**

Place the strawberries in a liquidiser or food processor with the icing sugar and lemon juice. Purée until smooth, then push the pulp through a sieve to remove any pips.

Whip the cream until soft peaks form, then fold into the purée. Pour into a rigid container and freeze until slushy. Whisk well with an electric whisk, then freeze again until hard. Remove from the freezer 10 minutes before serving.

ORANGE BOODLE

SERVES 6

Rich cream makes this famous pudding.

**110 g (4 oz) sponge cake
The grated rind and juice of 2 oranges
The grated rind and juice of 1 large lemon
85 g (3 oz) caster sugar
280 ml (½ pt) double cream
Candied orange slices or fresh orange
segments, to decorate
6 long-stemmed glasses**

Cut the cake into 1 cm (½ in) strips and put into the glasses. Mix the grated rind and juice of the oranges and lemon with the caster sugar – you should have about 200 ml (7 fl oz) liquid. Whip the cream until thick then gradually beat in the juice, rind and sugar, keeping the mixture thick.

Pour into the glasses and chill for several hours, preferably overnight. Decorate with slices or segments of orange, and serve.

The sponge can be sprinkled with orange liqueur if wished.

SUSSEX POND PUDDING

SERVES 6

The 'pond' is the tangy, buttery sauce that oozes out of the pudding when first cut.

**395 g (14 oz) self-raising flour
A pinch of salt
200 g (7 oz) vegetarian shredded suet
The grated rind and juice of 1 lemon
140 g (5 oz) unsalted butter, cut into cubes
140 g (5 oz) soft, light brown sugar
1 lime, scrubbed
1 lemon, scrubbed
6 kumquats
Mint leaves, to decorate
A 1.45 litre (2½ pt) pudding basin, greased**

Sift the flour and salt into a bowl, then mix in the suet and lemon rind. Add cold water to the lemon juice to make 280 ml (½ pt). Add the liquid to the flour mixture, a little at a time, to form a soft but not sticky dough. Knead the dough lightly and roll out on to a lightly floured work surface to a circle about 6 mm (¼ in) thick. Trim one quarter of the pastry from the circle and reserve for the lid.

Line the greased pudding basin with the circle of pastry. Bring the edges together and dampen with cold water to seal. Place half the butter and half the sugar in the base of the pastry followed by the lime, lemon and kumquats. Pack the remaining butter and sugar around the fruit and over the top.

Roll out the reserved pastry on a lightly floured work surface and brush the edges with water. Place the pastry lid over the pudding and trim the edges. Cover the basin with greaseproof paper and foil that has been pleated to allow for expansion. Tie securely with string around the rim and across the top to form a handle.

Steam the pudding in a pan filled with boiling water to the depth of 4 cm (1½ in) for 3½ to 4 hours. Top up with boiling water from time to time so that the pan doesn't boil dry. Remove from the pan carefully and leave to stand for about 5 minutes.

Remove the greaseproof paper and foil, and carefully turn the pudding out on to a serving dish. Decorate with mint and serve with custard or clotted cream.

RIGHT *Sussex Pond Pudding.*

VICTORIA PLUM LATTICE TART

SERVES 8

For the pâte sucrée:
170 g (6 oz) plain flour
A pinch of salt
85 g (3 oz) unsalted butter, softened
85 g (3 oz) caster sugar
3 egg yolks, size 3
For the filling:
680 g (1½ lb) Victoria plums, halved and stoned
60 g (2 oz) golden caster sugar
30 g (1 oz) unsalted butter, melted
For the almond topping:
110 g (4 oz) unsalted butter
40 g (1½ oz) golden caster sugar
60 g (2 oz) plain flour
85 g (3 oz) ground almonds
1 egg, size 3, beaten
Icing sugar for dusting (optional)
A 23 cm (9 in) loose-based, fluted flan tin
A large piping bag fitted with a
6 mm (¼ in) plain No. 4 nozzle

To make the pâte sucrée, sift the flour with the salt on to a cool work surface. Make a large well in the centre, then add the butter, sugar and egg yolks. With the tips of your fingers work the ingredients in the well together until they resemble scrambled eggs. Still using your fingers, draw in the flour from all sides until it binds together. Using a pastry scraper or your hands, bring the pastry together to form a ball. Lightly knead until smooth. Wrap and chill for 20 to 30 minutes.

Roll out the pastry on a lightly floured work surface into a circle and use to line the flan tin. Prick the pastry case and chill for a further 15 minutes.

Set the oven at Gas Mark 5, 375°F, 190°C. Place a baking tray in the oven to heat.

Line the pastry with greaseproof paper, fill with baking beans and stand the flan tin on the hot baking tray. Bake 'blind' for 10 minutes, then remove the baking beans and greaseproof paper. Return to the oven for a further 5 minutes.

To make the filling, place the plums and sugar in a pan and cook gently for 5 minutes. Leave to cool slightly, then drain well using a slotted spoon. Arrange in the pastry case and drizzle over the melted butter.

To make the topping, cream the butter with the sugar until light and fluffy. Work in the flour, almonds and egg to form a stiff dough. Continue to work the dough with your hands until soft enough to pipe. Place in the piping bag and pipe over the plum filling to make a lattice top (see page 35). Bake in the oven for 25 to 30 minutes, until the plums are soft and the almond topping is golden brown. Dust with icing sugar, if liked and serve with lightly whipped cream or custard.

PEARS IN PUFF PASTRY WITH CARAMEL SAUCE

SERVES 6

For the filling:
30 g (1 oz) unsalted butter, softened
30 g (1 oz) soft, light brown sugar
60 g (2 oz) ground walnuts
1 egg yolk, size 3
The grated rind of 2 oranges
3 large Conference pears, peeled, halved, cored
and brushed with lemon juice
1 tablespoon lemon juice
455 g (1 lb) puff pastry, thawed if frozen
Beaten egg, to glaze
For the caramel sauce:
170 g (6 oz) sugar
140 ml (¼ pt) single cream

To make the filling, beat the butter, sugar, ground walnuts, egg yolk and orange rind together until smooth. Cover and chill until ready to use – up to 4 hours. Fill the hollow of each pear half with a teaspoon of the walnut mixture. Brush with a little lemon juice to prevent the pears from browning.

Divide the puff pastry into 6 portions and place 1 portion on a lightly floured work surface. Wrap and chill remaining 5 portions until ready to use. Cut off a third of the pastry and roll out into an oval about 1 cm (½ in) larger than the pear half, cutting a stalk shape at the top (see photograph on left).

Place a stuffed pear half, cut side down, on to the rolled-out pastry. Mould the edges of the pastry up around the sides of the pear. Brush with cold water. Roll out the remaining pastry. Cut out a leaf shape and cut the remaining pastry into thin strips. Lay the strips of pastry over the pear in a lattice. Secure the ends of the strips of pastry to the base, and moisten with a little cold water. Secure the pastry leaf as shown in opposite.

Carefully transfer to a baking tray and chill for at least 15 minutes, while making the rest of the puff pastry pears in the same way. Glaze with beaten egg and cook for 25 to 30 minutes or until golden and crisp.

To make the caramel sauce, melt the sugar slowly in 5 tablespoons of cold water in a heavy-based pan and heat until the mixture starts to bubble and turn brown. Standing well back, pour over another 4 tablespoons of water and stir in the cream. Leave the sauce to cool.

Serve the pastry pears hot with a little of the caramel sauce.

LEFT *Pears in Puff Pastry with Caramel Sauce.*

CHELSEA BUNS

MAKES 9 BUNS

A London delicacy sold from the old
Chelsea Bun Shop in Pimlico which sadly no longer exists.

230 g (8 oz) strong white bread flour
½ teaspoon caster sugar
½ sachet of easy-blend yeast
150 ml (¼ pt) milk, warmed to blood heat
½ teaspoon salt
1 egg yolk, size 3, beaten
30 g (1 oz) butter, melted

85 g (3 oz) currants
30 g (1 oz) chopped mixed peel
60 g (2 oz) soft, light
brown sugar
1 tablespoon clear honey, to glaze
Caster sugar for sprinkling
An 18 cm (7 in) square cake tin, greased

Gently warm the flour and a mixing bowl. Mix 60 g (2 oz) of the flour with the sugar and yeast. Stir in the milk to form a smooth batter. Leave in a warm place for about 30 minutes until frothy.

Mix the remaining flour with the salt. Rub in the butter with your fingertips until the mixture resembles fine breadcrumbs. Stir in the egg and the yeast mixture, using a round-bladed knife. Mix to a soft dough. Turn out onto a floured work surface and knead thoroughly for 10 minutes until very smooth and elastic. Put the dough into an oiled bowl. Turn the dough over, cover with oiled cling film, then leave in a warm place until doubled in size – about 45 minutes to 1 hour.

Knock down the proved dough, then turn out on to a floured work surface and roll to a 30.5 by 23 cm (12 by 9 in) rectangle. Brush the dough with the melted butter, then mix the currants, peel and brown sugar together and sprinkle over the surface, leaving a clear 1.5 cm (½ in) border of dough all round.

Roll up the dough like a Swiss roll, starting at one long side. Cut the roll into 9 equal pieces, and place them close together, cut side up, in the tin. Cover the tin with oiled cling film and leave in a warm place for 20 to 30 minutes until doubled in size. Meanwhile, set the oven at Gas Mark 5, 375°F, 190°C.

Bake in the preheated oven for about 30 minutes, until golden brown. Turn out of the tin, and while the buns are still hot, brush them with honey (use a wet brush) and sprinkle with caster sugar. Set aside to cool slightly before separating the buns.
TO FREEZE: freeze until firm, then wrap in cling film and foil.
TO USE FROM FROZEN: thaw uncovered on a wire rack for 3 to 4 hours.

FAR RIGHT Use redcurrants, together
with morello cherries, in Cherry Jam – and
serve with High Rise Scones (page 101).

KENTISH HUFFKINS

MAKES ABOUT 10

These are soft, oval rolls with a dent
in the middle.

735 g (1 lb 10 oz) strong white bread flour
1½ teaspoons salt
60 g (2 oz) lard or white fat
1 sachet easy-blend yeast
Flour for dusting
Greased baking trays

Sieve the flour and salt into a large warmed, mixing bowl. Rub in 30 g (1 oz) of the fat. Stir in the yeast. When the mixture is thoroughly blended, stir in about 430 ml (¾ pt) warm (blood heat) water, and mix to a soft, pliable but not sticky dough, adding a little more water as necessary.

Turn the dough out on to a floured work surface and knead thoroughly for 10 minutes – this is important for a good result and should not be skipped. Shape the dough into a ball, place in a lightly oiled bowl, then turn the dough over in the bowl. Cover the bowl with oiled cling film and leave to prove in a warm place until doubled in size, about 45 minutes to 1 hour.

Knock back the proved dough, and work in the remaining lard. Shape into a ball, return to the bowl, cover and leave to rise in a warm place for about 30 minutes.

Turn out the dough on to a floured work surface and roll out to 2 cm (¾ in) thick. Cut into rounds 10 cm (4 in) in diameter. Arrange, well-spaced, on the baking trays and dust well with flour. Cover lightly with a tea towel and leave in a warm place until it has doubled in size. Meanwhile, set the oven at Gas Mark 7, 425°F, 220°C.

Bake for 15 to 20 minutes, turning them over halfway through the cooking time. As soon as they are cooked, remove from the baking trays, wrap in a clean tea towel and leave to cool.
TO FREEZE: open-freeze until firm, then wrap in polythene bags, and seal.
TO USE FROM FROZEN: thaw on a wire rack, uncovered, for 2 to 3 hours.

CHERRY JAM

MAKES SIX 340 G (12 OZ) JARS

0.9 kg (2 lb) redcurrants, rinsed
1.8 kg (4 lb) morello cherries, stoned
1.8 kg (2 lb) sugar with pectin
The juice of 3 lemons
30 g (1 oz) butter
A jelly bag
Warm, sterilised jam jars,
covers and labels

Put the redcurrants in a preserving pan with 280 ml (½ pt) cold water. Bring slowly to the boil, reduce the heat and simmer until softened – about 4 minutes. Mash the fruit against the side of the pan, then pour into a jelly bag suspended over a large bowl. Leave overnight to allow the juice to drip into the bowl.

Place the juice in a preserving pan. Put the cherry stones in a plastic bag and crack with a rolling pin. Put the stones in a saucepan with 280 ml (½ pt) cold water. Bring to the boil. Strain the liquid into the preserving pan. Add the sugar, lemon juice and the butter and dissolve the sugar slowly. Bring to the boil, then add the cherries and boil rapidly until setting point (225°F, 110°C) in 7 to 10 minutes.

Spoon into the warmed jars, cover and label. Store in a cool, dark place.

TRADITIONAL MARMALADE

MAKES 4.1 KG (9 LB)

To make this chunky marmalade darker and richer, add 30 g (1 oz) of black treacle before potting, in the approved Oxford fashion.

1.35 kg (3 lb) Seville oranges
2 large lemons

2.7 kg (6 lb) granulated sugar, warmed
Warm sterilised jars, covers and labels

Wipe the fruit with a damp cloth, then score the rind into quarters and remove the peel. Remove as much pith as possible. Shred the peel as finely or as coarsely as you wish and place in a large, non-metallic bowl. Add 3.45 litres (6 pt) cold water. Stir well, cover and leave to soak overnight.

Next day, chop up the fruit pulp and tie in a muslin bag with the pips. Put into a preserving pan or large saucepan with the minced peel and its soaking water. Bring the mixture slowly to the boil (this should take about an hour), then simmer gently until the peel is very soft (1 to 1½ hours). Remove the muslin bag, squeeze between two plates to extract all the juice, then discard. Add the warmed sugar to the pan, and stir over a very gentle heat until the sugar has completely dissolved. Bring to a rolling boil, and boil until the marmalade has reached setting point (this will take about 1½ to 2 hours). Turn off the heat and leave to stand for 10 to 15 minutes.

Pour the marmalade into the warmed jars, then cover, seal and label. Store the marmalade in a cool, dark cupboard until ready to use.

East Anglia

The flat, arable farmlands of the Eastern Counties are the bread basket of Britain. Although the soils vary from country to county – ranging from rich and peaty in the Fens to sandy near the coast, with belts of forest and heath scattered in between – the crops are always similar. For, as far as the eye can see across the flat, featureless landscape of Eastern Britain, stretch fields of wheat, barley, sugar-beet and oil-seed rape.

Horticulture is an important industry here, too, and the farms in East Anglia help keep the country's salad bowls and vegetable racks filled with fresh produce. Potatoes, pears, cauliflowers and soft fruit grow easily on the rich farmland in the shadow of the processing and packaging plants.

Shellfish thrive in the warm waters off the eastern coast. Colchester in Essex produces some of the finest native flat oysters available in this country, while further up the coast, at Brancaster and Morston in Norfolk, Pacific oysters are farmed. Pink and brown shrimps are caught in the Wash, Cromer is famous for its crabs, while lobsters, mussels, cockles and whelks are found in abundance all round the coast.

Talking turkey, millions of birds are reared in Norfolk and Suffolk, now the national headquarters for the production of poultry. And Essex, home of Tiptree and Elsenham, is the manufacturing centre for marvellous English jams and preserves.

ASPARAGUS SOUP

SERVES 6

2 tablespoons sunflower oil
1 medium onion, chopped
455 g (1 lb) asparagus, trimmed and
cut into 4 cm (1½ in) pieces
170 g (6 oz) potato, peeled and chopped

430 ml (15 fl oz) skimmed milk
430 ml (15 fl oz) chicken stock
Salt and freshly ground black pepper
60 ml (2 fl oz) sherry (optional)
2 tablespoons chopped fresh herbs

Heat the oil in a saucepan, and fry the onion until just softened but not coloured. Add the asparagus pieces (reserving the spears), potato, milk and stock with a little seasoning. Bring to the boil, and simmer for 30 minutes. Blanch or steam the reserved spears for 2 minutes. Drain. Process the soup in a liquidiser until smooth. Sieve to remove any fibrous pieces and return to the rinsed-out pan. Add sherry (if using) and reserved spears. Reheat, taste and adjust seasoning. Sprinkle with the herbs and serve.

WINTER VEGETABLE SOUP

SERVES 4 TO 6

1 medium onion, finely chopped
2 cloves garlic (or to taste), crushed
2 sticks celery, thinly sliced
1 to 2 tablespoons sunflower oil
1 teaspoon ground coriander
2 medium carrots, finely chopped
230 g (8 oz) celeriac,
finely chopped

2 medium parsnips, finely chopped
170 g (6 oz) potato, chopped
1.15 litres (2 pt) vegetable stock
A large bouquet garni
2 tablespoons tomato purée
1 tablespoon Worcestershire sauce
Salt and pepper
Chopped parsley, to garnish

In a large saucepan, fry the onion, garlic and celery in the oil for 5 minutes or until softened, but not coloured. Stir in the coriander and cook gently for a minute. Add the remaining vegetables and stock, mix well and bring to the boil. Add the bouquet garni to the soup with the tomato purée, Worcestershire sauce and seasoning. Reduce the heat and simmer gently for 20 to 25 minutes or until the vegetables are tender. Remove the bouquet garni. Taste and adjust seasoning as required. Garnish with parsley and serve with freshly baked soda bread (see page 155).

This soup can also be puréed in a blender or processor before serving.

TO FREEZE: follow directions on page 48 for Harvest Soup.

LEMONY POTATO SALAD

SERVES 4 TO 6

Use firm, slightly waxy, small salad potatoes that won't fall apart when cooked.

680 g (1½ lb) potatoes such as Rose Fir
or Belle de Fontenay, scrubbed
115 ml (4 fl oz) good-quality mayonnaise
115 ml (4 fl oz) Greek-style yogurt
1 small onion, finely chopped

The grated rind of 1 lemon
1 tablespoon lemon juice,
or to taste
Salt and freshly ground black pepper
2 tablespoons freshly chopped coriander

Boil the potatoes in a large pan of salted water for 8 to 12 minutes or until they are just tender. Drain well and leave to cool for 10 minutes. Cut into small dice, or slice. Place in a large bowl, mix with the mayonnaise, and cool completely.

Stir in the yogurt, chopped onion, lemon rind and juice, salt, freshly ground black pepper and coriander. Mix well and chill until ready to serve, or for up to 2 hours.

WARM LIVER SALAD WITH BALSAMIC VINEGAR

Although expensive, Balsamic vinegar has a wonderfully powerful and unique flavour – a little goes a long way.

170 g (6 oz) fresh young spinach
110 g (4 oz) mange tout,
topped and tailed
110 g (4 oz) unsalted butter
1 onion, finely chopped
340 g (12 oz) lambs' liver,
cut into strips
170 g (6 oz) button mushrooms, sliced
2 tablespoons Balsamic vinegar

Wash and dry the spinach thoroughly, then arrange on individual salad plates. Blanch the mange tout in boiling water for 1 minute, then drain and plunge into cold water. Drain again, cut them in half diagonally and arrange on top of the spinach leaves.

Heat the butter in a frying pan. Add the onion and cook until softened but not coloured. Add the liver and cook over a high heat until just cooked. Add the mushrooms and toss them for a few seconds. Using a slotted spoon, remove the liver and mushrooms from the pan and arrange on top of the spinach. Deglaze the pan with the Balsamic vinegar over a high heat for 1 minute, stirring constantly, then spoon over each salad. Serve at once.

EAST ANGLIA

67

LEFT *Warm Liver Salad with Balsamic Vinegar (top) and Lemony Potato Salad.*

CLASSIC SUMMER SALAD

SERVES 6 TO 8

Choose from the large selection of salad leaves to create this colourful dish. Add the dressing just before serving or the leaves will become limp.

1 small Iceberg lettuce
1 endive or lollo rosso lettuce
1 bunch watercress or
oak leaf lettuce
1 radicchio lettuce
1 bunch Lamb's lettuce
1 punnet mustard and cress
1 green pepper, deseeded
and diced
½ cucumber, diced
1 avocado (optional)
1 tablespoon lemon juice
For the dressing:
3 tablespoons olive oil
1 tablespoon tarragon vinegar
A pinch of caster sugar
Salt and freshly ground
black pepper
2 tablespoons freshly chopped
mixed herbs

Thoroughly wash the lettuce leaves, then dry by gently spinning in a salad spinner or pat dry on a large, clean tea towel. Tear any of the larger leaves into bite-sized pieces and arrange them in an attractive serving dish with the mustard and cress, green pepper and cucumber. Peel and slice the avocado (if using), then dip it into the lemon juice, and add it to the salad.

To make the dressing, place all the ingredients in a screw-topped jar and shake vigorously until well emulsified. Taste and adjust the seasoning. Just before serving, pour the dressing over the salad and toss gently.

CRISP APPLE SALAD

SERVES 4 TO 6

More than one third of all the vegetables and salad crops come from this area of the country. Use the freshest ingredients possible to make this crisp and crunchy salad.

1 head of celery
230 g (8 oz) crisp, red dessert apples
The juice of ½ lemon
115 ml (4 fl oz) good-quality mayonnaise
5 tablespoons double cream
85 g (3 oz) walnut halves
60 g (2 oz) raisins (optional)
Salt and freshly ground white pepper
A few sprigs of flat-leaf parsley,
to garnish

Wash and slice the celery. Core and dice the apples, then toss in the lemon juice to prevent them turning brown. Blend the mayonnaise with the cream in a large mixing bowl, add the walnut halves and raisins (if using) and mix well. Season to taste with salt and freshly ground white pepper. Cover the bowl and chill the mixture until ready to serve, or for up to 4 hours.

To serve, arrange the salad in an attractive glass serving dish and garnish with a few sprigs of flat-leaf parsley.

HONEY CHICKEN SALAD

SERVES 6

Honey and ginger combine perfectly to give a sweet and spicy taste to this delicious salad.

340 g (12 oz) mixed salad leaves, such as
lollo rosso, frisée, Lambs' lettuce
4 cooked chicken breasts, free from
skin and bone
6 slices prosciutto
For the honey dressing:
6 tablespoons sunflower oil
2 tablespoons red vinegar
1 tablespoon clear honey
A 2.5 cm (1 in) piece of root ginger,
peeled and grated
Salt and freshly ground black pepper
Toasted almonds, chopped

Thoroughly wash the lettuce leaves, then dry by gently spinning in a salad spinner, or pat dry on a large, clean tea towel. Tear the leaves into bite-sized pieces and arrange them on individual serving plates.

Slice the cooked chicken breasts and arrange attractively with the prosciutto on top of the salad leaves.

To make the dressing, place all the ingredients in a screw-topped jar and shake vigorously until well emulsified. Pour the dressing over the salad, scatter a few toasted almonds on top to garnish, and serve immediately.

OPPOSITE *Classic Summer Salad (top) and Crisp Apple Salad.*

PRAWNS IN GINGER HERB CREAM

SERVES 4

An unusual but delicious starter – perfect for a special dinner.

1 small onion, finely chopped
A 2.5 cm (1 in) piece root ginger,
peeled and grated
15 g (½ oz) unsalted butter
4 tablespoons dry white wine
1 tablespoon lemon juice
140 ml (¼ pt) double cream
1 teaspoon each of chopped fresh dill,
parsley and tarragon
230 g (8 oz) peeled, cooked prawns,
thawed if necessary
Salt and freshly ground
black pepper
A few lettuce or Chinese leaves
To garnish:
A few slices of lemon
Sprigs of dill

Gently cook the onion and ginger in the butter until softened – about 5 minutes. Stir in the wine and simmer gently until the liquid has reduced by half. Remove from the heat, stir in the lemon juice and leave to cool. When cold, add the cream, herbs, prawns and seasoning. Taste, and adjust the seasoning. Chill until ready to serve – up to an hour.

To serve, arrange the salad leaves on small plates. Spoon the prawn mixture on top. Garnish with lemon slices and sprigs of dill.

CRAB SOUFFLÉ

SERVES 4 TO 6

For extra flavour replace the paprika with curry powder. If crab meat is unavailable, an equal quantity of flaked, cooked, smoked haddock can be substituted.

40 g (1½ oz) butter
1 shallot, very finely chopped
1½ teaspoons paprika
30 g (1 oz) flour
210 ml (7½ fl oz) milk
230 g (8 oz) white crab meat, thawed
if necessary
4 egg yolks, size 3
Salt, pepper and Tabasco, to taste
6 egg whites, size 3
A 1.7 litre (3 pt) soufflé dish, buttered and
sprinkled with fine brown breadcrumbs

Set the oven at Gas Mark 6, 400°F, 200°C. Melt the butter. Add the shallot and paprika and cook gently for one minute. Stir in the flour and cook, stirring, for a few seconds. Pour in the milk and bring to the boil, while stirring continuously, to make a thick, lump-free sauce. Remove from the heat and stir in the crab meat and egg yolks. Add seasoning and Tabasco to taste – the mixture should be well-flavoured.

Stiffly whisk the egg whites. Stir a quarter into the crab mixture. When thoroughly blended, tip on to the remaining egg whites and carefully fold in using a large metal spoon. Pour into the prepared soufflé dish. Bake for 15 to 20 minutes until puffed, golden brown and just firm. Serve immediately.

SMOKED TROUT WITH AVOCADO MOUSSE

SERVES 2

Smoked trout makes a delicious and substantial first course served with thick, creamy avocado mousse.

2 smoked trout fillets, weighing
about 85 g (3 oz) each
For the avocado mousse:
1 small avocado
2 tablespoons soured cream or yogurt
1 tablespoon mayonnaise
¼ teaspoon creamed horseradish sauce,
or to taste
Salt and freshly ground black pepper
Thin slices of lemon and sprigs of fresh
dill, to garnish

Put the smoked trout on 2 individual serving plates, then peel and halve the avocado and remove the stone.

In a liquidiser or processor, purée the avocado with the soured cream or yogurt, mayonnaise, horseradish sauce and plenty of seasoning to taste.

Spoon half the avocado purée on to each plate, at one end of the fish. Garnish with lemon twists and a sprig of fresh dill.

CREAM OF LOBSTER SOUP

SERVES 8

Fresh lobster is available from May to September. Use it to make this starter for a special dinner party.

1 small cooked lobster
60 g (2 oz) butter
1 large onion, chopped
110 g (4 oz) carrots, chopped
2 sticks celery, diced
110 g (4 oz) mushrooms, chopped
60 ml (2 fl oz) dry white wine
60 g (2 oz) flour
2 tablespoons brandy
A bouquet garni
1.15 litres (2 pt) fish stock
1 teaspoon paprika
Salt and pepper
570 ml (1 pt) milk
2 egg yolks, size 3
140 ml (¼ pt) double cream

Halve and clean the lobster. Remove the flesh from body and claws, then dice. Crush all the shells and claws using a meat mallet or rolling pin.

Melt the butter in a heavy pan. Add the vegetables and cook slowly over low heat for 10 minutes until softened and golden. Add the crushed shells and stir-fry for 1 minute. Add the wine and simmer gently for 10 minutes. Stir in the flour and cook for 2 minutes stirring constantly. Pour in the brandy and ignite. When the flames die down add the bouquet garni, fish stock, paprika and seasoning. Cover and simmer gently for 30 minutes. Strain the soup, pressing the shells and vegetables well to extract all the juices and flavour.

Gently heat the lobster flesh in the milk. Stir in the strained soup and reheat. Mix the egg yolks with the cream and then blend into the soup. Taste, and adjust the seasoning. Reheat the soup carefully, stirring constantly – but do not boil or the soup will curdle.

TROUT WITH SAGE AND BRANDY

SERVES 4

This quick and simple recipe for cooking trout is adapted from Antonio Luciano's Italy: A Culinary Journey .

4 trout, each weighing about 230 g (8 oz)
30 g (1 oz) plain flour for dusting
85 g (3 oz) unsalted butter
4 bay leaves

8 to 10 sage leaves or
1½ teaspoons dried sage
60 ml (2 fl oz) dry white wine
60 ml (2 fl oz) brandy

Wash the trout and pat dry. Lightly coat with the flour. Heat the butter in a heavy-based frying pan, add the bay leaves and sage and sauté until the butter is golden brown, then add the trout. Fry over a high heat, turning only once, until the skins are crunchy and golden. Add the wine and brandy, cook for a further 5 minutes.

Serve immediately on warm plates with the sage and bay leaves which will, by now, be crunchy and delicious.

HERBY STUFFED PLAICE

SERVES 4

Plaice is easily identifiable from the large reddish-orange spots on its skin. Along with cod, it is the all-time British favourite; easy, economical and naturally tender. Here's a new way to serve it.

For the stuffing:
60 g (2 oz) unsalted butter
3 spring onions, finely chopped
85 g (3 oz) mushrooms, chopped
60 g (2 oz) wholemeal breadcrumbs
3 tablespoons freshly chopped parsley
Salt and freshly ground black pepper
For the fish:
4 plaice fillets
85 ml (3 fl oz) white wine
4 tablespoons double cream

Set the oven at Gas Mark 6, 400°F, 200°C. To make the stuffing, heat the butter in a heavy-based pan, add the spring onions and mushrooms and cook gently for about 2 to 3 minutes. Add the remaining ingredients and mix together. Place a spoonful of the stuffing mixture on each plaice fillet and roll up from the head towards the tail. Put the fish in an ovenproof dish, pour over the wine, bake for 15 to 20 minutes.

Place the fish on a warmed serving plate, strain the cooking juices into a small pan and reduce, add the cream and reheat. Pour the sauce over the fish and serve with seasonal vegetables.

CRUNCHY TROUT WITH LIME

SERVES 4

A very simple recipe for trout, with a truly marvellous flavour.

4 large trout fillets
1 onion, finely chopped
1 clove garlic (or to taste), crushed
1 stick celery, finely chopped
1 tablespoon sunflower oil
60 g (2 oz) fresh wholemeal breadcrumbs
The grated rind of 1 lime
1 tablespoon lime juice
1 tablespoon chopped
fresh parsley
Salt and pepper
15 g (½ oz) unsalted butter

Rinse the fillets if necessary and pat dry with absorbent kitchen paper. Gently fry the onion, garlic and celery in the heated oil for 5 minutes, or until they are softened but not coloured. Remove the frying pan from the heat and mix in all the remaining topping ingredients except the butter.

Divide the mixture into 4 and spread one portion on top of each fillet. Dot with the butter. Line the grill pan with foil. Arrange the trout fillets in the pan and grill for 10 to 12 minutes. Turn the fillets around occasionally whenever necessary, but do not turn over until the fish is tender and the topping crunchy. Serve immediately.

BONED NORFOLK TURKEY WITH THYME AND TARRAGON STUFFING, GRAVY, AND VEGETABLES

SERVES 6 TO 8

If the idea of boning the turkey is overfacing, most butchers will do it for you, providing they are given plenty of warning. The turkey can be boned, stuffed and frozen for up to one month in advance, providing you use a fresh turkey. Do make sure that the bird and stuffing are thoroughly thawed before cooking.

A 6.75 kg (15 lb) turkey
2 large onions, finely chopped
3 cloves garlic, crushed
A 2.5 cm (1 in) piece fresh root ginger, peeled and finely chopped
3 tablespoon sunflower oil
60 g (2 oz) unsalted butter
3 sticks celery, washed and chopped
0.9 kg (2 lb) good quality sausagemeat

455 g (1 lb) no-need-to-soak dried apricots, chopped
230 g (8 oz) fresh white breadcrumbs
The grated rind of 2 lemons
4 tablespoons each of chopped thyme, tarragon and parsley
Salt and freshly ground black pepper, to taste
30 g (1 oz) unsalted butter, melted

To bone the turkey, turn the bird on to its breast. Using a small, sharp knife make a slit along the backbone. Keeping the knife against the bone, carefully remove the flesh from the carcass. Then work around to the legs and wings, staying close to the rib cage, until the joints are reached. Continue working to expose the socket joint, and force the thigh out of the socket. Cut through the tendons to leave the legs still attached. Do the same with the wings. Now, work down towards the breastbone. Remove the carcass (use to make stock). Using a cleaver or heavy sharp knife, chop off the leg end and beyond the drumstick, and the pinion and middle joint of each wing. Remove these bones carefully, working from inside the bird. Cut off any large sinews. Push the leg and wing flesh into the bird through the boning 'hole'. Alternatively ask your local butcher to do this for you!

Set the oven at Gas Mark 5, 375°F, 190°C. To make the stuffing, fry the onion, garlic and chopped ginger in the oil and butter until soft and golden. Add the celery and cook gently for 2 to 3 minutes more. Remove from the heat and leave to cool.

Mix together the sausagemeat, apricots, breadcrumbs, lemon rind and herbs. Add the onion mixture, and seasoning, mix well.

Put the boned turkey skin-side down on a work surface and trim off any excess skin. Spread the stuffing over the bird. Carefully tuck the neck and vent end in towards the filling. Shape the turkey into a roll, then sew up the join with a trussing needle and thin string. Weigh to calculate the cooking time – allow 20 minutes per 455 g (1 lb) plus 20 minutes.

Place the turkey in a roasting tin with the seam underneath. Brush over the melted butter and a little seasoning. Baste occasionally for the calculated time until the juices run clear. If serving the turkey hot, leave to stand for 15 to 20 minutes to allow the meat to 'set' before carving. To serve cold, leave the bird to cool then chill overnight before carving.

Interesting accompaniments for the turkey are Carrot and Ginger Purée (see page 74) and Gravy with Kick, and Curried Creamed Sprouts (see right).

TO FREEZE: the boned stuffed turkey can be wrapped in cling film and foil and frozen for up to 1 month. Do not refreeze a previously-frozen turkey.

TO USE FROM FROZEN: thaw the bird for 3 days in the refrigerator before cooking.

LEFT *Boned Norfolk Turkey with Thyme and Tarragon Stuffing, Gravy with Kick, Curried Creamed Sprouts, and Carrot and Ginger Purée (page 74).*

GRAVY WITH KICK

SERVES 8

Ideal to serve with roast poultry.

30 g (1 oz) flour
About 430 ml (¾ pt) good-quality chicken stock
3 to 4 tablespoons port or sherry
Salt and freshly ground black pepper

Spoon off all the fat from the turkey roasting tin, leaving the sediment and meat juices. Stir in the flour and heat gently for 1 minute, stirring constantly. Add the port or sherry and seasoning and continue simmering gently for about 1 to 2 minutes. Taste and adjust the seasoning if necessary. Serve piping hot in a warmed gravy boat.

CURRIED CREAMED SPROUTS

SERVES 8

This is the most unusual and delicious sprout recipes I have ever tasted.

1.35 kg (3 lb) Brussels sprouts
2 tablespoons olive oil
570 ml (1 pt) double cream
1 teaspoon hot curry paste, or to taste
Salt and freshly ground black pepper
60 g (2 oz) toasted flaked almonds, to garnish

Remove the stalks and slice the sprouts. Heat the oil in a heavy based pan, add the sprouts and stir-fry for 5 minutes until softened. Add the cream and curry paste and continue cooking for about 5 to 10 minutes. Season with salt and freshly ground black pepper to taste. Serve immediately, garnished with the flaked almonds.

CARROT AND GINGER PURÉE

SERVES 8

Colourful, full of flavour and freezes very well.

A 2.5 cm (1 in) piece fresh root ginger
1 large onion, chopped
2 tablespoons olive oil
1.35 kg (3 lb) carrots, peeled and chopped

850 ml (1½ pt) good quality vegetable
or chicken stock
Salt and freshly ground
black pepper

Peel and chop the fresh ginger, then fry it with the onion in the oil in a large, heavy-based pan for 5 minutes until softened but not coloured. Add the carrots and cook for a further 5 minutes, stirring frequently. Add the stock, bring to the boil, and simmer for about 30 minutes until the carrots are very soft. Transfer the mixture to a liquidiser or food processor and process until smooth. Return the mixture to the rinsed out pan, heat gently. Season to taste and serve with turkey.

TO FREEZE: place the purée mixture in a rigid plastic container and freeze for up to 1 month.

TO USE FROM FROZEN: thaw overnight in the fridge before reheating.

TRADITIONAL ROAST PHEASANT WITH TOASTED OATMEAL STUFFING

SERVES 4 TO 6

A simple roast with a moist stuffing of apple, onion and oatmeal.

1 brace of young pheasants, with giblets
1 small onion
60 g (2 oz) tart eating apple
60 g (2 oz) medium oatmeal
30 g (1 oz) shredded suet
1 egg yolk, size 3
Salt and freshly ground black pepper

30 g (1 oz) butter, melted
170 g (6 oz) streaky
bacon rashers
2 tablespoons plain flour
280 ml (½ pt) game stock
60 ml (2 fl oz) port or red wine
Watercress, to garnish

Set the oven at Gas Mark 7, 425°F, 220°C. Wipe the pheasants inside and out with a damp cloth and season the cavity. The birds will be much easier to carve if the wishbone is removed before cooking. This can be done by the butcher or game dealer, or at home using a small, sharp knife to cut the bone free from the flesh, Make sure to lift the skin off the meat so that it is not pierced.

To prepare the stuffing; peel and finely chop the onion, peel, core and finely chop the apple, then lightly toast the oatmeal until golden. Mash the reserved pheasant liver (optional). Mix all these ingredients together with the suet and egg yolk, and season well. Spoon the stuffing into the pheasants then truss with fine string or secure the legs with skewers. Stand the birds in a roasting tin and brush liberally with the butter. Season with pepper, then wrap the bacon rashers over the birds to cover the breast meat completely.

Roast for 45 minutes, basting frequently, then remove the bacon, baste, and dredge the birds with a little of the flour. Return to the oven and roast for a further 10 minutes. Transfer the pheasants to a warmed serving dish, remove the trussing string or skewers, and keep hot.

To make the gravy, add the remaining flour to the juices in the roasting tin and cook, stirring constantly, over a low heat for a minute. Whisk in the stock and port or wine and bring to the boil. Simmer for 2 minutes or until the gravy is of the right thickness. Add any meat juices from the pheasants, season to taste, then strain into a warmed gravy boat. Garnish the pheasants with watercress and serve with fried breadcrumbs, bread sauce and game chips.

HONEY-GLAZED GAMMON

Nothing can beat the delicious taste of succulent home-cooked ham.

A 3.85 kg (8½ lb) knuckle gammon joint –
whole middle gammon on the bone
1 small onion, peeled
1 small carrot, quartered
1 bay leaf
5 black peppercorns
570 ml (1 pt) dry cider
For the glaze:
3 tablespoons ready-made English mustard
3 tablespoons demerara sugar
60 ml (2 fl oz) clear honey
Whole cloves
Watercress, to garnish

Weigh the gammon to calculate the cooking time – allow 20 minutes per lb, plus 20 minutes. Soak the ham overnight in enough cold water to cover.

Place the gammon in a large saucepan with the onion, carrot, bay leaf, peppercorns and cider. Cover with cold water, bring to the boil and simmer for the calculated time.

Remove the gammon from the pan and drain well. Remove the skin and cut away any excess fat.

Set the oven at Gas Mark 5, 375°F, 190°C. To glaze, place the ham in a roasting tin and spread with the made mustard. Sprinkle over the demerara sugar, then brush with the honey. Stud with cloves and roast for 25 minutes until golden. Serve hot or cold.

RIGHT *Honey-glazed Gammon with a selection of cheeses, photographed at Kenwood House.*

ROAST DUCK WITH CHEAT'S ORANGE SAUCE

SERVES 4

Painting the duck skin with soy sauce and marmalade makes it especially delicious, while the well-flavoured sauce complements the rich meat perfectly.

1 large duck
Salt and pepper
3 tablespoons marmalade
2 tablespoons soy sauce
1 small onion, chopped
1 small carrot, chopped
1 tablespoon flour
2 tablespoons frozen concentrated orange juice, thawed
1 tablespoon lemon juice
280 ml (½ pt) chicken stock
1 tablespoon brandy or orange liqueur (optional)

Set oven at Gas Mark 6, 400°F, 200°C. Wipe the duck inside and out, prick with a fork and rub all over with salt. Stand on a rack in a roasting tin and cook for 1½ hours, turning the duck twice during cooking. Then pour off all the fat that has collected in the tin, but leaving the meat juices at the bottom. Mix the marmalade with the soy sauce, and brush half over the duck's skin. Put the onion and carrot into the roasting tin and return duck to the oven for a further 15 to 20 minutes. Remove the duck from the oven, and keep it warm while making the orange sauce.

Add the flour to the vegetables and juices in the roasting tin and cook for 2 minutes, stirring constantly. Add the orange and lemon juice and stock and bring to the boil, stirring all the time. Simmer for 2 minutes, then strain into a small pan. Stir in the remainder of the marmalade and soy sauce mixture, and add the brandy. Reheat, then taste and adjust the seasoning as necessary.

Serve the duck and the sauce piping hot, with a rice pilaff and seasonal green vegetables – peas are traditional.

CIDER-COOKED PIGEONS WITH GRAPES

SERVES 6

An unusual and delicious dish cooked with good English cider.

6 wood pigeons, each about 230 g (8 oz)
230 g (8 oz) seedless white grapes, peeled
60 g (2 oz) butter
1 tablespoon oil
170 g (6 oz) onions
170 g (6 oz) carrots
170 g (6 oz) turnips
Salt and pepper
1 tablespoon fresh basil, or
1 teaspoon dried basil
570 ml (1 pt) dry cider
6 slices wholemeal bread
A little oil and butter, for frying

Set the oven at Gas Mark 4, 350°F, 180°C. Wipe the birds inside and out and put a few grapes inside each.

Heat the butter and oil in a heavy, flameproof casserole. Brown the birds, two at a time, drain and remove. Peel and chop the onions, carrots and turnips and add to the casserole. Cook very gently until soft, stirring frequently. Season lightly and stir in the basil. Arrange the birds, breast side down, on top of the vegetables. Pour over the cider, bring to the boil, cover and cook the casserole in the oven for 1 hour.

Reduce the oven temperature to Gas Mark 2, 300°F, 150°C, and cook for a further 1½ to 2 hours, or until very tender. Remove the birds and cut the breast meat off the carcasses. Keep warm.

Boil the liquid in the casserole until reduced by half. Strain, pressing down on the vegetables to extract all the juices. Add the remaining grapes to the sauce and reheat, then taste, and adjust the seasoning.

Trim the slices of bread into heart shapes, circles or triangles, then fry in the hot butter and oil until golden and crispy. Drain on kitchen paper.

To serve, arrange the pigeon breasts on the fried bread, and spoon over some of the sauce. Serve the remaining sauce separately in a sauceboat.

JUGGED HARE

SERVES 6

Hare, often regarded as the poor man's meat and fit only for the peasant-pot, has a powerful pungent flavour. Try it for a casual Saturday night supper. Most good butchers sell hare that has been hung, but you could also use rabbit instead.

1 hare, paunched and jointed, with its blood (keep this for the gravy)
60 g (2 oz) seasoned flour
110 g (4 oz) rindless streaky bacon, diced
60 g (2 oz) butter
1 large onion, skinned and stuck with cloves
2 medium carrots, quartered
2 sticks celery, sliced
A bouquet garni
1 teaspoon ground allspice
The grated rind of ½ lemon
Salt and pepper
850 ml (1½ pt) beef stock
2 teaspoons flour
15 g (½ oz) butter
85 ml (3 fl oz) port
2 tablespoons redcurrant jelly

Set the oven at Gas Mark 3, 325°F, 170°C. Toss the hare in the seasoned flour. Fry the bacon in an ovenproof, flameproof casserole and remove. Add the butter and brown the hare joints two at a time. Drain and remove. Add the vegetables, bouquet garni, allspice, lemon rind and seasoning. Stir-fry for 2 minutes. Pour over the stock and bring to the boil. Replace the bacon and hare joints. Cover and cook in the oven for about 2½ to 3 hours or until the hare is really tender.

Transfer the hare to a serving dish, cover and keep warm. Discard the onion and the bouquet garni. Strain the gravy into a pan. Mash the flour and butter to a paste and whisk into the hot gravy. Bring to the boil, whisking constantly until smooth and thickened. Mix the reserved blood from the hare together with the port. Whisk into the gravy with the redcurrant jelly. When the gravy is smooth and glossy, taste and adjust the seasoning as necessary. Pour the gravy over the hare and serve.

HOT GAME PIE

A handy recipe for using up any game that may not be of good enough quality to roast.

For the pastry:
200 g (7 oz) strong plain flour
A pinch of salt
110 g (4 oz) butter
15 g (½ oz) lard or white fat
For the filling:
2 to 3 game birds to yield 455 g (1 lb) meat, free of skin and bone
340 g (12 oz) lean venison or stewing steak, cubed
140 ml (¼ pt) red wine
30 g (1 oz) dripping or white fat
170 g (6 oz) onions, finely chopped
110 g (4 oz) celery, chopped
110 g (4 oz) rindless back bacon, roughly chopped
2 tablespoons plain flour
230 g (8 oz) mushrooms
2 tablespoons chopped parsley
¼ teaspoon dried rubbed sage
2 tablespoons redcurrant jelly
280 ml (½ pt) well-reduced game stock
Salt and freshly ground pepper
Beaten egg to glaze
A 1.7 litre (3 pt) pie dish with a pie funnel

To make the pastry, sift the flour with the salt into a mixing bowl. Dice the fats and rub into the flour, using fingertips, until the mixture resembles fine breadcrumbs. Bind to a soft but not sticky dough with about 100 ml (3½ fl oz) icy water. Turn out on to a floured surface and knead lightly. Roll out to a rectangle about 30.5 by 10 cm (12 by 4 in). Fold the lower third of the pastry up to cover the middle third, then fold the top third down to make a square of pastry 3 layers thick. Press the edges of the pastry with a rolling pin to seal, then turn the square so that the 'fold' is on the left – like a book. Repeat this rolling and folding of the pastry twice more, then cover and chill for about 20 minutes. Roll and fold 3 times more, so the pastry has been rolled out and folded 6 times. Wrap and chill while preparing the filling.

To make the filling, remove all the flesh from the game birds, discarding the skin and any damaged areas. Cut into bite-sized pieces. Put into a non-metallic bowl with the cubed venison, pour over the wine and mix well. Cover and marinate for half an hour.

Heat the dripping in a heavy-based pan and gently fry the onions, celery and chopped bacon until soft and golden. Lift the meat out of the marinade on a slotted spoon (reserve the marinade) and pat dry with absorbent kitchen paper. Add the meat to the ingredients in the pan and stir-fry until browned. Stir in the flour, mushrooms, herbs, redcurrant jelly, wine marinade, stock and seasoning. Bring to the boil, stirring continuously, and simmer gently for about an hour or until the meat is tender. Taste and adjust the seasoning. Pour into the pie dish and cool.

Set the oven at Gas Mark 7, 425°F, 220°F. Roll out the pastry on a floured surface to a rectangle about 5 cm (2 in) larger all round than the top of the pie dish. Cut off a strip of pastry the width of the rim of the dish, moisten, and stick to the rim (damp side down). Carefully lift the pastry over the pie to cover without stretching. Press the edges firmly to seal. With a sharp knife, trim off the excess and use for decoration. 'Knock-up' the edges of the pastry with the back of a knife, then flute. Brush lightly with beaten egg. Make sure the steam-hole in the pie funnel is clear. Bake for 30 minutes, then reglaze with beaten egg. Reduce the oven temperature to Gas Mark 5, 375°F, 190°F, and bake for a further 10 to 15 minutes until the pastry is crisp and golden. Serve immediately.

CLASSIC BREAD AND BUTTER PUDDING

SERVES 4 TO 6

Leaving the dish to stand before cooking allows the liquids to be evenly and thoroughly absorbed by the bread, giving a deliciously light, moist pudding.

110 g (4 oz) sultanas
3 tablespoons brandy
10 slices of medium white bread,
crusts removed
60 g (2 oz) butter, softened
140 g (5 oz) apricot jam
570 ml (1 pt) single cream
3 tablespoons golden caster sugar
A few drops vanilla essence
4 eggs, lightly beaten
2 tablespoons demerara sugar
A 1.15 litre (2 pt) ovenproof dish, buttered

Place the sultanas in a small bowl, pour over the brandy, cover and leave to soak for 4 hours or overnight. Spread each slice of bread with butter, then with jam. Make into sandwiches and cut each into 4 triangles.

Arrange a layer of triangles on the base of the prepared dish. Scatter over some of the sultanas, followed by another layer of bread, then another of sultanas. Continue layering until all the ingredients are used.

Heat the cream and sugar gently, until the sugar has dissolved, then add the vanilla essence. Pour the hot cream mixture on to the beaten eggs in a long, slow steady stream, beating constantly. Pour on to the bread and leave to soak for 1 to 1½ hours.

Set the oven at Gas Mark 5, 375°F, 190°C. Place the bread and butter pudding in a bain-marie. Sprinkle the top of the pudding with the demerara sugar and bake for 35 to 40 minutes or until just set and golden. Serve at once.

SPOTTED DICK

MAKES ONE 18 CM (7 IN)
ROUND LOAF

Also known as Spotted Dog, this popular recipe is made for breakfast as well as the traditional brown soda bread.

680 g (1½ lb) flour
110 g (4 oz) sugar
A pinch of salt
2 teaspoons bicarbonate of soda
60 g (2 oz) butter
340 g (12 oz) raisins
1 egg, size 3, beaten
430 ml (¾ pt) soured milk

Set the oven at Gas Mark 7, 425°F, 220°C. Sift the flour, sugar, salt and bicarbonate of soda together, and rub in the butter with your fingertips until the mixture resembles fine breadcrumbs. Stir in the raisins. Make a well in the centre. Mix in the beaten egg and the milk gradually, drawing in the flour from the sides.

Turn it out on to a lightly floured work surface and knead lightly to form a soft dough. Shape into an 18 cm (7 in) round and cut a cross on the top. Place on a greased baking tray and bake for 40 to 45 minutes. Transfer to a wire rack and leave to cool.

Serve cold or lightly toasted with butter and marmalade.

PREVIOUS PAGE *Place the pudding in a bain-marie. Sprinkle the top of the pudding with the demerara sugar.*

The West Country

D uring the summer, tourists flock to the West Country which, with its seas warmed by the Gulf Stream, enjoys the mildest climate in Great Britain. Most holiday-makers return home a few pounds heavier after a week or two spent enjoying Cornish pasties, Devon cream teas, Somerset cider and the well-flavoured treasures of a West Country cheeseboard.

The rich green grazing land gives milk in the South West a high butterfat content, which is ideal for making cream, cheese and butter. Cheddar, the world's most popular hard cheese, was first made centuries ago only in Somerset but – without the cloak of copyright with which the French protect national treasures like Champagne – is now made all around the globe. Double Gloucester cheese, Blue Vinney, Devon Garland, Cornish Yarg and the sublime Sharpham cheese from Totnes are all excellent reasons to celebrate the cheesemaker's art.

Spring arrives here before anywhere else in the Britain, ripening fruit and vegetables ready for market. Orchards abound, and when the apples are pulped and allowed to ferment naturally in barrels, they produce the drink which - from rough strong farmhouse scrumpies to smooth, dry, yuppie ciders - is the hallmark of this region's drinking.

Pig farming is traditional, especially in Wiltshire, and huge areas of wheat, barley and oats are grown in Gloucestershire.

Oysters
Smoked Mackerel Salad
Mussels with Cream
and Saffron Sauce
– ∗ –
Macaroni Cheese
Cheese and Ale
Cornish Pasties
Individual Chicken Puff Pies
Rich Cheese Soufflés
– ∗ –
Crab Thermidor
Summer Fish Kebabs
Hake with Tartare Sauce
– ∗ –
Boned Chicken with Thyme
and Tarragon Stuffing
Gingered Sauté of Pork
Roast Pork Loin with Apple
Cider Sauce
Piquant Lamb Casserole
Dartmouth Pie
Caudle Chicken Pie
– ∗ –
Spicy Fruit Crumble
Shortbread Galette
Cornish Fairings
Strawberry Meringue Parfait
Clotted Vanilla Ice-cream
– ∗ –
Saffron Cake
Penzance Cake
Apple Pear Cake
Sheer Luxury Cherry Cheesecake
Saffron Bread
High Rise Scones
Traditional Heavy Cake

OYSTERS

Oysters are irresistible – served chilled on the half shell on a bed of finely chopped ice.

Allow 4 to 6 oysters per person

Scrub the oyster shell with a small stiff brush to remove all sand and grit.

To open the oyster, wrap a thick tea towel around your hand, or wear an oven glove. Hold the oyster in the protected hand, round shell facing upwards. Insert a knife with a short, strong blade into the hinge and twist it until the oyster starts to open. Cut through the muscles that lie above and below the oyster.

Continue running the knife blade between the shells to open and discard the rounded shell.

Serve the oysters accompanied by thinly sliced, buttered wholemeal bread and lemon wedges, and add a dash of Tabasco sauce, if wished.

PREVIOUS PAGE LEFT *West Country fishermen provide a wealth of seafood for the tables of Europe.*

PREVIOUS PAGE RIGHT *Mussels with Cream and Saffron Sauce, served with Saffron Bread.*

BELOW *A barrel of fine oysters – all they need is a sprinkle of freshly ground black pepper.*

OPPOSITE *Checking oysters at the Helford Oyster Farm in Cornwall.*

Smoked Mackerel Salad

SERVES 6

A deliciously simple first course. The tart, creamy dressing counter-balances the richness of the fish.

4 fillets smoked mackerel
2 red eating apples
2 tablespoons lemon juice
4 sticks celery, washed
and sliced
60 g (2 oz) walnuts, roughly chopped
For the dressing:
2 tablespoons good-quality mayonnaise
3 tablespoons fromage frais, soured
cream or yogurt
1 to 2 tablespoons chopped fresh dill
Lemon juice to taste
Freshly ground black pepper
To serve:
A few lettuce leaves, thoroughly washed
and dried
Lemon wedges
Brown bread and butter

Carefully remove the skin and any bones from the mackerel fillets. Flake the fish into large pieces. Core and roughly chop the apples, then dip in the lemon juice to prevent browning.

Mix the flaked mackerel, chopped apples, lemon juice, sliced celery and nuts together.

To make the dressing, beat all the ingredients together in a small bowl. Spoon over the mackerel, and toss the fish gently to coat it with the dressing. Cover the bowl and chill for up to 2 hours before serving.

To serve, spoon a little mackerel mixture into each lettuce leaf, and serve with wedges of lemon and thinly sliced brown bread and butter.

Mussels with Cream and Saffron Sauce

SERVES 4 TO 6

2 kg (4½ lb) mussels
30 g (1 oz) butter
2 tablespoons sunflower oil
1 large onion, finely chopped
2 to 3 cloves garlic (or to taste), crushed

430 ml (15 fl oz) dry white wine
1 teaspoon saffron strands
30 g (1 oz) chopped fresh parsley
140 ml (¼ pt) double cream
Freshly ground white pepper

As soon as you get home with the mussels, transfer them to a bucket or a sink, and cover well with cold water. Sprinkle over a little oatmeal (or flour), and leave them in a cool place for up to 2 days, changing the water frequently.

Before cooking, scrub the mussels thoroughly. Remove any barnacles with a knife, and scrape away any seaweed and remove the hairy beard. Rinse in several changes of water to remove all traces of grit. Discard all shells that are in any way damaged, or do not shut when tapped. Drain mussels well and set aside.

Heat the butter and oil in a large pan until foaming, and gently cook the onion and garlic until softened but not coloured. Add the mussels to the pan with the wine and saffron, and cover with a lid. Cook over a high heat until the mussels open (about 5 or 6 minutes), shaking the pan occasionally. Once the shells have opened, transfer the mussels to a warmed serving dish, using a slotted spoon. Cover with a lid or a piece of buttered foil (to prevent the mussels from drying out). Keep warm.

Boil the liquid left in the pan until reduced by half. Add the parsley and cream and simmer very gently for 1 to 2 minutes. Season with freshly ground white pepper to taste. Arrange the mussels in a large soup tureen and allow everyone to help themselves, eating the mussels from soup bowls, with the creamy sauce poured over the top. Serve with good bread such as Saffron Bread (see recipe on page 100), to mop up the juices.

MACARONI CHEESE

SERVES 4

Use strong mature Cheddar to make this family favourite.

850 ml (1½ pt) milk	½ teaspoon English mustard
1 small onion, stuck with 6 cloves	A few drops Worcestershire sauce
6 black peppercorns	230 g (8 oz) mature Cheddar
1 bay leaf	cheese, grated
230 g (8 oz) macaroni	2 tablespoons grated Parmesan cheese
60 g (2 oz) butter	110 g (4 oz) ham, diced
60 g (2 oz) flour	85 g (3 oz) fresh breadcrumbs
Salt and pepper	An ovenproof dish

Pour the milk into a pan and add the onion, peppercorns and bay leaf. Bring slowly to the boil. Remove from the heat and leave to infuse for 15 minutes. Meanwhile, cook the macaroni according to instructions on the packet. Drain and keep warm. Set the oven at Gas Mark 4, 400°F, 200°C.

Strain the milk. Melt the butter, add the flour and cook for 1 minute, stirring. Remove from the heat and gradually stir in the milk. Return the saucepan to the heat, stirring constantly, bring to the boil and simmer gently for 1 to 2 minutes. Remove from the heat and stir in the salt, pepper, mustard and Worcestershire sauce.

Add 170 g (6 oz) of the Cheddar and half the Parmesan, the macaroni and the ham and mix well. Pour into the dish. Sprinkle over the remaining Cheddar and Parmesan and the breadcrumbs, and bake the Macaroni Cheese in the preheated oven for about 20 to 25 minutes until golden and bubbling.

ABOVE *Mussels with Cream and Saffron Sauce.*

CHEESE AND ALE

SERVES 2

Dating from the Middle Ages, this dish can be made from Double Gloucester or Cheshire cheese – both have a mild mellow flavour and melt easily.

110 g (4 oz) Double Gloucester or
Cheshire cheese
English mustard to taste (optional)
60 ml (2 fl oz) ale
2 slices wholemeal or granary bread,
toasted

Cut the cheese into thin slices and put in a heavy-based pan, then dot with mustard, if using. Pour over the ale and heat very gently until the mixture melts and is like a thick custard. Spoon the mixture on to the hot toast and serve immediately.

The cheese mixture can be prepared in a very low oven if you don't have a heavy-based pan.

CORNISH PASTIES

MAKES 4 PASTIES

Originally made for Cornish farmers and miners to take to work, pasties are made with a wrapping of crisp pastry around a filling of lean meat, mixed with herby potato.

For the basic shortcrust pastry:	1 medium onion, diced
375 g (12 oz) plain flour	230 g (8 oz) potato, diced
75 g (3 oz) butter	Salt and pepper
75 g (3 oz) white fat	1 tablespoon stock or water
For the filling:	1 tablespoon chopped mixed herbs
455 g (1 lb) lean topside or rump steak	A little beaten egg to glaze

To make the shortcrust pastry, sift the flour into a mixing bowl. Add the fats, cutting them into small pieces with a knife. Then rub into the flour with your fingertips until the mixture resembles fine breadcrumbs. Using a round-bladed knife, mix in enough cold water to make a firm dough. The dough should be firm, and not sticky or crumbly. Wrap and chill for 15 to 20 minutes before using.

To make the filling, cut the meat into bite-sized pieces and mix with the onion, potato, salt, pepper, stock or water, and herbs.

Roll out the pastry dough and cut out four 20.5 cm (8 in) circles. Divide the meat mixture into four and place in the centre of each pastry circle. Brush the rim with water. Bring up the pastry edges to meet above the filling and pinch firmly together. Flute the edges.

Place the pasties on a baking tray and chill while setting the oven at Gas Mark 6, 400°F, 200°C. Glaze with beaten egg and bake for 20 minutes. Reduce the heat to Gas Mark 4, 350°F, 180°C, and bake for a further 30 minutes. Serve hot or cold.

TO FREEZE: open-freeze the uncooked pasties until firm.

TO USE FROM FROZEN: cook from frozen for 10 minutes longer, until piping hot.

INDIVIDUAL CHICKEN PUFF PIES

SERVES 6

These little pies make a spectacular first course for a special meal.

For the filling:
6 baby onions, unpeeled
2 to 3 tablespoons sunflower oil
1 small onion, finely chopped
1 clove of garlic, crushed
110 g (4 oz) button mushrooms, halved
110 g (4 oz) carrots, finely diced
3 boneless chicken breasts, cooked
140 ml (¼ pt) dry cider
140 ml (¼ pt) double cream
¼ teaspoon thyme
Salt and pepper
340 g (12 oz) packet frozen puff pastry
Beaten egg to glaze
6 large ramekin dishes, lightly greased

Put the baby onions in a small pan of cold water. Bring to the boil, then drain and peel. Heat a tablespoon of the oil in a saucepan, fry the whole onions until well browned. Put one in each ramekin.

Add the remaining oil to the pan and cook the chopped onion, the garlic, mushrooms and carrots for 5 minutes.

Cut the chicken into small dice and add to the pan with the cider, double cream, thyme and seasoning to taste. Bring to the boil, stirring constantly, then carefully divide the filling between the ramekins. Stand the ramekins on a baking tray. Cool.

Set the oven at Gas Mark 6, 400°F, 200°C. Roll out the thawed pastry on a lightly floured work surface. Cut out 6 circles each 2.5 cm (1 in) larger than each ramekins, using a saucer or pan lid as a guide. Brush the rim of each of the ramekin with a little beaten egg, then place a pastry circle over the top of each ramekin. Smooth the pastry over the top of the dishes and a little way down the sides. Press well to seal to the dishes.

Brush the pastry with beaten egg to glaze, and make a small steam hole. Use any trimmings to make small leaves, if wished. Chill for 10 minutes. Bake in the preheated oven for 25 to 30 minutes or until the pastry is puffed and golden. Serve immediately.

RICH CHEESE SOUFFLÉS

SERVES 6

Individual light-as-air soufflés are ideal for supper, a light lunch or a first course.

2 tablespoons Parmesan cheese, grated
140 ml (¼ pt) dry cider
85 ml (3 fl oz) milk
1 onion, quartered
1 carrot, quartered
1 stick celery, quartered
1 bay leaf
6 peppercorns
30 g (1 oz) butter
30 g (1 oz) flour
1 teaspoon Dijon mustard
Salt, cayenne pepper and grated nutmeg
110 g (4 oz) Cheddar cheese, grated
4 eggs, size 3, separated
6 ramekin dishes, well greased.

Set the oven at Gas Mark 4, 350°F, 180°C. Use the Parmesan to cover the insides of the ramekins completely. Put the cider, milk, onion, carrot, celery, bay leaf and peppercorns in a saucepan and bring almost to boiling point, then remove, cover and leave to infuse for 15 minutes. Strain.

Melt the butter in a saucepan, stir in the flour and cook over a low heat for about 1 minute or until straw-coloured. Remove the saucepan from the heat and gradually whisk in the cider and milk mixture. Return the pan to the heat and bring to the boil, stirring constantly to make a smooth, thickened sauce. Add the mustard, salt, pepper, nutmeg and grated cheese and mix well. Taste and adjust the seasoning.

Remove the saucepan from the heat and leave the sauce to cool for a few minutes, then beat in the egg yolks, one at a time. Whisk the egg whites until stiff but not dry. Carefully fold a third of the egg whites into the mixture to loosen, and then gently fold in the remaining egg whites.

Spoon the mixture into the small ramekins, stand on a baking tray and bake for 20 to 25 minutes or until puffed and golden. Serve at once.

RIGHT *Cornish cheeses.*

CRAB THERMIDOR

SERVES 6

One of the best ways to serve crab hot – the sauce is enriched with cream and sharpened with mustard.

A blade of mace, a bay leaf, slice of onion,
a few parsley stalks,
6 peppercorns
280 ml (½ pt) milk
20 g (¾ oz) unsalted butter
20 g (¾ oz) flour
A little melted butter for dotting
680 g (1½ lb) cooked white crab meat
40 g (1½ oz) unsalted butter

1 tablespoon finely chopped shallots
4 tablespoons white wine
140 ml (¼ pt) single or double cream
1 tablespoon dry mustard powder
Salt and cayenne pepper, to taste
60 g (2 oz) freshly grated Parmesan
cheese
Fresh dill to garnish

To make the béchamel sauce, put the mace, bay leaf, onion slice, parsley stalks and peppercorns into a pan with the milk. Bring slowly to the boil, cover, remove from the heat and leave to infuse for 20 minutes. Strain and discard the flavourings.

Melt the butter in another pan, then stir in the flour, followed by the strained milk. Return the pan to the heat and stir constantly to make a smooth, thickened sauce. Leave to simmer gently for a minute, then remove the pan from the heat. Dot a little melted butter over the surface to prevent a skin forming.

Pick over the crab meat to remove any stray pieces of shell.

Heat the butter in a pan and cook the shallots gently for 2 minutes. Add the wine and simmer for 5 minutes. Stir in the béchamel sauce and add all but 1 tablespoon of cream. Reheat gently, stirring constantly. Simmer for a minute, then add the crab. Stir well and reheat gently but thoroughly. Mix the mustard powder with the remaining cream to a smooth paste. Remove from the heat and gradually stir the mustard paste into the crab mixture until it tastes right for you, adding salt and cayenne pepper to taste. Spoon into 6 shallow, heatproof dishes and sprinkle with Parmesan.

Cook under a hot grill until brown and bubbling. Garnish each dish with fresh dill and serve immediately with a salad.

SUMMER FISH KEBABS

SERVES 4 TO 6

Delicately coloured and succulent, summer kebabs are ideal for barbecuing or grilling.

12 jumbo prawns
455 g (1 lb) monkfish, skinned and boned
For the marinade:
3 tablespoons olive oil
1 tablespoon soy sauce
A clove of garlic, crushed
A 2.5 cm (1 in) piece root ginger, peeled and finely chopped.

To cook the prawns (this will be only necessary if they are fresh), plunge them into a pan of boiling water and simmer for about 2 to 5 minutes depending on their size. The prawns will turn from grey to pink. Peel prawns by holding the head between the thumb and forefinger of the right hand. Hold the tail with the left hand and gently pinch and pull off the tail shell. Holding the body gently, pull off the head, the body shell and claws. Using the point of a knife, remove and discard the black vein which runs down the back of the prawn.

Cut the monkfish into 2.5 cm (1 in) cubes. Thread the prawns and diced monkfish on to skewers.

Mix together all the ingredients for the marinade, then place the skewers of fish and prawns in a large, shallow, non-metallic dish. Pour the marinade over the top. Cover and chill for up to 12 hours, turning frequently.

Preheat the grill, then remove the skewers from the marinade and grill for about 2 to 3 minutes on each side, brushing with the remaining marinade occasionally. Serve hot with rice and a mixed green salad.

HAKE WITH TARTARE SAUCE

SERVES 6

A classic combination.

0.9 kg (2 lb) hake or cod fillets, free
from skin and bones
30 g (1 oz) unsalted butter, melted
For the sauce:
280 ml (½ pt) good quality mayonnaise
1 teaspoon French mustard
Salt and freshly ground white pepper
1 tablespoon capers, chopped
8 black olives, stoned and finely chopped
A 10 cm (4 in) piece of cucumber,
skinned and finely chopped
2 tablespoons freshly chopped parsley
A little salad, to garnish

To make the tartare sauce, mix all the
ingredients together in a bowl and
season to taste with salt and freshly
ground white pepper. Cover the bowl
and leave in the fridge for up to 4 hours.

Preheat the grill. Cut the fish fillets
into 6 or 8 pieces, removing any bones.
Cook the fish fillets under the grill for
5 minutes on each side, brushing with
melted butter. Serve garnished with a
little salad and a generous serving of
the tartare sauce.

LEFT *Hake with Tartare Sauce.*
OPPOSITE *Crab Thermidor.*

BONED CHICKEN WITH THYME AND TARRAGON STUFFING

SERVES 6 TO 8

Boning a chicken may sound difficult, but is actually very easy. It simplifies carving, and the hot or cold slices of stuffed chicken look impressive, particularly on a buffet table. The distinct aromatic flavours of thyme and tarragon show why these two herbs are the favourite, traditional accompaniments to roast chicken.

A 1.6 to 1.8 kg (3½ to 4 lb) corn-fed chicken
1 medium onion, finely chopped
1 clove garlic, crushed
A 2.5 cm (1 in) piece fresh root ginger, peeled and finely chopped
1 tablespoon oil
15 g (½ oz) butter
1 stick celery, chopped
110 g (4 oz) no-need-to-soak dried apricots, chopped
230 g (8 oz) good-quality sausagemeat
60 g (2 oz) fresh breadcrumbs
The grated rind of 1 lemon
1 tablespoon each of chopped thyme, tarragon and parsley
1 egg, size 3, beaten
Salt and pepper to taste
A 230 g (8 oz) piece boneless bacon, or gammon joint, cooked

To bone the chicken, turn the bird on to its breast. Using a small, sharp knife make a slit along the backbone. Keeping the knife against the bone, carefully remove the flesh from the carcass. Then work round to the legs and wings, staying close to the rib cage, until the joints are reached. Continue working to expose the socket joint, and force the thigh out of the socket. Cut through the tendons to leave the legs still attached. Do the same with the wings. Now, work down towards the breastbone. Remove the carcass (use to make stock). Using a cleaver or heavy sharp knife, chop off the leg end beyond the drumstick, and chop between the pinion and middle joint of each wing. Remove these bones carefully, working from inside the bird. Cut off any large sinews. Push the leg and wing flesh back into the bird through the boning 'hole'.

Set the oven at Gas Mark 5, 375°F, 190°C.

To make the stuffing, fry the onion, garlic and ginger in the oil and butter until soft and golden. Add the celery and cook gently for a further 2 to 3 minutes. Remove from the heat and leave to cool.

Mix together the apricots, sausagemeat, breadcrumbs, lemon rind and herbs. Add the onion mixture, egg and seasoning. Mix well.

Put the boned chicken skin side down on a work surface and trim off any excess skin. Spread the stuffing over the bird, then cut the bacon into strips to fit down the centre. Carefully tuck the neck and vent end in towards the filling. Shape the chicken into a roll, then sew up the join with a trussing needle and thin string.

Place the chicken in a roasting tin with the seam underneath. Brush over the melted butter and sprinkle with a little seasoning. Cook for about 1 hour 20 minutes, basting occasionally, until the juices run clear.

To serve the chicken hot, leave to stand for about 15 to 20 minutes, basting occasionally, until the juices run clear. To serve cold, leave to cool then chill overnight before carving.

GINGERED SAUTÉ OF PORK

SERVES 4

Fresh ginger, orange juice and cider combine to make an attractive, mouth-watering sauce to accompany lean strips of pork.

1 onion, finely chopped
A 5 cm (2 in) piece fresh root ginger, peeled and grated
2 tablespoons sunflower oil
680 g (1½ lb) pork fillet, cut into strips
The grated rind and juice of 1 orange
140 ml (¼ pt) dry cider
140 ml (¼ pt) chicken stock
¼ teaspoon rubbed sage (optional)
Salt and pepper
1½ teaspoons arrowroot or cornflour
Sprig of sage
To garnish:
orange segments

Fry the onion and ginger in the oil for 5 minutes or until softened but not coloured. Add the strips of pork and stir-fry over fairly high heat for about 5 minutes or until the pork is cooked through. Remove the pork to a warmed serving dish and keep warm.

Add the remaining ingredients (except the arrowroot) to the pan and bring to the boil. Reduce the heat and simmer gently for 5 minutes.

Meanwhile mix the arrowroot or cornflour to a smooth paste with a little cold water and whisk in the simmering liquid. Continue whisking until the mixture has thickened. Return the pork to the pan and cook gently for a further minute only, stirring all the time. Taste and adjust the seasoning.

Spoon into a warmed serving dish, garnish with orange segments and the sprig of fresh sage. Serve with rice.

ROAST PORK LOIN WITH APPLE CIDER SAUCE

SERVES 6 TO 8

A boneless pork roast, complete with crisp crackling and filled with a tasty stuffing, served in the French style accompanied by a slightly unusual sauce.

A 1.8 kg (4 lb) boneless pork loin, with rind left on
For the stuffing:
110 g (4 oz) dried apple rings, quartered
60 g (2 oz) dried apricots, quartered
140 ml (¼ pt) dry cider
15 g (½ oz) butter
1 small onion, chopped
A 2.3 cm (1 in) piece fresh root ginger, peeled and grated
60 g (2 oz) button mushrooms, halved
1 stick celery, chopped

60 g (2 oz) fresh wholemeal breadcrumbs
¼ teaspoon rubbed sage
1 egg, size 3, beaten
Salt and black pepper
For the apple sauce:
1 large onion, chopped
60 g (2 oz) butter
455 g (1 lb) cooking apples
4 tablespoons dry cider
280 ml (½ pt) good chicken stock
1 bay leaf
Salt and pepper

Put the apples and apricots in a bowl, pour over the cider and stir well, then cover and leave to soak overnight.

The next day, heat the butter in a frying pan and gently fry the onion, with the ginger, mushrooms and celery for 5 minutes until softened but not coloured. Add this vegetable mixture to the soaked fruits (and their liquid) along with the fresh breadcrumbs and sage. Stir well, adding the beaten egg and plenty of seasoning. Beat the mixture until thoroughly combined.

Set the oven at Gas Mark 7, 425°F, 220°C. Score the pork rind at evenly spaced intervals, using a very sharp knife (this will form the crackling). Open out the boned loin of pork and lay it, rind side down, on a chopping board. Using a sharp knife, cut the meat down the centre of the loin to within 5 mm (¼ in) of the rind. Slice the meat horizontally, cutting towards both edges of the loin, to within 1 cm (½ in) of the edge to form 2 flaps. Open the flaps and flatten with a tenderiser to make 1 large 'sheet' of meat of fairly even thickness. Arrange the stuffing evenly down the centre of the loin, cover with the meat flaps and re-roll the loin. Tie the meat securely with string at regular intervals to make a neatly shaped joint of meat. Brush the scored rind with a little oil and sprinkle with salt, rubbing it in well to ensure a crisp crackling.

Weigh the pork to calculate the cooking time. Allow 25 minutes per 455 g (1 lb). Put the pork into an oiled roasting tin and roast for 25 minutes, basting frequently. Reduce the oven temperature to Gas Mark 5, 375°F, 190°C, for the remainder of the cooking time.

To prepare the sauce, cook the onion in half the butter for 10 minutes, or until a deep caramelised colour (but not burnt), stirring well frequently. Peel, core and slice the apples and add to the onion with the cider, stock, bay leaf and seasoning. Cover and cook gently for 10 minutes. Blend the sauce in a food processor or liquidiser until smooth. Reheat gently with the remaining butter taste and adjust the seasoning. Keep the sauce warm until ready to serve.

Remove the strings around the meat and carve into fairly thick slices. Pour the sauce into a warmed gravy boat, and serve as gravy. A colourful selection of boiled and steamed vegetables are suitable accompaniments.

PIQUANT LAMB CASSEROLE

SERVES 4 TO 6

Luscious dried fruits, soaked in dry cider, add a pleasant, contrasting sharpness to the richness of lamb.

110 g (4 oz) large seedless raisins
110 g (4 oz) dried apricots, halved
570 ml (1 pt) dry cider
1.1 kg (2½ lb) boned shoulder of lamb
30 g (1 oz) flour
¼ teaspoon paprika
¼ teaspoon ground cumin (or to taste)
2 to 3 tablespoons sunflower oil
1 large onion, chopped
110 g (4 oz) button mushrooms, halved
1 green pepper, deseeded and diced
230 g (8 oz) potato, cubed
570 ml (1 pt) lamb stock
2 bay leaves
Salt and freshly ground black pepper

Put the raisins and apricots into a bowl, pour over the cider, then cover and leave to marinate overnight. The next day, cut the lamb into pieces 5 cm (2 in) square.

Mix together the flour, paprika and cumin. Toss the lamb in this seasoned flour, reserving any remaining flour.

Heat the oil in a heavy flameproof casserole then thoroughly brown the meat on all sides, in several batches. Drain and remove. Gently fry all the vegetables in the remaining oil in the casserole for 5 minutes until softened. Sprinkle over the remaining seasoned flour, and then cook gently, stirring constantly until golden.

Remove the pan from the heat and gradually stir in the lamb stock. Add the dried fruits, cider, as well as the meat, bay leaves and seasoning to the casserole. Bring to the boil, stirring, then reduce the heat and simmer gently, uncovered, for 1 hour or until the lamb is really tender, stirring from time to time. Remove the bay leaves, taste and adjust the seasoning.

Serve the casserole piping hot with rice and a green vegetable.

TO FREEZE: see on page 50.

DARTMOUTH PIE

SERVES 6

*This magnificent, tasty lamb pie, rich with fruit and spices, is
adapted from a recipe by Joyce Molyneux from the famed
Carved Angel restaurant in Dartmouth.*

0.9 kg (2 lb) very lean lamb, cut into
2.5 cm (1 in) cubes
Salt
40 g (1½ oz) dripping
2 teaspoons black peppercorns
1 teaspoon blade mace
1 teaspoon whole allspice
A 5 cm (2 in) cinnamon stick
2 teaspoons whole coriander seeds
455 g (1 lb) onions, thinly sliced
1 tablespoon flour
570 ml (1 pt) lamb or beef stock
140 g (5 oz) hunza apricots (from health food stores)
140 g (5 oz) dried prunes
110 g (4 oz) California raisins
The grated rind and juice of 1 orange (Seville if possible)
For the rough puff pastry:
140 g (5 oz) plain flour
A generous pinch of salt
15 g (½ oz) white fat
85 g (3 oz) butter
½ teaspoon lemon juice
Beaten egg to glaze

Set the oven at Gas Mark 6, 400°F, 200°C. Sprinkle the meat
with the salt. Heat the dripping in a heavy, flameproof
casserole, then brown the meat in batches. Remove from the
pan with a slotted spoon.

Meanwhile, roast the spices in the oven for about 1 minute,
then reduce the temperature to Gas Mark 1, 275°F, 140°C.

Whizz the roasted spices in a spice mill or (clean) coffee
grinder until finely ground. Add to the casserole and fry
briskly for a minute, stirring constantly, to cook out the
spices. Add the onions and cook gently for 5 to 10 minutes
until softened. Add the flour and the stock, and gradually
bring to the boil. Season to taste. Cover and cook for 1½ to
2 hours or until the meat is very tender, stirring occasionally.
Taste and adjust the seasoning as necessary. Cool, then cover
and chill overnight. (The mixture can also be frozen for up to
3 months. Defrost in the fridge overnight before continuing).

To make the pastry, sieve the flour and salt into a mixing
bowl. Cut the fat into small flakes. Stir into the flour using a
round-bladed knife, without breaking up the pieces, then add
85 ml (3 fl oz) ice-cold water with the lemon juice. Mix
quickly to form a fairly stiff, lumpy dough, and turn it out on
to a lightly floured work surface and roll into a rectangle
18 by 5 cm (7 by 2 in). Fold the pastry into 3 by folding the
lower third up over the middle third, then fold the top third
down to cover the remaining two-thirds. Lightly press the
edges together to seal. Wrap and chill for 15 minutes. Repeat
the rolling, folding and chilling process 3 more times, giving
the pastry a quarter turn clockwise each time. Wrap and chill.

The next day, set the oven at Gas Mark 6, 400°F, 200°C.
Spoon the meat mixture into the pie dish (if you wish, you can
remove the stones from the apricots). Roll the pastry out on to
a lightly floured work surface to an oval 5 cm (2 in) larger than
the pie dish. Trim off a narrow strip of pastry. Wet the rim of
the pie dish and then press on the strip of pastry. Dampen the
pastry rim, then carefully lift the pastry over the filling (use
the rolling pin to support the weight). Seal well, 'knocking
back' the sides with the back of a small knife. Decorate with
shapes cut from any pastry trimmings. Brush the pie lightly
with beaten egg to glaze and bake for 30 to 35 minutes until
the pastry is crisp and golden. Serve piping hot.

LEFT *West Country waterway.*
OPPOSITE *Len Hodges, Cornish
oyster farmer.*

CAUDLE CHICKEN PIE

SERVES 4 TO 6

The caudle is the cream and egg mixture which is poured into the pie towards the end of cooking. Some Cornish cooks prefer to cook the chicken filling first, and then add the pastry topping.

30 g (1 oz) butter
1 medium onion, finely chopped
3 chicken breasts, free from skin and bone
15 g (½ oz) chopped fresh parsley
4 spring onions, trimmed and chopped
Salt and freshly ground black pepper
140 ml (¼ pt) milk
280 g (10 oz) good-quality puff pastry
Beaten egg to glaze
To complete:
140 ml (¼ pt) double cream
1 egg, size 3, beaten
An 850 ml (1½ pt) pie dish

Melt half the butter in a frying pan until foaming, then add the onion and cook gently until softened but not coloured. Using a slotted spoon, transfer to the pie dish. Add the remaining butter to the pan.

Cut the chicken into 2.5 cm (1 in) pieces and fry in batches in the hot fat, until lightly browned. Transfer the chicken to the pie dish. Add to the pan the chopped parsley, spring onions, plenty of seasoning and the milk. Stir well (scraping up all the juices). Bring slowly to the boil. Reduce the heat and simmer gently for 2 to 3 minutes, stirring occasionally. Pour over the chicken in the pie dish, then carefully arrange the meat so it is mounded in the centre (or use a pie-raiser). Leave the mixture to cool.

Set the oven at Gas Mark 7, 425°F, 220°C.

Roll out the pastry on a lightly floured work surface, to an oval 2.5 cm (1 in) larger than the pie dish. Cut a pastry strip long enough to fit the rim of the dish. Moisten the rim of the dish with water and attach the pastry strip to the rim. Dampen the pastry rim, then carefully place the pastry lid on top. Seal the edges of the pastry firmly, then knock back and flute all around. Carefully cut a steam hole in the top of the pie and (if not using a pie raiser) Insert a small funnel made of foil in the top. Decorate the pie with any remaining pastry trimmings and brush thoroughly with beaten egg to glaze. Bake for about 20 to 25 minutes or until the pastry is golden, then remove the pie from the oven.

Reduce the oven temperature to Gas Mark 4, 350°F, 180°C. Beat the cream and egg together and pour into the pie through a funnel (or through the foil funnel). Carefully shake the pie to disperse the cream and egg mixture. Return the pie to the oven and bake for a further 10 to 15 minutes. Leave to stand for 5 minutes before serving hot or cold.

SPICY FRUIT CRUMBLE

Seasonal fruits, and the last of the summer berries, are given a spicy, oaty topping for this quick-and-easy pudding.

For the base:
230 g (8 oz) Bramley apples
230 g (8 oz) plums, halved and stoned
230 g (8 oz) blackberries
170 g (6 oz) blueberries
170 g (6 oz) raspberries
60 to 85 g (2 to 3 oz) soft, light brown sugar
A pinch ground allspice
For the topping:
280 g (10 oz) plain flour
140 g (5 oz) unsalted butter
60 g (2 oz) rolled oats
110 g (4 oz) demerara sugar
1 teaspoon ground allspice
A 1.15 litre (2 pt) ovenproof dish

Set the oven at Gas Mark 5, 375°F, 190°C. Peel, core and slice the apples. Place the apples in the ovenproof dish with the prepared plums, blackberries, blueberries and raspberries.

Sprinkle over the sugar, allspice and 6 tablespoons of cold water.

To make the topping, sift the flour into a bowl. Rub in the butter until the mixture resembles fine breadcrumbs, then stir in the oats, sugar and allspice. Sprinkle the mixture over the fruit and bake for 50 minutes. Serve hot with home-made custard or cream.

This recipe freezes well, so it is a good idea to make several and enjoy them later in the year.

TO FREEZE: leave to cool completely, then cover with cling film and freeze for up to 2 months.

TO USE FROM FROZEN: thaw at room temperature, covered with a clean tea towel, overnight. Reheat at Gas Mark 5, 375°F, 190°C for 20 to 25 minutes or until piping hot.

SHORTBREAD GALETTE

Strawberries are the essence of the English summer. What better way to serve them than sandwiched between rich buttery shortbread and thickly whipped double cream!

170 g (6 oz) unsalted butter
85 g (3 oz) caster sugar
230 g (8 oz) plain flour
30 g (1 oz) rice flour (or fine semolina)
To complete:
570 ml (1 pt) double cream, lightly whipped
455 g (1 lb) strawberries, hulled
Icing sugar, for dusting

Cream the butter until soft. Add the sugar and beat until pale and light. Mix in the flour and rice flour until the mixture binds together. Knead lightly to form a smooth dough. Divide the mixture into 3. Roll each piece of dough on a baking tray to a 23 cm (8 in) round. Using your fingers, flute the edge. Prick two of the shortbread bases with a fork. Mark the final shortbread round into 8 segments. Chill in the refrigerator for 15 minutes.

Set the oven at Gas Mark 4, 350°F, 180°C. Bake the shortbread for about 15 to 20 minutes, until pale golden and just firm to the touch. Transfer to a wire rack and leave to cool.

To complete, place a shortbread disc on to a serving plate, then pipe a rope of cream around the edge and place half of the strawberries in the centre. Place a second disc on top and pipe a rope of cream around the edge. Arrange the remaining strawberries on top. Place the remaining segments of shortbread at an angle on top, and dust with icing sugar.

LEFT *Spicy Fruit Crumble with Cream.*

CORNISH FAIRINGS

MAKES ABOUT 22

Slightly spicy, gingery biscuits with an attractive 'crazed' finish.

170 g (6 oz) self-raising flour
A pinch of salt
¼ teaspoon bicarbonate of soda
2 teaspoons ground ginger
1 teaspoon ground mixed spice
85 g (3 oz) butter
85 g (3 oz) golden caster sugar
3 tablespoons golden
syrup, warmed
1 tablespoon mixed peel,
very finely chopped

Set the oven at Gas Mark 6, 400°F, 200°C. Sift the flour, salt, bicarbonate of soda and spices into a mixing bowl. Rub in the butter until the mixture resembles fine breadcrumbs. Stir in the sugar, followed by the warm syrup and finely chopped mixed peel. Mix well.

Shape the mixture into evenly-sized balls, each about the size of a walnut. Place the balls well apart on several greased baking trays and bake for about 5 to 8 minutes. Cool slightly, then lift on to wire racks to cool complete. Store in an airtight tin.

TO FREEZE: open-freeze until firm. Store in sealed polythene bags.
TO USE FROM FROZEN: thaw the biscuits, uncovered, on a wire rack at room temperature for 2 to 3 hours.

STRAWBERRY MERINGUE PARFAIT

SERVES 8

A scrumptious, ice-cream-like combination of crushed meringues, strawberries and cream.

2 egg whites, size 3
110 g (4 oz) caster sugar
680 g (1½ lb) strawberries, hulled
570 ml (1 pt) double cream, lightly whipped
Extra strawberries, to decorate
A 1.1 kg (2½ lb) terrine, oiled and lined

Set the oven at Gas Mark 1, 275°F, 140°C. To make the meringues, whisk the egg whites until stiff but not dry, in a spotlessly clean, grease-free bowl. Gradually whisk in the sugar, whisking well after each addition, until the meringue is stiff and glossy. Spoon the mixture into mounds on to a baking tray greased and line with baking parchment. Bake for 1 to 1½ hours or until crisp and slightly golden. Transfer to a wire rack and leave to cool completely.

Roughly crush the meringues. Purée half the strawberries in a blender or a food processor. Quarter the remaining strawberries. Fold the purée and the chopped strawberries into the lightly whipped cream with the crushed meringues. Mix gently but thoroughly. Pour into the prepared terrine and freeze for about 12 hours or until firm. Transfer to the refrigerator 30 minutes before serving. Serve sliced, decorated with extra strawberries.

OPPOSITE *From left: Cornish Fairings, Penzance Cake, Traditional Heavy Cake and Saffron Cake.*

CLOTTED VANILLA ICE-CREAM

SERVES 6 TO 8

This classic rich dairy ice has been a British favourite for many years. Serve it with a selection of fresh summer berries for a truly scrumptious dessert.

570 ml (1 pt) milk
280 ml (½ pt) double cream
1 vanilla pod
6 egg yolks, size 3
110 g (4 oz) golden caster sugar
230 g (8 oz) clotted cream
A selection of summer berries,
to decorate

Heat the milk and double cream in a heavy-based pan. Split the vanilla pod in half lengthways, scrape out the seeds and place both pod and seeds in the pan. Bring the milk mixture to just below boiling point, then remove from the heat. Leave to infuse for 10 minutes, and then strain.

Whisk the egg yolks and sugar together until pale, thick and light. Pour the hot milk mixture on to the egg and sugar mixture in a steady stream, whisking all the time. Return to the rinsed out pan and stir over a low heat with a wooden spoon until the mixture coats the back of the spoon. Do not overheat or the custard will curdle. Strain and leave to cool. Carefully fold in the clotted cream and place in a rigid plastic container and freeze until slushy. Beat well in a food processor and freeze again. Repeat this process twice more. Transfer the ice-cream to the fridge to soften, then scoop onto foil-lined trays and firm for 30 minutes in the freezer before serving.

To serve, arrange scoops of ice-cream in chilled dishes and then decorate with summer berries.

SAFFRON CAKE

MAKES ONE 0.9 KG (2 LB) LOAF

Saffron was originally added to this 'cake' (which is actually a rich, yeast-raised fruit bread) to make it look wonderfully rich and buttery, as well as to add flavour.

2 teaspoons saffron strands
455 g (1 lb) strong plain flour
½ teaspoon salt
170 g (6 oz) butter
2 sachets easy-blend yeast

85 g (3 oz) sugar
230 g (8 oz) mixed dried fruit
170 ml (6 fl oz) lukewarm milk
A 0.9 kg (2 lb) loaf tin, about 22 by 12.5 by
9 cm (8 ¾ by 5 by 3 ½ in), greased

Soak the saffron in 1 tablespoon cold water for at least 4 hours, preferably overnight.

Sift the flour and salt into a bowl. Rub in the fat until the mixture resembles fine breadcrumbs. Stir in the yeast, sugar, mixed dried fruit and saffron with its liquid (if any), and mix well. Add enough warm milk to make a soft but not sticky dough. Turn out on to a lightly floured work surface and knead thoroughly for 10 minutes.

Turn the dough into an oiled bowl, cover with oiled cling film and leave in a warm place to prove until doubled in size, preferably overnight. (The dough is very heavy, and therefore slow to rise.)

Knock back the risen dough and shape in the prepared tin. Cover with oiled cling film and leave to prove in a warm place until almost doubled in size (1½ to 2 hours).

Meanwhile, set the oven at Gas Mark 5, 375°F, 190°C and bake for 40 minutes, then reduce the oven temperature to Gas Mark 4, 350°F, 180°C. Bake for a further 50 minutes. Leave to cool in the tin for 15 minutes, then turn out and cool on a wire rack before serving, sliced and buttered. Eat within 3 days.

Please note that the high proportion of yeast is needed because the loaf is enriched with so much butter.

PENZANCE CAKE

MAKES A 20.5 CM (8 IN)
ROUND CAKE

Easy-to-make, like a large rock cake.

455 g (1 lb) self-raising flour
A pinch of salt
2 teaspoons ground cinnamon
110 g (4 oz) butter
455 g (1 lb) currants, washed and dried
60 g (2 oz) mixed peel, very finely chopped
85 g (3 oz) stem ginger, finely chopped
85 ml (3 fl oz) clear honey, warmed
85 ml (3 oz) milk, warmed
3 eggs, size 3, beaten
A 20.5 cm (8 in) round, deep cake tin,
greased and lined

Set the oven at Gas Mark 4, 350°F, 180°C. Sift the flour, salt and cinnamon into a bowl. Rub in the butter until the mixture resembles fine breadcrumbs. Stir in the currants, the mixed peel and the stem ginger. Add the honey, milk and eggs and mix to a soft but not sticky dough.

Spoon into the prepared tin and bake for 1 to 1½ hours or until a skewer inserted into the centre comes out clean. Cool in tin, then store wrapped in greaseproof paper and foil. This cake is best kept for a day before cutting.

APPLE PEAR CAKE

MAKES ONE 19 CM (7 ½ IN) ROUND CAKE

85 g (3 oz) plain wholemeal flour	2 semi-ripe pears, weighing about
85 g (3 oz) plain white flour	280 g (10 oz), peeled and
1½ teaspoons baking powder	roughly sliced
170 g (6 oz) unsalted butter	Icing sugar for dusting
140 g (5 oz) caster sugar	A 19 cm (7½ in) deep, round cake tin,
3 eggs, size 3, beaten	greased and lined with
A little milk, if required	greaseproof paper tied
2 crisp dessert apples, weighing about	around the outside of the tin
230 g (8 oz), peeled and roughly sliced	to make a collar

Set the oven at Gas Mark 5, 375°F, 190°C. Sift the flours and baking powder into a bowl, returning any remaining bran to the bowl. Cream the butter and sugar together until pale and light. Alternately beat in the eggs and fold in the flour. Add a little milk to soften the mixture if necessary. Fold in the sliced fruit. Spoon the mixture into the prepared cake tin. Level the surface, making a dip in the centre.

Bake for 50 minutes to 1 hour or until cooked. The cake is cooked when it is firm to the touch, golden brown, and beginning to leave the sides of the tin. Cover the cake with greaseproof paper if it starts to brown to quickly. Remove from the oven and leave to cool in the tin. Store in an airtight container for up to 2 days. Dust with icing sugar and serve at tea time, or with whipped cream as a pudding.

SHEER LUXURY CHERRY CHEESECAKE

SERVES 12

For the base:	The grated rind and juice of 1 orange
110 g (4 oz) plain flour	230 ml (8 fl oz) milk
83 g (3 oz) unsalted butter	15 g (½ oz) powdered gelatine
40 g (1½ oz) icing sugar, sifted	340 g (12 oz) cream cheese
1 egg yolk, size 3	430 ml (¾ pt) double cream
For the filling:	*To decorate:*
340 g (12 oz) cherries, stoned	230 ml (½ pt) double cream, whipped
3 tablespoons Kirsch	A few cherries with stalks
3 egg yolks, size 3	A 21.5 cm (8½ in) loose-based
170 g (6 oz) caster sugar	spring-clip tin, greased
1 tablespoon plain flour	A piping bag fitted with a large star nozzle

Make the pastry as described on page 61 in the recipe for Victoria Plum Lattice Tart.

Set the oven at Gas Mark 6, 400°C, 200°C. Roll out the pastry on a lightly floured surface and use to line the base of the tin. Prick with a fork, then line with grease-proof paper and baking beans. Bake 'blind' for 10 minutes, remove the beans and paper and return to the oven for a further 10 minutes. Leave to cool.

To make the filling, place the cherries with the Kirsch in a heavy based pan and heat gently until the cherries are tender. Remove from the heat and leave to cool. Meanwhile in another heavy based pan, gently heat the egg yolks with the sugar, flour, grated orange rind and milk, stirring all the time. Cook until the mixture has thickened slightly to make a custard, but do not allow to boil. Leave to cool

Sprinkle the gelatine over the orange juice in a small heatproof bowl and leave for 5 minutes. Stand the bowl in hot water and heat gently to dissolve the gelatine.

Beat the cream cheese until soft, add the cream and beat until thick. Mix in the custard, stir in the gelatine, cherries and their liquid. Pour filling over pastry base and leave to set overnight in the fridge. To finish, remove from the tin, pipe a rope of cream around the sides and place cherries on the top. Serve within 12 hours.

OPPOSITE High Rise Scones. Serve them with home made jam, such as Cherry Jam (see recipe page 63) and whipped or crusted clotted cream.

SAFFRON BREAD

MAKES ONE LARGE LOAF
This light, golden, aromatic bread is delicious served warm with Mussels with Cream and Saffron Sauce.

680 g (1½ lb) strong, unbleached white
bread flour
1½ teaspoons salt
30 g (1 oz) fat (butter or lard)
1 sachet easy-blend yeast
1 teaspoon saffron strands, soaked in 1
tablespoon hot water
430 ml (15 fl oz) lukewarm milk
Beaten egg to glaze

Sieve the flour and salt into a large, warmed mixing bowl. Rub in the fat and stir in the yeast. When thoroughly blended, stir in the saffron (with any liquid) and lukewarm milk, and mix to make a soft but not sticky dough. Turn the dough out on to a lightly floured work surface and knead thoroughly for 10 minutes until smooth. Place the dough in an oiled bowl, cover with oiled cling film and leave in a warm place until doubled in size.

Knock back the proved dough with your knuckles. Roll out the dough to a large rectangle and carefully roll up like a Swiss roll. Tuck the ends under and place on a greased baking tray. Cover with oiled cling film and leave to prove in a warm place until doubled in size – about 30 to 45 minutes.

Meanwhile, set the oven at Gas Mark 8, 450°F, 230°C.

Brush the top of the bread with the beaten egg to glaze and bake for about 25 to 30 minutes until cooked through – the loaf will sound hollow when tapped underneath.

TO FREEZE: leave to cool, wrap in cling film and foil. Freeze for up to 5 months.

TO USE FROM FROZEN: thaw on a wire rack, uncovered, for 3 hours.

TRADITIONAL HEAVY CAKE

MAKES ONE 15 CM (6 IN) CAKE
This rich, scone-like flat cake is best eaten straight from the oven.

170 g (6 oz) plain flour
¼ teaspoon salt
85 g (3 oz) lard, chilled and diced
40 g (1½ oz) caster sugar
85 g (3 oz) currants
1 tablespoon mixed peel, finely chopped (optional)
To serve:
Caster sugar for dredging
Clotted cream

Set the oven at Gas Mark 5, 375°F, 190°C. Sift the flour and salt into a bowl. Rub in the lard until the mixture resembles fine breadcrumbs, then stir in the remaining ingredients. Mix with enough cold water to form a soft but not sticky dough.

Knead gently and roll out or pat out on a lightly floured work surface to a circle about 2.5 cm (1 in) thick and about 15 cm (6 in) across. Transfer to a greased baking tray. Using a sharp knife, make a criss-cross pattern on top of the cake. Bake for 35 to 40 minutes.

Leave to cool on the baking tray for about 5 minutes before turning out on to a wire rack. Dredge with caster sugar and serve warm with clotted cream. Heavy cake is best eaten the same day, but if you have any leftovers they can be kept in an airtight tin and warmed in the oven before serving again.

For an even richer, moister cake, omit the lard and water and add about 230 ml (8 oz) clotted cream, to make a soft but not sticky dough, then continue as before.

HIGH RISE SCONES

MAKES 6 SCONES
Serve with Cherry Jam (see page 63), whipped cream or Devon's crusted clotted cream.

For the dough:	60 g (2 oz) butter
115 ml (4 fl oz) milk	30 g (1 oz) caster sugar
1 teaspoon lemon juice	For the glaze:
230 g (8 oz) plain flour	1 egg, size 3
1½ teaspoons baking powder	1 teaspoon caster sugar
½ teaspoon salt	A 5.5 cm (2¼ in) round, fluted cutter

Set the oven at Gas Mark 7, 425°F, 220°C. Mix the milk and lemon juice. Sift the flour, baking powder and salt into a large bowl. Roughly cut up the butter and rub into the flour until the mixture resembles fine breadcrumbs. Mix in the sugar.

Make a well in the centre of the mixture and pour in the milk. Mix gently together with a palette knife – the mixture will be quite damp. Using your hands, gently bring the dough into a smooth ball. Place on a lightly floured work surface and gently press out to a 2.5 cm (1 in) thickness. Dip the cutter in a little flour and stamp out rounds, gently rerolling the trimmings as necessary.

To make the glaze, whisk the egg and sugar together. Brush the tops of the scones with the glaze. Place on a baking sheet dredged with flour and bake for 10 minutes or until well risen and golden. Transfer the scones to a wire rack and leave to cool.

To FREEZE: follow method for Cornish Fairings on page 98.

CHAPTER SIX

Scotland

Although Scotland is the most mountainous part of the United Kingdom, most of the country is in fact low lying and fertile, producing some of the finest and most famous food in the British Isles.

Scottish lamb and beef enjoy a worldwide reputation – Aberdeen Angus is a byword for excellence – and the black-faced breeds of sheep which graze on the heather are particularly well-suited to life on the exposed windy hillsides.

The land of Robert the Bruce has long been famous for game. The term is defined as wild birds and animals – like pheasant, venison, hare and grouse shot for sport during the shooting season – found on the moors and in the forests which cover half the country.

Huge catches of herring, haddock, halibut, whiting, cod, mackerel and sole are landed at the busy seaports. Crabs and lobsters are caught in creels off the coast of Fife. Scallops and winkles are found in the Western Isles and anglers love fishing for the beautiful salmon and trout in the pure waters of the deep lochs and fast flowing rivers that criss-cross the land.

Potatoes, peas, turnips and leeks, as well as many of Britain's finest fruits, grow well in the Scottish climate. And if the best blended whiskies are Scotland's answer to claret, then the finest malts are the kingdom's equivalent of Cognac or Champagne. Whisky is not just the national drink of Scotland – it is also one of the best-selling spirits in the world.

CREAMY SCOTCH PORRIDGE

SERVES 12

Surely the best porridge ever. Made with lashings of cream and served with plenty of brown sugar, honey and malt whisky, it will certainly warm many a heart.

170 g (6 oz) jumbo porridge oats
A pinch of salt
850 ml (1½ pt) warmed milk
850 ml (1½ pt) double cream
To serve:
Soft, dark brown sugar
Honey
Malt whisky

The night before, put the oats, salt, milk and cream in a heavy-based saucepan, bring slowly to the boil, remove from the heat, cover with a tightly fitting lid and leave overnight.

Next morning, stir the porridge, place the pan on the hob and cook gently for 10 minutes. Serve piping hot with the brown sugar, honey and malt whisky.

KINNAIRD COCK-A-LEEKIE SOUP

SERVES 4

A recipe from the 16th Century. The prunes are an innovation, adding flavour to the broth.

60 g (2 oz) carrot, very finely chopped
60 g (2 oz) celery, very finely chopped
230 g (8 oz) leeks, very finely chopped
1.15 litres (2 pt) good quality chicken stock
4 black peppercorns
230 g (8 oz) chicken leg,
free from fat, minced
2 egg whites, size 3

A pinch of salt
To complete:
12 small carrots, turned
30 g (1 oz) cooked leek,
cut into thin strips
60 g (2 oz) cooked chicken breast, free from skin and bone, cut into thin strips
12 ready-to-eat prunes

Mix the finely chopped vegetables with the stock, peppercorns, minced chicken, egg white and a pinch of salt in a pan large enough to leave plenty of room to spare.

Place the mixture on a medium heat and stir well. Once the mixture reaches a simmer do not stir but reduce heat to give a steady rolling simmer – this will not break up the crust which should have formed. Simmer gently for 1½ hours. Very carefully, strain through a jelly bag, avoiding the crust if possible. You should now have a pale amber-coloured liquid with a good flavour of chicken and leeks.

To complete, cook the carrots in a pan of salted boiling water for 10 minutes, drain and refresh with cold water. Set aside. Pour the liquid into a pan, then add the carrots, chicken, leeks and prunes. Serve the soup hot.
NOTE: to 'turn' the carrots, cut into 5 cm (2 in) lengths. If necessary, halve each piece lengthways. Using a small paring knife and working from top to bottom, trim off all the sharp edges – curving and turning the vegetables as you cut.

SCOTCH WOODCOCK

SERVES 6

This delicious dish dates back to Victorian times. It was always eaten at the end of the meal but nowadays can be enjoyed at breakfast time.

40 g (1½ oz) unsalted butter, softened
1 to 2 tablespoons chopped parsley
Ground pepper and lemon juice to taste
1 large uncut loaf of white bread
Oil for shallow frying
12 mushrooms

4 eggs, size 3
3 tablespoons single cream
Salt and pepper
30 g (1 oz) unsalted butter
A 6.5 cm (2½ in) round cutter
A 2.5 cm (1 in) round cutter

To make the parsley butter, mash the butter with the parsley, pepper and lemon juice to a smooth paste. Place on a piece of kitchen foil and shape into a cylinder about 2.5 cm (1 in) in diameter. Roll up in the foil and chill until firm.

Cut the bread into slices 4 cm (1½ in) thick. Using the larger cutter, cut out 6 rounds from the slices. Place the smaller cutter on the centre of each circle and cut two-thirds of the way down, as if making a vol-au-vent case (do not remove the centres). Fry the bread cases, a few at a time, in the hot oil until golden brown and nicely crisp, turning frequently. Drain on kitchen paper. When cool enough to handle, remove the centre portion of bread with a small sharp knife. Reserve the cases until ready to serve, then warm gently in a low oven. Grill the mushrooms; keep warm.

Beat the eggs with the cream and a little seasoning. Heat the butter in a heavy pan, add the eggs and scramble over a very low heat, stirring constantly. Spoon the scrambled eggs into the bread cases, top each with two cooked mushrooms, and finish with a slice of parsley butter. Flash under a hot grill for a few seconds, then serve.

The mushrooms may be replaced by 6 anchovy fillets, soaked in a little milk for 10 minutes, then drained, or a little cooked flaked Finnan haddock or kipper.

ABROATH SMOKIES IN CREAM

SERVES 4 TO 6

These are made from small haddock, with heads removed, that have been salted and smoked. Available in most fishmongers and supermarkets.

0.9 kg (2 lb) Arbroath smokies
280 ml (½ pt) double cream
Pepper and cayenne pepper to taste
A few tablespoons dried breadcrumbs
20 g (¾ oz) Scottish Cheddar, grated
4 or 6 ramekins or a small ovenproof baking dish, greased

Set the oven at Gas Mark 6, 400°F, 200°C. Remove the flesh from the fish, and flake into bite-sized pieces. Divide the fish between the small ramekins, or arrange in the base of the baking dish.

Gently heat the cream together with the seasoning until slightly thickened. Stir, then pour over the fish.

Mix the breadcrumbs with the cheese and sprinkle evenly over the top of the ramekins, or arrange in the base of the baking dish. Stand on a baking tray and bake for 10 to 12 minutes until bubbling. Quickly brown under a hot grill, then serve immediately with hot toast or crusty bread, and a salad.

As a delicious variation, you could add 2 tablespoons chopped fresh herbs to the Arbroath smokies before pouring over the cream.

PREVIOUS PAGE LEFT *Lord and Lady Macdonald's Kinloch Lodge, on Skye.*
PREVIOUS PAGE RIGHT *Rosette of Smoked Salmon with Quail's Eggs (recipe page 108).*
LEFT *Highland view from Kinnaird House.*

SMOKED SALMON QUICHE

SERVES 8

Use smoked trout for a cheaper alternative to smoked salmon.

For the pastry:	1 tablespoon freshly chopped parsley
170 g (6 oz) plain flour	The grated rind of 1 lemon
85 g (3 oz) unsalted butter	Salt and freshly ground
For the filling:	black pepper
280 ml (½ pt) whipping cream	340 g (12 oz) smoked salmon
140 ml (¼ pt) soured cream	or smoked trout
140 ml (¼ pt) milk	A 30.5 by 20.5 by 4 cm(12 by 8 by 1½ in)
6 eggs, size 3, beaten	baking tin, greased and base-lined
1 tablespoon freshly chopped dill	with foil

Set the oven at Gas Mark 6, 400°F, 200°C. Place a baking tray in the oven to heat.

To make the pastry, sift the flour into a bowl and rub in the butter with the tips of your fingers, until the mixture resembles fine breadcrumbs. Add enough cold water to make soft but not sticky dough. Wrap and chill for 10 minutes.

Roll out the pastry on a lightly floured surface and use to line the baking tin. Lightly prick the pastry case and chill for a further 10 minutes.

Line the pastry with greaseproof paper and fill with baking beans. Stand the tin on the hot baking tray and bake 'blind' for 10 minutes. Remove the baking beans and greaseproof paper, and bake the quiche for a further 10 minutes. Reduce the oven temperature to Gas Mark 5, 375°F, 190°C.

To make the filling, beat together the whipping cream, soured cream, milk, eggs, dill, parsley and lemon rind. Season with salt and pepper.

Chop the smoked salmon or trout into strips and arrange on the pastry base. Pour over the cream mixture and bake for 40 to 45 minutes, until puffed, golden and set.

Carefully loosen the quiche from the edge of the tin, cut it into 8 pieces and serve it either hot or cold, with a little green salad if wished.

CULLEN SKINK

SERVES 6

Finnan haddock (named after the Aberdeenshire village of Findon) are split, dipped in brine, then cold-smoked until they are a light golden colour. This traditional Scottish fish soup-stew comes from the shores of the Moray Firth.

3 Finnan haddock	230 g (8 oz) potato, peeled and diced
1.15 litres (2 pt) milk	Pepper to taste
30 g (1 oz) unsalted butter	5 tablespoons double cream
230 g (8 oz) onions, finely chopped	Chopped chives, to garnish

Skin and bone the haddock, and cut the flesh into chunks. Put the skin and bones into a large pan with the milk and simmer gently for 15 minutes.

Melt the butter in a large, heavy-based pan, add the onions and cook over a low heat until softened and transparent – do not allow to colour. Pour on the strained milk and add the haddock chunks, the potato and a little pepper. Bring to the boil, then simmer for 10 to 12 minutes or until the potato is cooked. Taste and adjust the seasoning. Serve in warmed bowls, with the cream swirled in and a sprinkling of chopped chives, to garnish.

BAKED KIPPERS

SERVES 2

Fish has been dried and smoked for centuries. This is a delightfully simple way of cooking kippers.

One pair undyed kippers
A knob of butter
Black pepper

Set the oven at Gas Mark 5, 375°F, 190°C. Cut off the heads, tails and fins of the kippers, using kitchen scissors. Lay one kipper, skin side down, on a lightly greased roasting tin and place a knob of butter on top. Season the fish with pepper.

Place the second kipper on top of the first, with the skin side uppermost. Pour enough boiling water into the tin to half cover the first kipper. Cover the tin and bring to the boil on top of the stove, then bake in the oven for about 10 minutes until the backbone lifts easily from the flesh. Serve the kippers at once with creamy scrambled eggs.

JUGGED KIPPERS

SERVES 2

One pair undyed kippers

Put the kippers, head first into a jug, or lay them in a roasting tin. Pour boiling water into the jug up to the fish tails, or cover with boiling water if using a tin. Leave for 10 to 12 minutes, depending on the size of the kippers. Drain and serve immediately.

OMELETTE ARNOLD BENNETT

SERVES 4

Look out for Langskaill – a rich mature cheese that combines perfectly with the haddock and eggs to make this classic Scottish dish.

680 g (1½ lb) smoked haddock fillets
280 ml (½ pt) milk and water mixed
6 eggs, size 3
60 g (2 oz) Langskaill or Cheddar cheese, grated

Pepper
15 g (½ oz) unsalted butter
140 ml (¼ pt) double cream, lightly whipped
A 23 to 25.5 cm (9 to 10 in) frying pan

Set the oven at Gas Mark 4, 350°F, 180°C. Arrange the smoked haddock fillets in a roasting tin and pour over the milk and water. Cover and cook for 10 to 15 minutes until just cooked. Cool. Remove skin and bones and flake the flesh. Beat the eggs with one tablespoon of the fish cooking liquid. Stir in the fish and half the cheese. Add pepper to taste.

Heat the butter in the frying pan, then pour in the egg mixture and cook until the bottom is lightly browned. Put the pan under the grill for a few minutes until the top is puffed up and set. Spread over the whipped cream and sprinkle with the remaining cheese. Brown under a hot grill until golden and bubbling.

HAM AND HADDIES

SERVES 3 TO 4

Finnan haddocks are salted and smoked at Finnan. They are very pale in colour since no dye is used in the process.

2 Finnan haddock
140 ml (¼ pt) milk
110 g to 170 g (4 to 6 oz) cooked gammon, bacon or ham, diced
15 g (½ oz) unsalted butter
Freshly ground black pepper
140 ml (¼ pt) single cream, warmed

Set the oven at Gas Mark 5, 375°F, 190°C. Put the haddock in a shallow ovenproof dish. Pour over the milk, cover and bake for 10 to 15 minutes. Remove the fish from the milk. Discard the skin and bones, flake the flesh into large pieces and keep warm. Fry the gammon, bacon or ham in the butter for about 2 to 3 minutes, then put into a heatproof dish and cover with the fish pieces. Season with black pepper. Pour over the single cream and place the dish under a hot grill for 3 to 5 minutes. Serve with plenty of crusty bread.

ROSETTE OF SMOKED SALMON WITH QUAILS' EGGS

SERVES 4

What a nicer and more appropriate way to include fish in a Burns' Night dinner than with Scottish smoked salmon and quails' eggs served with a creamy sauce.

14 quails' eggs
1 medium shallot, finely chopped
115 ml (4 fl oz) dry white wine
60 ml (2 fl oz) double cream
340 g (12 oz) smoked salmon, thinly sliced
110 g (4 oz) unsalted butter
A pinch of cayenne pepper
Salt and freshly ground black pepper
The juice of 1 lemon
To garnish:
A mixture of cooked courgette, carrot
and leek, chopped
Sprigs of fresh chervil

Boil the quails' eggs in a large pan of salted, boiling water for 3½ minutes, then drain and immediately refresh with cold water. Shell the eggs, starting at the pointed end, and set aside in warm, salted water.

Put the finely chopped shallot into a small pan, cover with the wine and simmer gently, stirring occasionally, until reduced by two-thirds. Add the cream and return to the heat to continue simmering until reduced by one-third.

Meanwhile, arrange the slices of smoked salmon on 4 warm plates, forming a rose-like shape in the centre of each. Take the warm quails' eggs and place a whole one in the centre of each of the salmon rose patterns, and surround by 5 half eggs.

Preheat the grill.

Add the unsalted butter in small lumps to the reduced shallot sauce and shake, adding seasonings and lemon juice to taste.

To serve, place each plate under the grill for a few seconds to heat (the salmon should be served warm, not hot) and coat with a little of the sauce. Sprinkle over the chopped vegetable garnish, and top with sprigs of fresh chervil. Serve at once.

HAGGIS TARTLETS

SERVES 4

Robert Burns was instrumental in making the haggis the national Scottish dish. This is a delightful way of serving haggis – and in traditional fashion, it should be accompanied by a dram of whisky.

2 large sheets filo pastry
85 g (3 oz) butter, melted
1 haggis, weighing about 455 g (1 lb)
340 g (12 oz) cooked potatoes, mashed
340 g (12 oz) cooked swede, mashed
A little butter
Salt and freshly ground black pepper
Sprigs of fresh chervil
4 small brioche tins

Set the oven at Gas Mark 6, 400°F, 200°C. Brush each piece of filo pastry with butter, fold in half and then in half again to give a sheet of pastry 4 layers thick. Cut the layered filo down the middle to make 2 squares. Repeat with the other sheet of filo.

Line each brioche tin with a square of layered pastry, pushing the pastry well into the sides of the mould and trimming the top with a sharp knife. Bake the tartlets for 7 to 10 minutes or until they are a light golden brown. Cool. The cooked tartlets will keep up to a week in an airtight tin.

Meanwhile, steam the haggis gently for 1½ hours. When the haggis is cooked, place the mashed potato and swede in separate pans, each with a little butter, and heat gently, stirring frequently. Season as required. Shape a little of each purée with separate spoons and set next to each other on a warm plate beside the filo pastry tartlets. Garnish with chervil sprigs.

Cut open the hot haggis and fill the tartlets, mounding it up in the filo cases. Serve with a dram of whisky.

LEFT *From left, clockwise: Kinnaird Cock-a-Leekie Soup (recipe page 104), Poached Scotch Fillet Steak with Horseradish Dumplings (page 110), Haggis Tartlets (recipe at right) and Rosette of Smoked Salmon with Quails' Eggs (recipe at left).*

POACHED SCOTCH
FILLET STEAK WITH
HORSERADISH DUMPLINGS

Scottish beef has a fullness of flavour which combines well with this rich Madeira and port sauce. The steak is poached gently in the sauce (which must not boil) and cooked to tender perfection. Arrange the turned vegetables (see note for Kinnaird Cock-a-Leekie Soup) and horseradish dumplings around each of the fillet steaks.

For the dumplings:	60 ml (2 fl oz) port
85 g (3 oz) flour	60 ml (2 fl oz) dry Madeira
40 g (1½ oz) beef suet	16 small carrots, turned
Salt and freshly ground black pepper	16 small turnips, turned
½ teaspoon freshly chopped parsley	16 small courgettes, turned
1½ teaspoons horseradish relish	1 teaspoon arrowroot
For the sauce:	1 to 2 tablespoons olive oil
280 ml (½ pt) good veal stock	Four 170 g (6 oz) fillet steaks,
280 ml (½ pt) beef consommé	well trimmed

To make the dumplings, mix all the ingredients together in a bowl and add enough cold water to make a soft but not sticky dough. Roll into walnut-sized balls. The dumplings may be made up to an hour in advance, or frozen, if required.

To make the sauce, place the stock, consommé, port and Madeira in a pan and bring to the boil. Boil rapidly until reduced by half.

Meanwhile, cook the carrots and turnips for 10 minutes in separate pans of salted, boiling water. Drain the vegetables and refresh with cold water, and set aside. Blanch the courgettes in a pan of salted, boiling water. Drain and refresh again with cold water, and set aside.

Mix the arrowroot with a little cold water and stir into the reduced sauce. Continue cooking gently, stirring constantly, until the sauce has thickened and is smooth and glossy. Remove the pan from the heat.

Heat the oil in a heavy-based frying pan until hot, add the steaks and fry to seal – taking care to give all sides a good colour without overcooking.

Return the sauce to the heat and bring to the boil; skim, if required. Add the dumplings and simmer gently for 4 minutes. Add the steaks to the pan, reduce the heat and poach without boiling (once the meat is added to the sauce it must not boil or the meat will toughen and spoil the finished dish). Cook the steaks for a further 5 to 6 minutes, keeping the meat pink. Add the vegetables and continue cooking for about a minute to warm through.

Arrange each steak on a warm plate surrounded by the dumplings and vegetables, all sitting in a generous measure of sauce. Serve immediately.

110

RIGHT *Poached Scotch Fillet Steak with Horseradish Dumplings.*

LEFT *Lady Maclean's house is set in acres of glorious woodland in Argyllshire.*

HAGGIS IN A BOWL

SERVES 4

This is probably the best known Scottish meat dish. It is made from minced offal and usually served on Burns' Night.

230 g (8 oz) lamb's liver
1 lamb's heart
2 large onions
110 g (4 oz) pinhead oatmeal
60 g (2 oz) shredded beef suet
1½ teaspoons salt
2 teaspoons freshly ground black pepper
Cayenne pepper, ground mace and ground nutmeg, to taste
A 1.15 litre (2 pt) pudding basin, greased

Rinse the liver and heart thoroughly. Peel and quarter the onions and put into a pan with the liver and heart. Cover with water, bring to the boil and cook gently for 40 minutes. Leave until cool. Reserve the liquid. Process or mince the liver, heart and onions, using the medium cutter of the mincer. Remove any tubes from the meat.

Put the oatmeal into a heavy frying pan and stir over a low heat until lightly browned. In a bowl, mix the oatmeal with the minced ingredients, the suet, salt, pepper and spices. Add enough of the reserved liquid to make a dropping consistency.

Fry one spoonful of the mixture, taste, and adjust as necessary. Place the mixture into a greased heatproof pudding basin and cover with a lid or greaseproof paper securely tied with string. Steam the haggis in a pan of water (with the water coming halfway up the sides of the basin) for 2 hours.

Turn out and serve with mashed swede and creamed potatoes.

SPICY VENISON CASSEROLE

SERVES 4

Scottish venison, perhaps, the best in the world, is now widely available.

1 tablespoon black peppercorns
1 tablespoon juniper berries
1 tablespoon whole allspice
280 ml (½ pt) red wine
2 bay leaves
0.9 kg (2 lb) stewing venison, trimmed and cut into 5 cm (2 in) cubes
4 cloves garlic, crushed

4 to 5 tablespoons sunflower oil
170 g (6 oz) shallots
110 g (4 oz) baby carrots
110 g (4 oz) baby turnips
2 tablespoons flour
280 ml (½ pt) good-quality beef stock
Salt and freshly ground black pepper
A large, heavy-based, flameproof casserole

Finely grind the peppercorns, juniper berries and allspice berries together using a pestle and mortar or a coffee grinder. Mix the red wine with the ground spices and bay leaves in a non-aluminium pan. Bring to the boil very gently, remove the pan from the heat and leave to cool completely.

Place the venison and 3 crushed cloves of garlic in a glass bowl. Pour over the cooled wine mixture, cover and leave to marinate in the refrigerator for 48 hours, turning occasionally.

On the day of serving, drain the cubes of venison, strain the marinade through a sieve and reserve. Set the oven at Gas Mark 3, 325°F, 170°C.

Heat half the oil in the large flameproof casserole dish, add the remaining crushed garlic clove, the shallots, carrots and turnips, then cook until well browned, stirring from time to time. Remove from the casserole using a slotted spoon, drain on absorbent kitchen paper. Set aside.

Pat the venison dry with absorbent kitchen paper. Add the remaining oil to the casserole and cook the venison in batches until well browned and sealed on all sides. Remove from the casserole using a slotted spoon and reserve. Add the flour to the casserole, stir into the juices and cook over a gentle heat for 2 minutes, stirring constantly. Return all the ingredients to the casserole, stir well and season with salt and pepper to taste. Cover and cook in the oven for 1½ hours, stirring from time to time, until very tender. Serve with hot jacket potatoes or creamed celeriac and a selection of lightly steamed green vegetables.

TO FREEZE: see instructions on page 50.

CLAPSHOT

SERVES 4

Turnips in the north are the coarse-skinned root vegetable with an orange flesh which, in the south, is known as swede. The combination of mashed turnip and potato is often eaten as an accompaniment to haggis.

455 g (1 lb) potatoes, peeled and
boiled until tender
455 (1 lb) swedes or turnips, peeled and
boiled until tender
60 g (2 oz) butter
1 tablespoon chopped chives
Salt and freshly ground
black pepper

Mash together the hot potatoes and swedes or turnips. Beat in the butter. Stir in the chives and season with plenty of salt and pepper. Serve immediately.
TO FREEZE: place the mixture in a rigid plastic container and freeze for up to 1 month.
TO USE FROM FROZEN: thaw the dish overnight in the fridge before reheating.

BASHED NEEPS

SERVES 4

Serve with baked, steamed or boiled haggis.

680 g (1½ lb) swede or turnip, peeled
30 g (1 oz) butter
3 tablespoons double cream
Salt, pepper and nutmeg

Dice the swede or turnip and boil for 20 to 30 minutes until tender. Drain well, turn on to a large chopping board and stir in the butter, cream, salt, pepper and nutmeg. Beat until creamy, then pile the piping hot mixture into a warmed dish and serve immediately.
TO FREEZE: place the mixture in a rigid plastic container and freeze for up to 1 month.
TO USE FROM FROZEN: thaw the dish overnight in the fridge before reheating.

ATHOLL BROSE

SERVES 4

Scottish farm workers accepted oatmeal, milk and salt as part of their wages, and so combined these ingredients to make a bowl of brose. Sometimes they bulked it out with barley for a main course or hedgerow fruits for a dessert. The Duke of Atholl introduced a richer version which used malt whisky and Scottish heather honey.

For the tuiles:
60 g (2 oz) icing sugar
30 g (1 oz) golden syrup
30 g (1 oz) flour
35 g (1¼ oz) butter, softened
For the brose:
40 g (1½ oz) medium oatmeal, dusted
with 1 teaspoon icing sugar
280 ml (½ pt) double cream
2 tablespoons clear honey
2 tablespoons whisky
A few drops freshly squeezed lemon juice
Fresh fruit to decorate;
for example, fresh redcurrants
A baking tray, greased and lined with
non-stick baking parchment

To make the tuiles, place all ingredients together in a large bowl, mix well, cover and leave aside for 30 minutes. Meanwhile, set the oven at Gas Mark 6, 400°F, 200°C.

Place teaspoons of the tuile mixture, well spaced out, on to the prepared baking tray and bake for 4 to 6 minutes or until golden brown around the edges. Remove from the oven and leave to cool for 2 to 3 minutes on the baking tray.

Wrap each biscuit around the handle of a greased wooden spoon. Cool on a wire rack. If the dough is too brittle, return to the oven for a few seconds to soften. Store the tuiles in an airtight container for 1 to 2 days.

To make the Atholl Brose, preheat the grill. Cook the oatmeal and icing sugar mixture under the grill until the oats are lightly toasted. Remove from the heat and leave to cool. When the cold, add the cream, honey, whisky and a couple of drops of lemon juice to taste. Whisk until the mixture forms soft peaks. Serve in bowls or wine glasses, decorated with the fruit of your choice and accompanied by the tuiles.

CLOUTIE DUMPLING

SERVES 8

Traditionally cooked in a cloutie (cloth).

280 g (10 oz) sultanas
230 g (8 oz) raisins
170 g (6 oz) currants
60 g (2 oz) glacé cherries, quartered
340 g (12 oz) plain flour
1 teaspoon baking powder
1 teaspoon mixed spice
1 teaspoon ground ginger
110 g (4 oz) fresh wholemeal breadcrumbs
230 g (8 oz) vegetarian shredded suet
230 g (8 oz) soft, light brown sugar
2 tablespoons golden syrup
2 tablespoons black treacle
1 tablespoon milk
2 large carrots, grated
2 eggs, size 3, beaten

Wash the fruit thoroughly and drain well. Leave to dry on a tray lined with absorbent kitchen paper for 4 hours.

Sift the flour, baking powder and spices into a large bowl, then add the remaining ingredients and the dried fruit. Mix to make a fairly firm mixture. Put a clean pudding cloth or large tea towel into a pan of boiling water and boil for 1 minute. Drain, and when cool enough to handle, squeeze dry. Lay the sterilised cloth on a work surface and sprinkle liberally with flour – this forms the important seal or crust around the pudding during boiling. Place the fruit mixture into the middle of the cloth and shape it into a neat round. Gather up the 4 corners and the edges of the cloth and tie them securely, leaving room for the pudding to swell slightly.

Bring a large pan of water to the boil. Place the dumpling in the pan, standing it on either a trivet or upturned saucer. Cover the pan and simmer the dumpling for 3 hours, topping up with boiling water as necessary.

The dumpling can be made up to 2 days in advance. Leave it to cool completely, unwrap and rewrap in greaseproof paper and foil. Store in a cool, dry place. To reheat, wrap in a sterilised tea towel and cook as above for 1 hour. Any leftover dumpling can be served cold and cut like a cake.

OATCAKES FOR CHEESE

MAKES ABOUT 10

These are served with a selection of Scottish cheeses, such as Mull of Kintyre Cheddar, Langskaill, Lanark Blue, Robrock with Sage, Bonchester or Smoked Arran.

110 g (4 oz) medium oatmeal
15 g (½ oz) butter, melted
A pinch of salt

A baking tray,
greased and lined
with greaseproof paper

Set the oven at Gas Mark 5, 375°F, 190°C. Place oatmeal, butter and salt in a large bowl. Add enough boiling water to mix into a stiff dough. Leave to cool slightly and then roll out on to a lightly floured work surface until 3 mm (⅛ in) thick. Cut out the oatcakes using a 5 cm (2 in) plain round cutter. Place on the prepared baking tray and cook for 3 to 5 minutes, or until lightly golden.

SCOTS PANCAKES

MAKES ABOUT 30

These quick and simple pancakes are also known as dropped scones because you 'drop' the mixture on to a hot griddle or frying pan.

230 g (8 oz) self-raising flour
A pinch of salt
60 g (2 oz) unsalted butter
30 g (1 oz) caster sugar
1 egg, size 3, beaten
230 ml (8 fl oz) milk
Oil or lard to grease griddle

Sift the flour and salt into a mixing bowl. Rub in the butter until the mixture resembles fine breadcrumbs, then stir in the sugar. Make a well in the centre of the flour and add the egg and a little milk. Mix together from the middle, gradually working in the flour from the sides, adding more milk as necessary – the final consistency should be that of double cream.

Heat the griddle or heavy-based frying pan until very hot and add a little oil or lard. Drop tablespoons of the mixture on to the griddle. For round pancakes, drop from the point of the spoon; for oval pancakes, drop from the side of the spoon.

Cook for about 2 to 3 minutes until the scones are slightly puffy and the surface bubbles. Turn the scones over and cook for a further 2 to 3 minutes until both sides are golden. Place the scones between clean tea towels while cooking the remainder of the mixture. Serve warm, spread with butter and a selection of honey, syrup and jams.

PREVIOUS PAGE *Hebridean shore.*
LEFT *Oatcakes are the perfect accompaniment for Scottish cheeses.*

DARK STICKY GINGERBREAD

MAKES ONE 455 G (1 LB) LOAF
*Try this deliciously spicy, sticky bread
served with lashings of butter.*

40 g (1½ oz) black treacle
40 g (1½ oz) golden syrup
85 g (3 oz) unsalted butter
85 g (3 oz) soft, dark brown sugar
130 g (4½ oz) plain flour
A pinch of salt
¾ teaspoon bicarbonate of soda
2 teaspoons ground ginger
¾ teaspoon ground cinnamon
1 egg, size 3, beaten
85 ml (3 fl oz) milk
A 455 g (1 lb) loaf tin, greased and lined

Set the oven at Gas Mark 2, 300°F, 150°C. Place the treacle, syrup, butter and sugar in a heavy-based pan. Stir over a gentle heat until the butter has melted and the sugar dissolved. Sift the flour with the salt, bicarbonate of soda and the spices, and beat into the butter mixture with the egg and milk. Pour the mixture into the prepared tin and bake for 1 hour 10 minutes until well risen and firm to the touch. Leave to cool in the tin as this helps keep the gingerbread moist. Remove from the tin, wrap in greaseproof paper and foil and store for 2 days before serving.

TO FREEZE: freeze, wrapped, for up to 3 months.

TO USE FROM FROZEN: loosen the wrapping and thaw for 4 to 5 hours at room temperature.

TODDY CAKE

MAKES ONE 28 BY 18 CM
(11 BY 7 IN) CAKE
*This light cake has a warming whisky
syrup poured over it. Cut into tiny squares
for tea, or cut into slabs and serve warm
with whipped cream for a
luxurious pudding.*

140 g (5 oz) unsalted butter
110 g (4 oz) soft, light brown sugar
140 g (5 oz) clear honey
2 eggs, size 3, beaten
200 g (7 oz) self-raising flour
For the syrup:
60 g (2 oz) sugar
3 tablespoons of whisky, or to taste
A 28 by 18 cm (11 by 7 in) cake tin,
greased and base-lined

Set the oven at Gas Mark 4, 350°F, 180°C. Place the butter, sugar and honey with 1 tablespoon of water in a pan and heat gently until melted and smooth. Leave to cool completely, then beat in the eggs. Sift in the flour and fold in to form a smooth batter. Pour into the prepared tin and bake for about 30 to 35 minutes or until golden and springy to the touch.

Meanwhile, to make the whisky syrup, dissolve the sugar in 85 ml (3 fl oz) water over a low heat. Remove from the heat and add the whisky.

As the cake comes out of the oven, prick the surface with a fork or skewer and pour over the warm syrup. Cool completely before removing from the tin. Eat the cake within 1 week.

TO FREEZE: do not add the syrup before freezing. Wrap the sponge in greaseproof paper and foil and freeze for up to 2 months.

TO USE FROM FROZEN: thaw at room temperature for about 2 hours before pouring over the syrup.

ROCK CAKES

MAKES ABOUT 15
*Use butter to make these spicy little cakes
found in most tea rooms. As a variation,
replace the raisins with sultanas or
currants, or a mixture of both, and
sprinkle with a little demerara sugar
before baking.*

230 g (8 oz) self-raising flour
1 teaspoon mixed spice
¼ teaspoon grated nutmeg
110 g (4 oz) unsalted butter
110 g (4 oz) demerara sugar
110 g (4 oz) raisins
3 tablespoons milk
Caster sugar for sprinkling

Set the oven at Gas Mark 5, 375°F, 190°C. Sift the flour with the spices into a mixing bowl. Rub in the butter with your fingertips until the mixture resembles fine breadcrumbs, then stir in the sugar and raisins. Add the milk and mix to form a fairly stiff dough, similar to that of shortcrust pastry.

Place large teaspoons of the mixture on greased baking trays and bake for 10 to 15 minutes. Leave on the trays for a minute, then transfer to a wire rack to cool completely. Store in an airtight tin and eat within 2 days.

TO FREEZE: open-freeze, then pack in polythene bags and stir in the freezer for up to 2 months.

TO USE FROM FROZEN: thaw at room temperature for an hour.

CELTIC CAKES

MAKES 8 TO 10

These traditional little cakes have light, crisp pastry bases, covered with jam and topped with vanilla-flavoured cake mixture.

85 g (3 oz) plain flour
40 g (1½oz) unsalted butter
For the filling:
85 g (3 oz) raspberry or strawberry jam
30 g (1 oz) unsalted butter
30 g (1 oz) golden caster sugar
1 egg, size 3, beaten
85 g (3 oz) plain flour
½ teaspoon vanilla essence
A 7.5 cm (3 in) round,
fluted cutter
10 patty tins

Set the oven at Gas Mark 5, 375°F, 190°C. Sift the flour into a bowl and rub in the butter until the mixture resembles fine breadcrumbs. Add enough water to make a soft but not sticky dough. Wrap and chill for 15 minutes.

Roll the pastry out on to a lightly floured work surface and use it to line the patty tins. Reserve any trimmings for decoration.

For the filling, place a little jam in the bottom of each pastry case. Cream the butter with the sugar until pale and light, then gradually beat in the egg, beating well after each addition. Fold in the flour and vanilla essence, then fill the pastry cases with this mixture.

Roll out the reserved pastry and cut into strips. Place 2 strips on the top of each cake to make a cross. Bake for 25 to 30 minutes until golden. Serve warm the same day as baking.

PITCAITHLY BANNOCK

MAKES ONE 23 CM (9 IN) ROUND

Traditionally, this decorated form of shortbread was broken above the bride's head as she entered her new home, with the intention of bringing health and happiness to the newly married couple.

30 g (1 oz) unblanched almonds
15 g (½oz) citron peel
110 g (4 oz) unsalted butter
85 g (3 oz) caster sugar
170 g (6 oz) plain flour
30 g (1 oz) rice flour or semolina

Set the oven at Gas Mark 3, 325°F, 170°C. Blanch the almonds in boiling water for 1 minute. Drain and, when cool enough to handle, 'pop' the almonds from their skins by pinching between the thumb and index finger. Finely chop the almonds and the citron peel.

Beat the butter until soft add the sugar and continue beating until light and fluffy. Sift the flours together and fold into the butter mixture with the chopped almonds and citron peel. Work the mixture until it forms a dough like that of shortbread.

Roll the pastry out on a lightly floured work surface to a 23 cm (9 in) round. Carefully transfer to a baking tray. Crimp the edges and prick all over with a fork. Lightly mark into triangles and bake for 20 to 30 minutes until golden. Leave on the tray for 5 minutes, then carefully transfer to a wire rack to cool completely. Store the bannocks in an airtight container for up to 3 days.

TO FREEZE: open-freeze, then wrap tightly in greaseproof paper and foil and freeze for up to 2 weeks.

TO USE FROM FROZEN: thaw the bannocks, uncovered, for 1 to 2 hours at room temperature, then crisp in a warm oven if necessary. Cool before serving.

OATY FLAPJACK

MAKES 10 FINGERS OR 20 SQUARES

Oats are used widely in Scottish baking since it is one of the few cereals that can survive the harsh weather conditions and poor soil.

85 g (3 oz) unsalted butter
30 g (1 oz) soft, light
brown sugar
3 tablespoons golden syrup
170 g (6 oz) rolled oats
A pinch of salt
30 g (1 oz) raisins
An 18 cm (7 in) square, shallow cake tin,
greased and base-lined.

Set the oven at Gas Mark 4, 350°F, 180°C. Heat the butter, sugar and syrup in a small, heavy-based saucepan until the sugar has dissolved.

Stir in the remaining ingredients and mix thoroughly. Spoon into the prepared tin and flatten with the back of a wooden spoon.

Bake for about 15 to 20 minutes or until golden brown. Leave in the tin to cool for 5 minutes, and then mark it into fingers or squares and loosen around the edges of the tin. When firm, remove from the tin and transfer to a wire rack to cool completely. When cold, break into fingers or squares, and store in an airtight tin for up to 4 days.

DUNDEE CAKE

MAKES ONE 20.5 CM (8 IN)
ROUND CAKE

*This traditional fruit cake is named after
the city where it originated.*

30 g (1 oz) whole unblanched almonds
280 g (10 oz) plain flour
A pinch of salt
A pinch of ground mixed spice
230 g (8 oz) unsalted butter
230 g (8 oz) soft, light
brown sugar
The grated rind of 1 orange
The grated rind of 1 lemon
4 eggs, size 1, beaten
230 g (8 oz) currants, washed
230 g (8 oz) sultanas, washed
170 g (6 oz) raisins, washed
110 g (4 oz) glacé cherries, chopped
2 tablespoons whisky or orange juice
A 20.5 cm (8 in) deep, round cake tin,
greased and lined

Set the oven at Gas Mark 3, 325°F, 160°C. Wrap a sheet of brown paper around the outside of the cake tin and tie securely with string.

Blanch the almonds and chop half of them, reserving the other half. Sift the flour, salt and mixed spice together. Cream the butter with the sugar until pale and light. Add the grated orange and lemon rind. Gradually beat in the eggs, beating well after each addition – if necessary add a little flour after each addition of egg to prevent the mixture from curdling. Fold in the flour using a large metal spoon.

Mix in the remaining ingredients, including the chopped almonds. Spoon into the prepared tin, smooth the top and arrange the remaining whole almonds in one circle neatly on top. Bake for 3 hours or until a skewer inserted into the centre of the cake comes out clean. After 1½ hours, cover the top of the cake with greaseproof paper to prevent it from overbrowning. Leave to cool in the tin.

Wrap the cake in greaseproof paper and foil and store in a cool, dry place for at least a week before cutting to bring out the flavour. The cake can be stored for up to a month.

BLACK BUN

MAKES ONE 20.5 CM(8 IN) ROUND CAKE

A rich and spicy cake baked in a pastry case to keep it moist.

For the pastry crust:
340 g (12 oz) plain flour
A pinch of salt
170 g (6 oz) unsalted butter
For the filling:
280 g (10 oz) plain flour
A pinch of salt
¼ teaspoon freshly ground
black pepper
1 teaspoon cream of tartar
½ teaspoon ground allspice
1 teaspoon ground cloves
1 teaspoon ground ginger
¾ teaspoon bicarbonate of soda

140 g (5 oz) demerara sugar
455 g (1 lb) muscatel raisins, washed
455 g (1 lb) currants, washed
60 g (2 oz) mixed peel, finely chopped
110 g (4 oz) blanched almonds,
chopped
3 eggs, size 3, beaten
6 tablespoons milk
2 tablespoons black treacle
1 tablespoon brandy
1 tablespoon rum
Beaten egg to glaze
A 20.5 cm (8 in) deep, round cake tin,
greased and lined.

Set the oven at Gas Mark 4, 350°F, 180°C. To make the pastry crust, sift the flour and salt into a mixing bowl and rub in the butter until the mixture resembles fine breadcrumbs. Add enough ice-cold water to make a soft, but not sticky dough. Roll out two-thirds of the pastry and use to line the tin. Put the prepared tin and the remaining pastry into the refrigerator to chill while preparing the filling.

To make the filling, sift the flour with the salt, pepper, cream of tartar, the spices and bicarbonate of soda into a large mixing bowl. Stir in the demerara sugar, and the prepared fruit and nuts. Add the eggs, milk, black treacle, brandy and rum. Mix well until thoroughly combined. Place the mixture in the chilled cake tin, pressing the filling down well.

Roll the reserved pastry into a 20.5 cm (8 in) round, brush the edge of the pastry lid with a little water and place on top of the filling, pressing firmly around the edge. Prick lightly all over with a fork, and brush with beaten egg.

Bake for 3 hours or until a skewer inserted into the centre of the cake comes out clean. After an hour, cover the top of the cake with a sheet of greaseproof paper to prevent the top from overbrowning. Leave to cool in the tin for 30 minutes then transfer to a wire rack to finish cooling. Wrap in greaseproof paper and foil and store in a cool, dry place for 3 to 5 weeks before cutting.

SCOTLAND

119

CHAPTER SEVEN

Wales

As anyone who has visited the principality knows only too well, Wales is, culturally and agriculturally, two nations. In the north, where the rugged mountains support nothing but sheep and oats, Welsh-speaking farmers have had to struggle against the hostile elements to scrape a living from the land. Down south, where they are more likely to watch 'EastEnders' and 'Emmerdale' than 'Pobol-y-Cwm', beef and dairy cattle thrive and, inevitably, milk, butter, cheese and cream, together with leeks, lamb and oats, feature heavily in traditional Welsh cooking.

Welsh lamb is lean and tender with a marvellously delicate flavour; and mutton pie is a tasty local delicacy well worth trying when you cross Offa's Dyke.

Salmon are caught in the rivers Teifi, Tywi and Taf in west Wales, where you can still see coracles at work and, on the Gower Peninsular, they still take ponies and traps out on the sands to bring back cockles.

Caerphilly, originally a favourite lunchtime snack down the mines, is the most popular cheese from the principality, but in the past few years many small producers have revived long-neglected types like Llangloffan, Llanboidy and Caws Fferm, while Teifi – Welsh goats' cheese – sells well throughout Britain.

CAERPHILLY AND LEEK BUNDLES

These delicate bundles look impressive but are not tricky to make. They have a delicious filling of leeks and Caerphilly cheese.

8 large sheets of filo pastry
60 g (2 oz) unsalted butter, melted
For the filling:
30 g (1 oz) unsalted butter
1 clove garlic, crushed
230 g (8 oz) leeks, washed and
finely chopped
110 g (4 oz) Caerphilly cheese, crumbled
Salt and freshly ground black pepper
A little salad, to garnish

Set the oven at Gas Mark 5, 375°F, 190°C. To make the cheese filling, melt the butter in a large, heavy-based pan, add the garlic and leeks, and cook until the leeks are softened but not coloured – about 5 minutes. Remove from the heat, add the Caerphilly cheese and season with salt and freshly ground black pepper.

Take a sheet of filo pastry and cut into 8 squares. Use 4 squares for each bundle, placing them on top of each other at a slight angle. Place a teaspoon of the leek mixture in the centre of the pastry, brush a little melted butter around the edges, and pinch the sides up to create a bundle. Continue making the bundles until all the mixture has been used up. Bake in the oven for about 5 minutes until golden. Serve garnished with a tossed green salad.

TO FREEZE: allow the bundles to cool completely, carefully transfer to a rigid, plastic container and freeze for up to 1 month.

TO USE FROM FROZEN: thaw at room temperature for 1 hour, then warm through gently in a low oven.

WALES

122

TANGY SMOKED FISH SALAD

SERVES 8

If possible use the wonderful locally-smoked trout and salmon from Dyfed to make this dish.

455 g (1 lb) smoked fish, preferably half trout, half salmon
110 g (4 oz) mixed salad leaves, washed
4 limes
For the dressing:
6 tablespoons sunflower oil
2 tablespoons lime juice
Salt and freshly ground black pepper
¼ teaspoon dry mustard
A pinch of caster sugar

Flake the trout and cut the salmon into strips. Arrange on 8 chilled serving plates with the salad leaves. Pare the peel from the limes and cut into fine strips. Segment the limes and reserve. Blanch the lime strips in boiling water for 1 to 2 minutes. Drain well, then plunge into cold water. Drain well and arrange the strips and segments of lime over the smoked fish.

To make the dressing, place all the ingredients in a screw-topped jar and shake vigorously until well emulsified. Drizzle over the fish before serving.

LEFT *Caerphilly and Leek Bundles and Tangy Smoked Fish Salad.*
PREVIOUS PAGE LEFT *Wales is one of the world's great sheep-rearing areas.*
PREVIOUS PAGE RIGHT *A selection of Welsh cheeses.*

LIKKY PIE

SERVES 6 TO 8

A great dish to serve on St David's Day.

For the suet pastry:	170 g (6 oz) rindless back bacon, diced
340 g (12 oz) self-raising flour	340 g (12 oz) leeks, washed and sliced
A large pinch each salt and pepper	A large pinch of dried thyme
170 g (6 oz) shredded vegetable	1 teaspoon flour
or beef suet	140 ml (¼ pt) single cream
For the filling:	Pepper
60 g (2 oz) butter	Beaten egg to glaze
1 onion, finely chopped	A 23 cm (9 in) deep, loose-based flan tin

To make the suet pastry, sift the flour, salt and pepper into a mixing bowl. Stir in the suet and mix to a soft dough with about 280 ml (½ pt) icy water. Turn out on a floured work surface. Roll out two-thirds of the pastry to a large circle and use to line the base and sides of the flan tin. Set the oven at Gas Mark 7, 425°F, 220°C.

To make the filing, melt half the butter in a frying pan. Add the onion and diced bacon and cook gently for 5 minutes, stirring frequently. Add the leeks with the remaining butter and the thyme and continue cooking gently until the vegetables are soft. Stir in the flour, and then gradually add the cream. Mix well, and season with plenty of pepper. Pour the filling into the lined flan tin and brush the pastry edges with a little cold water.

Roll out the remaining pastry to a circle large enough to fit the top of the flan. Cover the flan, sealing the edges firmly. Brush with beaten egg and decorate with pastry leaves cut from the trimmings, if wished. Bake for 15 minutes, then reduce the heat to Gas Mark 4, 350°F, 180°C, for a further 20 minutes. Serve hot.

WELSH RAREBIT

SERVES 4

Welsh creameries produce excellent Cheddar, Red Leicester and Cheshire cheeses. Any of them is ideal to use when making this traditional snack.

230 g (8 oz) mature Cheddar or similar
cheese, grated, plus a little for sprinkling
15 g (½ oz) butter
1 tablespoon Worcestershire sauce
1 tablespoon mustard
2 teaspoons flour
Pepper, to taste
4 to 5 tablespoons Guinness
4 slices of bread, toasted on one side only
Sprigs of parsley, to garnish

Put the cheese, butter, Worcestershire sauce, mustard, flour and pepper into a pan. Mix well, then add enough of the Guinness to moisten (the mixture shouldn't be too wet). Stir over a low heat until melted. When it forms a thickish paste, take out the spoon and swirl the mixture round the pan. Spread the mixture over the untoasted side of the bread. Quickly flash under a hot grill, then sprinkle lightly with a little grated cheese and garnish with sprigs of parsley. Serve immediately.

LAVERBREAD CROQUETTES

MAKES ABOUT 6
Wonderfully tasty, cooked with bacon rashers as a breakfast dish.

230 g (8 oz) cooked mashed potatoes
60 g (2 oz) laverbread (available in cans from health food shops)
1 tablespoon oil
30 g (1 oz) mixture of finely chopped leeks, carrots and celery, or
30 g (1 oz) finely diced bacon
Salt and pepper
To coat:
A little flour
1 egg, size 3, beaten
About 30 g (1 oz) dried breadcrumbs
Bacon fat or oil for shallow frying

Mix the potato and laverbread. Heat the oil, add the vegetables or bacon and cook until golden. Mix into the potato mixture, add seasoning to taste, then leave to chill for 1 hour.

When the mixture is firm enough to handle, shape into 6 sausage-shaped croquettes. Roll the croquettes in the flour, then dip in beaten egg, and finally coat in breadcrumbs. Chill until ready to cook, then shallow fry in hot bacon fat or oil until the croquettes are golden on all sides. Drain on absorbent kitchen paper and serve immediately.
TO FREEZE: freeze the uncooked croquettes between sheets of grease-proof paper for up to 1 month.
TO USE FROM FROZEN: cook from frozen, as above.

CELTIC PIE

SERVES 4 TO 6
A wonderfully flavoured savoury flan, made with an excellent oat base.

For the oat crumb base:
110 g (4 oz) butter
110 g (4 oz) oats
85 g (3 oz) wholemeal flour
A large pinch of salt
For the filling:
2 ripe tomatoes, sliced
2 tablespoons chopped fresh tarragon or basil
1 medium onion, sliced into thin rings
1 tablespoon olive oil
170 g (6 oz) farmhouse Cheddar cheese, sliced
A 213 g (7½ oz) can laverbread (from health food shops)
The grated rind and juice of 1 orange
140 ml (¼ pt) natural yogurt
2 eggs, size 3, beaten
4 tablespoons sweetcorn
Salt and freshly ground black pepper, to taste
Orange segments, to garnish
A 23 cm (9 in) flan dish

Set the oven at Gas Mark 6, 400°F, 200°C and put a baking tray into the oven to heat.

To make the base, melt the butter in a medium-sized pan. Add the oats, flour, salt and 2 tablespoons of cold water, and stir quickly with a wooden spoon: the mixture will look like putty. Using your fingers, press the oaty pastry into the flan dish to line the base and sides.

To make the filling, arrange the sliced tomatoes in an even layer on the base of the flan, and sprinkle with the chopped herbs. Gently fry the onion rings in the heated oil until softened but not coloured. Arrange the onion on top of the herbs, followed by the cheese. In a bowl mix together the laverbread, grated rind and juice of the orange, the yogurt, eggs, sweetcorn and plenty of seasoning. Spoon this mixture into the flan case, then set the flan on the heated baking tray and bake for about 40 to 50 minutes, or until set.

Garnish with orange segments if wished, and serve warm with salad and baked jacket potatoes.

LAVERBREAD QUICHE

MAKES ONE 25.5 CM (10 IN) QUICHE
Welsh laver is an edible seaweed. It is then processed commercially and made into a gelatinous purée called laverbread.

For the pastry:
100 g (3½ oz) plain flour
100 g (3½ oz) wholemeal flour
100 g (3½ oz) butter
For the filling:
2 tablespoons soya oil
230 g (8 oz) leeks, shredded
1 small carrot, finely diced
1 stick celery, diced
1 small onion, finely chopped
110 g (4 oz) streaky bacon, chopped (optional)
3 egg yolks, size 3
110 g (4 oz) low-fat cream cheese
280 ml (½ pt) milk or single cream
Half a 213 g (7½ oz) can laverbread
Pepper to taste
A 25.5 cm (10 in) loose-based flan tin

Set the oven at Gas Mark 5, 375°F, 190°C, and put a baking tray in the oven to heat.

To make the pastry, mix the flours, then rub in the fat until the mixture resembles fine breadcrumbs. Bind with 3 to 4 tablespoons iced water to make a soft but not sticky dough, then roll out the pastry and use to line the flan tin.

Heat the oil in a large frying pan. Add the vegetables and cook gently until tender. Remove and set aside. Cook the bacon (if using) in the pan until lightly browned and crispy. Mix the vegetables and bacon with the remaining ingredients. Taste, and adjust the seasoning. Pour the filling into the pastry case, then stand the quiche on the baking tray and bake for 40 to 45 minutes until the filling has set. Serve warm.

ANGLESLEY EGGS

SERVES 6 TO 8

A warming dish of leeks, potatoes and eggs with a cheesy sauce. Ideal for a light lunch or as a starter.

0.9 kg (2 lb) potatoes, peeled and diced
340 g (12 oz) leeks, green part only,
washed and coarsely chopped
For the sauce:
30 g (1 oz) butter
30 g (1 oz) flour
570 ml (1 pt) milk
Salt and white pepper, to taste
60 g (2 oz) mature Cheddar cheese, grated
To complete:
6 hard-boiled eggs, sliced or quartered
60 g (2 oz) mature Cheddar cheese, grated

Cook the potatoes and leeks in a large saucepan of salted, boiling water for 15 to 20 minutes, or until tender. Drain well. Tip into a processor and blend to the desired consistency. Season well. Spoon into a large ovenproof dish.

To make the cheese sauce, melt the butter in a heavy-based pan, stir in the flour and cook the mixture gently for about 2 minutes, stirring frequently. Remove the pan from the heat and gradually stir in the milk. Return the pan to the heat, and bring the sauce slowly to the boil, stirring to make a smooth, thickened sauce. Simmer the sauce for 2 minutes, still stirring, then remove the pan from the heat, stir in salt, pepper and nutmeg, followed by the grated cheese.

Arrange the hard-boiled eggs in a neat layer on top of the potato and leek mixture, then pour over the cheese sauce. Scatter the remaining grated cheese on top. When ready to serve, grill under a medium heat for 10 to 15 minutes, or until golden.

SOUFFLÉ OF PANTYSGAWN CHEESE

SERVES 4

Rich and creamy soufflés made with tangy Welsh goats' cheese.

For the béchamel sauce:
280 ml (½ pt) creamy milk
½ peeled onion
4 cloves
60 g (2 oz) butter
60 g (2 oz) flour
Salt and cayenne pepper,
to taste

To complete:
30 g (1 oz) Granary breadcrumbs
60 g (2 oz) Pantysgawn goats' cheese
4 egg whites, size 3
To serve:
115 ml (4 fl oz) whipping cream
30 ml (1 fl oz) hazelnut oil
4 ramekins, buttered

To make the béchamel sauce, put the milk in a heavy-based pan, stud the onion with the cloves and add to the pan. Slowly bring milk to just below boiling point, then remove from heat, cover and leave to infuse for 10 minutes. Strain and discard onion. Melt butter in a heavy-based pan, stir in flour and cook over a gentle heat for 2 minutes, stirring constantly. Remove from the heat and gradually stir in the milk. Return to the heat and cook gently for a minute, stirring constantly to make a smooth, thick sauce. Season to taste (the mixture should be well flavoured). Leave to cool, covered with buttered greaseproof paper to prevent a skin forming.

Set the oven at Gas Mark 5, 375°F, 190°C. Meanwhile, sprinkle the breadcrumbs in the base and up the sides of the buttered ramekins. Cut the cheese into 4. Whisk the egg whites until stiff but not dry and then fold into the gently warmed sauce in 3 batches. Spoon half of the mixture into the ramekins, pop a piece of goats' cheese on top, then spoon the remaining mixture on top of the cheese. Place the ramekins in a roasting tin half-filled with hot water and bake in the pre-heated oven for about 25 minutes or until fully risen and golden brown. Remove from the oven and turn out when cold. Wash and dry ramekins, then return soufflés to the ramekins and place in an ovenproof dish with sides.

When ready to serve, heat the oven to Gas Mark 8, 450°F, 230°C. Heat the cream almost to boiling point, remove the pan from the heat and gradually whisk in the oil, to form an emulsion. Season with salt and cayenne pepper, then pour the hot cream mixture carefully down the sides of the soufflés (between the edge of the ramekins and the cooked mixture) and bake again for 4 to 5 minutes.

NOTE: if using a fan-assisted oven, please consult the manufacturer's handbook for cooking instructions.

GLAMORGAN SAUSAGES

MAKES 12

Originally the poor man's sausage – these are ideal to serve to vegetarians.

140 g (5 oz) Caerphilly or Lancashire
cheese, grated
110 g (4 oz) fresh white breadcrumbs
2 tablespoons finely chopped
spring onion or leek
3 egg yolks
1 heaped tablespoon chopped parsley
½ teaspoon dried thyme
1 teaspoon mustard powder
Salt and pepper, to taste
1 egg white, lightly beaten
Dried breadcrumbs for coating
Lard or sunflower oil for shallow frying

Mix the cheese with the breadcrumbs and spring onions. Blend the yolks together with the herbs, mustard and seasonings, then add to the breadcrumb mixture to bind it.

Divide the mixture into 12, and then roll each piece into a small sausage shape about 5 cm (2 in) long. Dip them in egg white, then roll in the dried breadcrumbs and shallow fry, turning constantly in the fat until golden brown on all sides. Drain on absorbent kitchen paper and serve immediately.

WALES

127

FILLET OF TROUT WITH CROFFTA WINE SAUCE

SERVES 4

The Welsh Croffta wine can be replaced by elderflower wine or by any medium-dry white wine, and this recipe is equally good made with salmon fillets.

570 g (1¼ lb) trout	6 peppercorns
For the sauce:	70 ml (2½ fl oz) double cream
A few sprigs of parsley	70 ml (2½ fl oz) Croffta wine
½ small onion, sliced	*To complete:*
1 small carrot, sliced	30 g (1 oz) butter
1 stick celery, sliced	Sprigs of chervil and cucumber balls

Fillet and skin the trout, keeping the bones for the stock. Put the fish bones, parsley, onion, carrot, celery and peppercorns into a pan. Cover with 850 ml (1½ pts) cold water. Bring to the boil, and simmer for 20 minutes, then strain. Rapidly boil the liquid until it has reduced to about 140 ml (¼ pt) of thick, syrupy stock. Stir in the cream and wine and cook further until reduced to 85 ml (3 fl oz). Taste and adjust the seasoning if necessary.

Heat the butter until foaming, in a non-stick frying pan. Quickly sauté the trout fillets for about a minute on each side – don't allow to colour. Spoon the sauce on to warmed plates and arrange the salmon on top. Garnish with sprigs of chervil and cucumber balls (cut with a parisienne cutter or melon baller). Serve immediately.

Lamb with Almond and Parsley Sauce

SERVES 4

Ask your butcher to chine the lamb, and cut the bones down to a reasonable size.

2 best ends of Welsh lamb
(each with 6 cutlets)
The juice of 1 lemon
1 tablespoon chopped parsley
1 tablespoon chopped almonds
1 teaspoon chopped fresh rosemary
85 g (3 oz) butter
2 cloves garlic, crushed
For the sauce:
3 egg yolks, size 3
1 tablespoon chopped parsley
1 tablespoon chopped almonds
1 teaspoon grated lemon rind
1 clove garlic, crushed
Salt and pepper
170 g (6 oz) unsalted butter

Cut each best end of lamb in half, to give 4 portions of 3 cutlets. Remove the skin and trim down the bones. Score the fat with a sharp knife.

Mix the lemon juice with the chopped parsley, almonds, rosemary, butter and garlic to form a spreadable paste. Spread the paste over the meat and leave for 2 to 3 hours.

Set the oven at Gas Mark 7, 425°F, 220°C. Roast the lamb in the heated oven for 15 minutes, then reduce the temperature to Gas Mark 5, 375°F, 190°C, and cook for 25 to 30 minutes according to taste – the meat should still be slightly pink when cooked.

Meanwhile, prepare the sauce. Blend the egg yolks with the parsley, almonds, lemon rind, garlic and seasoning. Melt the butter until foaming, then pour on to the yolk mixture in a slow steady stream, whisking constantly, until the sauce is thick and creamy. The sauce must be served at once with the lamb – it cannot be reheated.

OPPOSITE *Classic Ratatouille, Welsh Lamb, Lamb with Almond and Parsley Sauce, Rosemary and Garlic Potatoes, Steamed Cauliflower, Banoffi Pie.*
ABOVE A *stone cottage in Wales.*

Honeyed Welsh Lamb

SERVES 6 TO 8

Welsh lamb is available nationwide. The meat is tender and lean with a delicious delicate flavour.

Salt and pepper
1 teaspoon ground ginger
2 sprigs of fresh rosemary
One 1.6 to 1.8 kg (3½ to 4 lb) leg
of Welsh lamb
(or a lean shoulder, boned and rolled)
170 g (6 oz) set honey
280 ml (½ pt) dry cider

Set the oven at Gas Mark 6, 400°F, 200°C. Line a roasting tin with foil. Rub salt, pepper and ginger into the lamb. Put the rosemary into the tin and set the lamb on top. Coat the meat with the honey and pour the cider around the joint.

Roast for 30 minutes, then reduce the heat to Gas Mark 3, 325°F, 170°C, and cook for a further 1½ to 1¾ hours (depending on the size of the joint), basting occasionally. Remove the meat from the roasting tin and keep warm.

Pour the meat juices from the tin into a saucepan and skim off the excess fat. Boil the juices until reduced and slightly syrupy, and add a little more cider if necessary. Taste the gravy for seasoning and serve with the lamb.

Welsh Lamb Cutlets in Cider Sauce

SERVES 4

Good with all roasts and cuts of lamb.

8 lamb cutlets or 4 lamb chops
For the sauce:
4 spring onions or 1 medium onion,
chopped
60 g (2 oz) mushrooms, sliced
1 clove garlic (optional), crushed
1 tablespoon oil
1 tablespoon lamb fat (see recipe)
1 tablespoon flour
1 tablespoon tomato purée
140 ml (¼ pt) sweet cider (or mead or wine)
140 ml (¼ pt) good meat stock
Salt and pepper

Grill, fry or roast the lamb according to your preference, reserving a tablespoon of the lamb fat for the cider sauce.

To make the sauce, fry the onions, mushrooms and garlic in the oil until tender but not browned.

Put the reserved fat into a small pan. Stir in the flour, tomato purée, cider and stock. Bring to the boil, stirring, to make a smooth sauce. Taste, and adjust the seasoning as necessary. Stir in the mushroom mixture and serve the sauce piping hot with the lamb.

PENTRE PORK

*Serve this piquant dish with boiled rice or
a lightly cooked fresh green vegetable.*

455 g (1 lb) pork fillet (tenderloin)
60 g (2 oz) butter
110 g (4 oz) mushrooms, sliced
½ green pepper, deseeded, cored
and chopped
½ red pepper, deseeded, cored
and chopped
1 tablespoon flour
280 ml (½ pt) good stock
2 to 3 tablespoons tomato purée
1 tablespoon demerara sugar
Salt and pepper
A small sprig of sage
140 ml (¼ pt) soured cream

Cut the pork into thin slices, and quickly
fry in the butter. Remove the meat from
the frying pan and set aside. Add the
mushrooms and peppers to the pan and
fry until softened. Stir in the flour,
followed by the stock, tomato purée,
sugar, seasonings and sage. Bring to the
boil, stirring constantly, then return the
meat to the pan. Simmer gently until the
pork is tender. Adjust the seasoning to
taste. Blend in the cream and serve.

WELSH VENISON

SERVES 6

An old-fashioned, very rich and delicious way to cook venison.

A 1.35 kg (3 lb) piece haunch of venison	*To complete:*
For the marinade:	15 g (½ oz) lard
280 ml (½ pt) claret	30 g (1 oz) butter
140 ml (¼ pt) port	2 onions, finely chopped
1 medium onion, sliced	140 ml (¼ pt) venison stock
2 carrots, sliced	(see recipe) or beef stock
8 peppercorns	Salt and pepper
1 bay leaf	15 g (½ oz) flour
	3 tablespoons double cream

Trim the venison (the trimmings and bones can be used to make the stock). Cut into
slices 1 cm (½ in) thick, then cut into large pieces. Put into a deep (not aluminium)
bowl with all the marinade ingredients. Stir well. Cover and leave to marinate for
3 days in the fridge or a cool larder.

When ready to cook, heat the lard and half the butter in a casserole. Add the
onions and cook slowly until softened. Lift the meat out of the marinade and drain
thoroughly. Add to the onions and cook over a high heat until brown on all sides.
Strain the marinade and add the liquid to the casserole with the stock and seasoning.

Cover and cook gently for 1 to 1½ hours until tender. Near the end of cooking
time, mix the remaining butter and the flour to a paste and whisk into the bubbling
venison sauce. Cook gently until the sauce thickens. Taste the sauce for seasoning
and stir in the cream just before serving.

WELSH LAMB WITH HERB CRUST

SERVES 4

*The breadcrumb mixture is pressed on to the meat during cooking to give a herby taste to
the succulent Welsh lamb. The gravy is equally delicious with plain roast lamb.*

For the gravy:	2 best ends of lamb, trimmed
About 0.9 kg (2 lb) lamb bones	2 sprigs rosemary
1 onion, quartered	*For the herb crust:*
1 clove garlic, peeled	1 tablespoon Dijon mustard
1 sprig rosemary	110 g (4 oz) fresh white breadcrumbs
1 teaspoon tomato purée	2 tablespoons freshly chopped parsley
For the lamb:	1 tablespoon freshly chopped rosemary
2 tablespoons olive oil	Salt and freshly ground black pepper

Set the oven at Gas Mark 8, 450°F, 230°C. Place all the ingredients for the gravy in
a roasting tin and roast for 20 minutes. Remove from the tin and place in a large,
heavy-based saucepan with enough cold water to cover. Bring to the boil, skim and
simmer for 15 minutes. Discard the lamb bones and strain the stock through a fine
sieve and reduce at a high boil to 280 ml (½ pt). Season to taste.

Set the oven at Gas Mark 7, 425°F, 220°C. To cook the lamb, heat the oil in a
large, heavy-based frying pan. Seal the lamb on both sides (about 3 to 5 minutes
each side), then place in the roasting tin with the sprigs of rosemary and roast for
about 10 minutes.

To make the herb crust, remove roasting tin from the oven and spread the Dijon
mustard over the lamb. Mix the remaining ingredients for the herb crust together and
press on to the lamb. Return to the oven for a further 20 to 25 minutes depending
how well cooked you like your lamb. Remove from the oven, cover with foil and
leave to stand for 5 minutes before carving.

SIMPLE STEAMED CAULIFLOWER

SERVES 6

If you've never steamed cauliflower you'll be delighted at how tender and delicious it becomes using this technique.

1.35 kg (3 lb) cauliflower florets
Salt and freshly ground black pepper
Freshly chopped parsley, to garnish

Steam the cauliflower in a steamer set over a pan of simmering water for 5 to 10 minutes. Season well, sprinkle with the parsley and serve immediately.

ROSEMARY AND GARLIC NEW POTATOES

SERVES 6

This flavoursome dish makes the most of the very first baby new potatoes of the year.

1.35 kg (3 lb) new potatoes, washed
4 sprigs rosemary
3 cloves garlic, peeled
110 g (4 oz) unsalted butter

Cook the potatoes with the sprigs of rosemary and garlic in a large saucepan of boiling, salted water for about 15 to 20 minutes or until tender. Drain and remove the rosemary and garlic, then toss in the butter just before serving.

CLASSIC RATATOUILLE

This colourful ratatouille can be made the day before and reheated just before serving. Here it is served hot, but it is also very good cold.

1 large aubergine
Salt
6 tablespoons extra virgin olive oil
1 red pepper, deseeded and diced
1 green pepper, deseeded and diced
1 yellow pepper, deseeded and diced
1 clove garlic, crushed
8 small onions, skinned and quartered

230 g (8 oz) courgettes, washed and sliced
680 g (1½ lb) tomatoes, skinned, deseeded and chopped
1 tablespoon tomato purée
1 tablespoon finely chopped marjoram
2 tablespoons finely chopped parsley
Freshly ground black pepper

Dice the aubergine into small pieces. Place in a colander and sprinkle with salt to extract the bitter juices. Leave for 30 minutes then rinse well and roughly dry on absorbent kitchen paper.

Heat the oil in a large, heavy-based casserole. Add the peppers, garlic and onions, and stir over a high heat for 3 minutes. Add the aubergine and courgettes and continue stirring for 2 minutes. When softened, add the tomatoes, tomato purée, herbs and seasoning, and cook for a further 2 minutes stirring constantly. Cover and simmer for 10 to 15 minutes, stirring occasionally.

ABOVE *Classic Ratatouille.*

BANOFFI PIE

MAKES A 20.5 CM (8 IN) ROUND FLAN

An ultra-rich pudding with an unusual filling of condensed milk that is boiled in the tin to create a gooey fudge. Serve in very small slices.

For the pastry:
170 g (6 oz) plain flour
85 g (3 oz) unsalted butter
For the filling:
A 397 g (14 oz) can of sweetened
condensed milk, unopened

2 medium-sized bananas
2 tablespoons lemon juice
280 ml (½ pt) double cream
Chocolate coffee beans,
to decorate
A 20.5 cm (8 in) loose-based flan tin

To make the pastry, sift the flour into a large mixing bowl. Rub in the butter, using your fingertips, until the mixture resembles fine breadcrumbs. Stir in enough ice-cold water to make a soft but not sticky dough. Wrap in cling film and chill for 10 minutes.

Meanwhile, set the oven at Gas Mark 6, 400°F, 200°C. Roll the chilled pastry out on a lightly floured work surface to a large circle and use to line the flan tin. Lightly prick the pastry. Line with greaseproof paper, fill with baking beans and bake 'blind' for 15 minutes. Remove the baking beans and greaseproof paper and bake for a further 10 to 15 minutes or until the pastry is cooked through. Leave to cool.

To make the filling, immerse the unopened tin of condensed milk in a pan of cold water. Bring to the boil, then partially cover and boil for 2 hours, topping up with boiling water as necessary. Remove the pan from the heat and run under cold water for 5 minutes. Leave to cool. Do not open the tin while the contents are still hot. When cool, carefully open the tin and transfer the condensed milk into a bowl. (It will have cooked to a thick caramel-coloured fudge sauce.)

Slice the bananas, toss in lemon juice and arrange over the base of the prepared pastry case. Spoon the condensed milk over the top and chill for up to 2 hours. Spoon or pipe the cream over the top. Decorate with chocolate coffee beans. Serve chilled. NOTE: take care never to allow the pan to boil dry or the can may explode!

TREACLE TART

SERVES 6
Every man's favourite pudding!

For the shortcrust pastry:
170 g (6 oz) plain flour
110 g (4 oz) butter
1 tablespoon caster sugar
1 egg yolk
For the filling:
280 g (10 oz) golden syrup
200 g (7 oz) fresh white breadcrumbs
The juice and rind of 1 large lemon
30 g (1 oz) demerara sugar
Glacé cherries, to decorate
A 20.5 cm (8 in) loose-based
deep flan tin.

To make the sweet shortcrust pastry, sift the flour into a mixing bowl. Add the butter, cut into small pieces with a knife, then rub into the flour with the tips of the fingers. Stir in the sugar. Mix the egg yolk with 1 tablespoon cold water and stir in, using a round-bladed knife, to make a firm but not sticky dough, adding a little more water as necessary. Wrap and chill the dough for 20 minutes before using.

Roll out the pastry on a floured work surface and use to line the flan tin, reserving the trimmings for the lattice. Chill while making the filling.

Set the oven at Gas Mark 6, 400°F, 200°C. In a bowl, mix together the syrup, breadcrumbs, lemon juice and rind. Spoon into the pastry case and sprinkle with demerara sugar. Cut the pastry trimmings into long strips and arrange in a lattice on top of the tart. Cut the cherries in half and place, cut side down in the latticed diamonds. Bake for 30 to 35 minutes until pale golden. Unmould and serve warm.

TO FREEZE: open-freeze until firm, then wrap in cling film and foil. Store for up to 2 months.

TO USE FROM FROZEN: thaw the tart, uncovered, for 4 hours. Warm through before serving if wished.

HONEY AND GINGER ICE-CREAM

MAKES 600 ML (½ PT) ICE-CREAM

An extremely quick, simple ice-cream made from Welsh honey.

170 g (6 oz) clear honey
430 ml (¾ pt) double cream
60 g (2 oz) stem ginger,
finely chopped

Whip the honey and cream together until thick, fold in the stem ginger and pour into a rigid, plastic container.

Freeze for 1 hour or until almost frozen, then blend in a food processor or liquidiser. Return to the freezer until ready to serve. Place the ice-cream in the fridge for about 10 minutes to soften before serving.

The ice-cream may be kept in the freezer for up to 2 weeks.

RIGHT *Honey and Ginger Ice-cream.*
OPPOSITE *Banoffi Pie*

WALES

133

SNOWDON PUDDING WITH SHERRY SAUCE

SERVES 8

Although traditionally cooked in a pudding basin, this delicious pudding can also be steamed in a loaf tin for easy slicing.

110 g (4 oz) large, seedless raisins
230 g (8 oz) fresh white breadcrumbs
230 g (8 oz) shredded suet
40 g (1½ oz) cornflour
170 g (6 oz) soft light brown sugar
The grated rind of 2 lemons
170 g (6 oz) lemon marmalade
A pinch of salt

6 eggs, size 3, beaten
A 1.15 litre (2 pt) pudding basin or loaf tin (base-lined)
For the sauce:
1 lemon
85 g (3 oz) granulated sugar
430 ml (¾ pt) medium sherry
110 g (4 oz) butter

Grease the basin and sprinkle a tablespoon of the raisins in the base. Combine the remaining ingredients and mix well. Spoon into the basin. Cover and steam for about 1½ to 1¾ hours until firm to the touch and cooked through. Turn out the pudding, and serve with sherry sauce.

To make the sauce, pare the lemon rind into strips, using a vegetable peeler. Put into a pan with the sugar and 140 ml (¼ pt) water. Heat slowly to dissolve the sugar, then boil for 10 minutes until syrupy. Mix with the sherry.

Melt the butter in another pan, stir in the flour, then the sherry mixture. Bring to the boil, stirring constantly, then simmer for 1 minute. Strain and serve.

WELSH CAKES

MAKES ABOUT 18

230 g (8 oz) self-raising flour
A pinch of salt
40 g (1½ oz) white fat
40 g (1½ oz) butter
85 g (3 oz) caster sugar
60 g (2 oz) currants, washed and dried
½ teaspoon ground mixed spice
1 egg, beaten
A little milk, to bind
Caster sugar for sprinkling
A 6.5 to 7.5 cm (2½ to 3 in) round biscuit cutter

Sieve flour and salt into a bowl. Rub in fats until the mixture resembles breadcrumbs. Stir in sugar, currants and mixed spice. Add egg and enough milk to make a firm but not sticky dough. Turn out on to a floured surface and roll to (3 to 5 mm ⅛ to ¼ in) thick. Cut into rounds with the biscuit cutter. Grease a frying pan and heat. Add the cakes, a few at a time, and gently cook until lightly browned on both sides. Dust with caster sugar while warm. Serve.

TO FREEZE: follow the directions for Cornish Fairings on page 98.

APPLE CAKE

MAKES ONE 20.5 CM (8 IN)
SQUARE CAKE

110 g (4 oz) butter
110 g (4 oz) soft, light brown sugar
2 eggs, size 3, beaten
The grated rind and juice of 1 lemon
230 g (8 oz) wholemeal self-raising flour
1 teaspoon ground cinnamon
455 g (1 lb) dessert apples, peeled,
cored and sliced
2 to 3 tablespoons honey or syrup
A 20.5 cm (8 in) square cake tin,
greased and lined

Set the oven at Gas Mark 4, 350°F,
180°C. Cream the butter and sugar
together until pale and light. Beat in
the eggs, lemon rind and juice. Fold in
the flour and cinnamon, to make a fairly
stiff mixture. Spoon into the tin and
spread evenly. Arrange the apples in a
neat layer on top of the cake, packing
them all on. Flick a little water over the
apples (this is very important), and
bake for 50 to 60 minutes. Warm the
honey or syrup and brush or drizzle
over the apple slices. Serve the Apple
Cake hot or cold.

BARA BRITH

MAKES A 0.9 KG (2 LB) LOAF
A famous Welsh teabread –
'Bara Brith' means 'speckled bread'.

170 g (6 oz) raisins
170 g (6 oz) sultanas
170 g (6 oz) currants
455 g (1 lb) strong, plain white flour
1 teaspoon salt
1 teaspoon ground cinnamon
1 teaspoon freshly ground nutmeg
1 teaspoon ground allspice
85 g (3 oz) unsalted butter,
cut into small pieces

280 ml (½ pt) milk
15 g (½ oz) fresh yeast
(available from supermarket
bakery counters or health food shops)
85 g (3 oz) dark, soft brown sugar
110 g (4 oz) mixed candied peel
For the sugar syrup:
60 g (2 oz) caster sugar
A 0.9 kg (2 lb) loaf tin, greased

Set the oven at Gas Mark ¼, 225°F, 110°C. Wash and dry the raisins, the sultanas and
the currants thoroughly. Sift the flour, salt and spices into a warm, ovenproof mixing
bowl and place in the oven for 10 minutes. Slowly melt the butter with the milk in a
small pan until it reaches blood heat.

Cream the yeast with a little of the warm milk mixture. Whisk in the brown
sugar, stirring well, then gradually add the remaining milk mixture.

Make a well in the centre of the flour mixture and pour in the yeast liquid. Using
a wooden spoon, mix well to make a soft, sticky dough. Transfer the dough to a
lightly oiled bowl and cover it with lightly oiled cling film. Leave the dough in a
warm place until it has doubled in size – this will take about 1½ to 2 hours. Turn the
dough out on to a lightly floured work surface and knead for 10 minutes.

Meanwhile, place the dried fruit and mixed peel in an ovenproof bowl and place
in the oven with the prepared loaf tin for 5 minutes. Knead the warmed fruit into the
dough. Set the oven at Gas Mark 6, 400°F, 200°C.

Shape the dough, place in the tin and cover with oiled cling film. Leave to rise
in a warm place until the dough comes to just above the top of the tin. Cut a slash
lengthways along the top of the dough.

Bake the loaf for about 1 hour and 10 minutes or until it sounds hollow when
gently tapped on the base. After about 20 minutes, cover with foil or greaseproof
paper to prevent the top from overbrowning.

Meanwhile, to make the sugar syrup, dissolve the caster sugar in 115 ml (4 fl oz)
of water in a heavy-based pan. Bring slowly to the boil, then remove from the heat.

Turn the loaf out on to a wire rack and immediately brush the top with the syrup.
When cold, wrap the loaf in greaseproof paper and foil. Store in a cool, dry place
for at least a day before cutting. Serve plain or buttered.

TO FREEZE: open-freeze until firm. Wrap in greaseproof paper and foil. Store for
up to 3 months.

TO USE FROM FROZEN: thaw, loosely covered, overnight.

ABOVE LEFT *Bara Brith.*

Northern Ireland

For centuries, traditional Irish cooking has been based on the good, whole-some, simple things in life – things like meat, butter, bread and, above all, potatoes. It's no surprise that Irish Stew is a simple but delicious casserole made with lamb, potatoes, onions and herbs!

Potatoes have not just been a staple crop and a vital part of the Irish economy since the 17th Century but they have also played a major part in political struggles over the years. Dunbar Standard, Pentland Dell, Kerr's Pinks, Maris Piper and Romano are the most popular varieties grown here. They aren't just roasted, boiled, baked in their jackets or mashed – but also used to make soup, pancakes and pies as well.

The wet climate encourages the grass in the Six Counties to grow green, rich and lush and so the region is famous for the quality of its milk, cream and butter.

Anglers flock to Northern Ireland for the salmon, trout, pike and perch. A quarter of the UK's bacon comes from Ulster and every high street has a bakery with shelves creaking with the weight of farls, loaves, barm brack, soda bread and, of course, potato bread.

If you're looking for authenticity, don't forget to serve a glass of creamy stout or a tumbler full of whiskey. (And never forget that, unlike Scotch, the Irish drink takes an 'e' between the 'k' and 'y' or, as they say in both Belfast and Derry, between 'the tumbler and the lips.')

Dilled Potato Salad
Curried Egg Mousse with
Rainbow Salad
– * –
Norah's Strawberry, Carrot
and Mint Soup
Leek and Potato Soup
– * –
Fadge
Fried Fish in Beer Batter
Bacon and Cabbage with Champ
Fish Pie
– * –
Glazed Roast Goose with Prune
and Orange Stuffing
Classic Liver and Bacon
A Traditional Irish Stew
Irish Colcannon
Beef in Guinness
– * –
Roast Vegetable Medley
Red Cabbage Apple and
Juniper Berries
Braised Celery with Bacon
– * –
Pears in Mulled Wine
Sheer Luxury Cherry
Cheesecake
Berry Glory
Assorted Fairy Cakes
– * –
Brandy Snap Baskets and
Butterscotch Sauce
Tiny Pastel Meringues
Fresh Fruit Tartlets
Tangy Lemon Sponge
Irish Porter Cake
– * –
Plum Chutney
Pear Chutney
Quick Spiced Fruit Chutney
– * –
Barm Brac
Soda Bread
Refreshing Lemonade

DILLED POTATO SALAD

SERVES 6

A favourite salad.

455 g (1 lb) small new potatoes, scrubbed
3 to 4 sprigs of fresh dill
Salt
For the dressing:
3 tablespoons olive oil
1 tablespoon wine vinegar
1 teaspoon chive-flavoured mustard
2 shallots or spring onions,
finely sliced
4 anchovy fillets, drained
and chopped
Salt and pepper, to taste
To garnish:
1 tablespoon fresh chopped dill

Put the potatoes and dill into boiling salted water and cook until tender – about 10 to 15 minutes. Meanwhile, place all the ingredients listed for the dressing in a screw-topped jar, with pepper to taste (salt may not be needed if the anchovies are salty). Shake the jar vigorously until emulsified. Taste for seasoning. Drain the cooked potatoes, place in a heat-proof, non-metallic bowl and pour the dressing over. Toss gently. When cool, cover the potato salad and chill for at least two hours.

When ready to serve, gently toss the potato salad, spoon into a serving bowl and garnish with fresh dill.

CURRIED EGG MOUSSE WITH RAINBOW SALAD

SERVES 4 TO 6

This light, interesting and mildly spiced mousse is accompanied by a crisp and crunchy rainbow salad.

¼ cucumber
1 dessert spoon coarse salt
One 11 g (0.4 oz) sachet gelatine
85 ml (3 fl oz) chicken stock
140 ml (¼ pt) mayonnaise
3 eggs, size 3, hard-boiled
and chopped
1 teaspoon curry powder
1 tablespoon lemon juice
Salt and freshly ground black pepper

85 ml (3 fl oz) double cream
To serve:
1 head of lettuce
4 tomatoes, sliced
1 cucumber, sliced lengthways
230 g (8 oz) carrots, grated
A few sprigs parsley, to garnish
A little French dressing
110 g (4 oz) feta cheese
4 to 6 small round ramekins, oiled

Peel the cucumber, cut in half lengthways and remove the seeds. Dice the cucumber, place in a colander and sprinkle over the salt. Leave to stand for 30 minutes to draw out some of the juices. Rinse thoroughly and pat dry with absorbent kitchen paper to remove excess moisture.

Sprinkle the gelatine over the stock and leave to soak for 5 minutes, then dissolve by placing the bowl in a pan of hot water.

Meanwhile, combine the mayonnaise, egg, curry powder, lemon juice and cucumber in a food processor or blender and process until smooth. Then add the dissolved gelatine and stock, season to taste, mix well and pour into a large jug. Leave in the refrigerator until just beginning to set. Fold the cream into the mixture and pour into the prepared ramekins.

Make individual rainbow salads using the lettuce, tomatoes, cucumber and carrot. Unmould a ramekin on top of each salad and garnish with a sprig of parsley. Sprinkle with French dressing and feta cheese.

PREVIOUS PAGE LEFT *Waterfall, Northern Ireland.*
PREVIOUS PAGE RIGHT *Brandy Snap Basket with Butterscotch Sauce.*
RIGHT *Curried Egg Mousse with Rainbow Salad.*
OPPOSITE *Norah's Strawberry, Carrot and Mint Soup.*

Norah's Strawberry, Carrot and Mint Soup

SERVES 6

This unusual soup is a light and refreshing way to start a meal. It may be served hot or cold.

2 tablespoons sunflower oil
30 g (1 oz) butter
2 medium onions, chopped
680 g (1½ lb) carrots, peeled and sliced
1 medium potato, peeled and sliced
1.7 litres (3 pt) good-quality chicken stock
340 g (12 oz) strawberries, hulled
16 large mint leaves
The juice of ½ lime or lemon
White pepper
280 ml (½ pt) single cream
To garnish:
strawberries, thinly sliced
mint leaves

Heat the oil and butter in a heavy-based pan and cook the onion until soft but not coloured. Add the carrots, potato and stock, bring to the boil and simmer gently until all the vegetables are completely soft. Leave to cool.

Pour the vegetables and stock into a food processor or liquidiser and work to a fine purée. Add the strawberries and mint to the food processor and whizz until smooth. Return to the rinsed-out pan. Stir in the lime or lemon juice and pepper, to taste.

When ready to serve, heat gently but thoroughly. Stir in the cream, but do not allow the soup to boil. Serve hot with fresh strawberries, thinly sliced, and mint leaves to garnish. The soup is also very refreshing on a hot day, served ice-cold in chilled bowls.

Leek and Potato Soup

SERVES 6

30 g (1 oz) butter
1 large onion, finely chopped
455 g (1 lb) leeks, washed
230 g (8 oz) potato, peeled
1.15 litres (2 pt) chicken stock
A bouquet garni
Salt, pepper and nutmeg, to taste

Melt the butter in a pan. Add the onion, cover, and cook gently until soft and golden, stirring frequently. Meanwhile, dice the leeks and potato, cutting the vegetables finely to make an elegant soup, or in larger chunks for a hearty soup. Add to the pan and cook over medium heat for about 8 minutes, stirring occasionally. Add the stock, bouquet garni and seasonings.

Bring to the boil, reduce the heat and simmer, stirring occasionally, 20 to 30 minutes until the vegetables are tender. Taste, adjust the seasoning, and remove the bouquet garni before serving.

To freeze: follow the directions for Harvest Soup on page 48.

Fadge

MAKES 18 TRIANGLES

Best fried in bacon fat and served with bacon, eggs and mushrooms, or simply on its own, buttered.

455 g (1 lb) cooked, mashed potatoes
½ teaspoon salt
30 g (1 oz) butter
About 110 g (4 oz) plain flour

Put the mashed potato into a bowl, sprinkle over the salt and dot with the butter. Knead in just enough flour to bind the potato together – do not add too much flour or the mixture will become tough. Cover the bowl and chill for several hours or overnight.

Roll out on a lightly floured work surface to 3 mm (⅛ in) thick. Cut into triangles or squares. Heat a little oil in a griddle or frying pan and cook the fadge until brown on each side – it will take about a minute. Spread out on a tea towel to cool. Serve warm or hot.

FRIED FISH IN BEER BATTER

SERVES 4

For an excellent way of deep frying, coat the fillets in this traditional Irish malty batter.

110 g (4 oz) plain flour
A pinch of salt
1 teaspoon dried, powdered yeast
1 tablespoon oil
200 ml (7 fl oz) beer
1 egg white
4 fillets skinned white fish,
each weighing 140 g (5 oz)
30 g (1 oz) seasoned flour
Oil for deep frying
lemon wedges, to serve

Sift the flour, salt and yeast into a bowl. Make a well in the centre, and pour in 2 tablespoons of warm water; leave for a few minutes until foaming. Mix it into the flour with the oil and beer to make a smooth, thick batter. Leave to stand in a warm place for 30 to 40 minutes, until it becomes frothy.

Whisk the egg white until stiff, then fold into the batter. Coat the fish fillets in seasoned flour, shaking off the excess. Dip in batter, coating the fillets completely and evenly. Deep fry in a pan one-third full of oil heated to 375°F, 190°C for 4 minutes or until golden brown and crispy. Thoroughly drain on absorbent kitchen paper and serve the fish immediately with chips, lemon wedges and tartare sauce.

BACON AND CABBAGE WITH CHAMP

SERVES 4

Stuffed cabbage parcels, fluffy potato champ, small bundles of carrot sticks and a good parsley sauce complement the succulent honey-roasted bacon to perfection.

A 0.9 kg (2 lb) joint of smoked gammon
A large bouquet garni
½ onion studded with cloves
1 carrot, quartered
1 tablespoon honey
2 teaspoons brown sugar
15 g (½ oz) butter
0.9 kg (2 lb) carrots, cut into sticks
1 teaspoon caster sugar
12 chives, blanched and cooled
4 large potatoes, peeled and quartered
60 g (2 oz) butter
60 ml (2 fl oz) milk
Salt and freshly ground black pepper
4 spring onions, finely chopped
½ head of Savoy cabbage
1 small onion, chopped
30 g (1 oz) mushrooms,
finely chopped
For the parsley sauce:
60 g (2 oz) butter
60 g (2 oz) flour
570 ml (1 pt) creamy milk
4 tablespoons chopped parsley
Salt and freshly ground black pepper
4 small round or oval ramekin dishes

Set the oven at Gas Mark 4, 350°F, 180°C. Put the gammon in a large pan with the bouquet garni, prepared onion and carrot. Bring to the boil and simmer for about 30 minutes (the gammon will not be completely cooked). Remove the skin from the gammon and put the joint into a roasting pan. Save the ham cooking liquid. Mix the honey, sugar and butter together and spread over the gammon. Roast the joint for a further 30 minutes.

Cook the carrots in a pan of boiling water with the sugar for 6 minutes. Drain, then tie them into tidy little bundles using the blanched chives. Keep warm.

Meanwhile, cook the potatoes until tender, then drain and mash them. Beat in 30 g (1 oz) of the butter and the milk, season to taste and beat in the spring onions – the mixture should be fluffy.

Blanch 4 of the outside leaves of the cabbage in the boiling ham cooking liquid and use to line the ramekin dishes. Finely chop the remaining cabbage. Fry the onion and chopped mushrooms in the remaining 30 g (1 oz) of butter for 5 minutes or until the cabbage is cooked. Use the mixture to fill the ramekins and then fold over the outer cabbage leaves. Place in a roasting pan half-filled with water and bake for about 5 to 6 minutes until ready to serve.

To make the parsley sauce, melt the butter in a small pan, stir in the flour and cook for a minute, then remove from the heat and gradually stir in the milk. Return the pan to the heat and slowly bring to the boil stirring all the time to make a smooth, thickened sauce. Add the chopped parley and seasoning to taste, and add any juices remaining from the gammon. To serve, arrange slices of the gammon in the centre of a large, warmed meat dish. Pipe or spoon a potato champ pyramid at the end of the dish, arrange the carrot bundles on one side and then turn out the cabbage ovals on the other. Serve with the parsley sauce.

LEFT *Bacon and Cabbage with Champ*

FISH PIE

Both sea fish and freshwater fish are found in abundance, and are deservedly popular with Irish cooks. We include several variations, using hard-boiled eggs or cheese.

680 g (1½ lb) white fish fillets,
such as haddock or cod
430 ml (¾ pt) milk
A bouquet garni
Salt and pepper
60 g (2 oz) butter
30 g (1 oz) flour
4 tablespoons chopped parsley
For the topping:
0.9 kg (2 lb) potatoes, peeled
60 g (2 oz) butter
2 tablespoons milk
Salt and pepper

Put the fish, milk, bouquet garni and a little seasoning in a pan. Bring slowly to the boil, then cover and simmer very gently for 10 to 15 minutes until the fish flakes easily. Strain the liquid and reserve. Flake the fish fillets into fairly large pieces.

Melt the butter, add the flour and cook for about 1 minute, stirring. Gradually stir in the strained fish liquid and bring the mixture to the boil, stirring constantly. Simmer for about 8 to 10 minutes, stirring occasionally, until the sauce is smooth and thickened. Taste and adjust the seasoning. Stir in the parsley and fish and turn the mixture into an ovenproof dish.

Boil the potatoes until tender, then drain thoroughly. Set the oven at Gas Mark 5, 375°F, 190°C. Beat the cooked potatoes with the butter, milk and the seasonings until light and fluffy. Cover the fish mixture with the potato. *Bake for about 15 to 20 minutes until golden.

As a variation to this recipe, you could add 2 chopped hard-boiled eggs to the fish mixture to make it go a little further, or sprinkle the potato topping with grated cheese before cooking, or add cheese to the sauce.

TO FREEZE: *open-freeze, unbaked, until firm, then wrap in clingfilm.

TO USE FROM FROZEN: thaw overnight in the fridge. Bake as above.

GLAZED ROAST GOOSE WITH PRUNE AND ORANGE STUFFING

SERVES 8

What could be more magnificent than succulent roast goose? The combination of this rich, dark meat with our light fruity stuffing is delicious. Order your goose well in advance from your butcher. Alternatively, fresh and frozen geese are available from most large supermarkets. If frozen, do make sure the bird is thawed thoroughly before cooking – 48 hours in the fridge for a 4.5 kg (10 lb) bird, for example. The recipes which appear later in this chapter, on page 145 – Roast Vegetable Medley, Braised Celery with Bacon or Red Cabbage, Apple and Juniper Berries – are all suitable accompaniments for this celebration dish.

1 oven-ready goose, about 4.5 kg (10 lb)
Salt and freshly ground black pepper
2 large bunches fresh sage
1 large onion, halved
For the stuffing:
30 g (1 oz) unsalted butter
2 medium onions, finely chopped
5 cm (2 in) piece fresh root ginger, peeled and grated
455 g (1 lb) pitted prunes, chopped
3 tablespoons concentrated orange juice

280 g (10 oz) fresh white breadcrumbs
2 tablespoons freshly chopped sage
Salt and freshly ground black pepper
To cook:
570 ml (1 pt) good-quality brown stock
For the gravy:
30 g (1 oz) shallots, finely chopped
200 ml (7 fl oz) red wine
570 ml (1 pt) good-quality brown stock
To garnish:
Flat-leaf parsley

Set the oven at Gas Mark 6, 400°F, 200°C. Prick the skin of the goose with a sharp fork and rub salt all over the skin. Put the sage leaves and onion in the 'parson's nose' cavity of the goose. Season the goose and put on a roasting rack set over a deep roasting tin. Cover with cling film and chill while preparing the stuffing.

To make the stuffing, melt the butter in a large, heavy-based pan. Fry the onions until softened but not coloured. Add the ginger and continue cooking for a further 2 minutes. Remove the pan from the heat and add the remaining ingredients for the stuffing. Mix well and leave to cool.

Stuff the neck end of the goose and sew it up or secure with a skewer, so that the stuffing doesn't spill out during cooking. Pour 570 ml (1 pt) good-quality stock over the goose. Cover with a sheet of buttered foil and roast for about 2 hours, basting the bird frequently. Finally, to crisp the skin, remove the foil and roast for a further 30 to 40 minutes or until the bird is cooked. The goose is cooked if the juices run clear when a skewer is inserted into the thickest part of the thigh. Remove the goose from the tin, cover it loosely with foil and leave to rest for 20 minutes – this will make carving easier.

To make the gravy, pour the fat from the roasting tin and reserve (it is delicious for roasting vegetables, and can be frozen, too), leaving the meat juices. Add the shallots to the roasting tin and cook gently until softened but not coloured. Add the wine and stock. Simmer the gravy for 15 to 20 minutes, then strain into a clean pan. Taste and adjust the seasoning as necessary and keep warm until required. Transfer the goose to a warmed serving platter and garnish with roast vegetables, and flat-leaf parsley. Serve with the suggested accompaniments.

RIGHT *Glazed Roast Goose with Prune and Orange Stuffing.*

CLASSIC LIVER AND BACON

SERVES 4

Pork has been a favourite meat in Ireland since the earliest times. Many traditional Irish meat dishes include some cuts of pork. Fine quality pig's liver was often used to make this classic dish, though you may prefer it with the milder lamb's liver.

455 g (1 lb) pig's or lamb's liver
3 tablespoons seasoned flour
340 g (12 oz) onions, sliced
3 tablespoons oil
230 g (8 oz) back bacon, rind removed
280 ml (½ pt) well-flavoured brown stock
1 tablespoon lemon juice
Salt and pepper
85 ml (3 fl oz) red wine or extra stock

Trim the liver as necessary, removing any membranes, and cutting out any ducts with kitchen scissors. Cut into wide strips and toss in the seasoned flour, reserving any extra flour. Fry the onions in 2 tablespoons of the oil until soft. Then raise the heat and cook, stirring constantly, until browned. Remove and keep warm. Grill the bacon until crispy and keep warm.

Heat the remaining tablespoon of oil in the pan and quickly fry the liver on both sides. Do not overcook; the liver should still be pink inside. Remove and keep warm. Remove the pan from the heat and sprinkle in the remaining seasoned flour. Gradually stir in the stock, lemon juice, seasoning and wine. Bring to the boil, stirring, and then reduce the heat and simmer for a couple of minutes more. Spoon the onions on to a warm serving plate and arrange the liver and bacon on top. Serve the gravy separately.

A TRADITIONAL IRISH STEW

SERVES 6

A favourite one-pot method of cooking.

1.35 kg (3 lb) old potatoes, peeled
680 g (1½ lb) onions, thinly sliced
455 g (1 lb) carrots, cut into thick matchsticks
Salt and pepper
About 1.35 kg (3 lb) middle neck of lamb chops
Stock or water (see recipe)
Chopped parsley for sprinkling

Set the oven at Gas Mark 2, 300°F, 150°C. Slice half of the potatoes thinly and put into a large casserole with the onions and carrots. Season well with salt and pepper. Trim the lamb chops and arrange on top. Cut the remaining potatoes in half and place around the meat. Season lightly. Half-cover the ingredients with stock or water. Cover and cook slowly in the oven for about 3 hours or until the meat is very tender. Slip any loose bones from the meat. Sprinkle with parsley and serve.

IRISH COLCANNON

SERVES 6

A traditional Hallowe'en dish.

280 g (10 oz) cooked roast beef
455 g (1 lb) cooked kale or cabbage, shredded or chopped
680 g (1½ lb) cold mashed potato
60 ml (2 fl oz) gravy
Salt and pepper
30 g (1 oz) dripping or white fat

Cut the roast beef into bite-sized pieces. Mix with the cabbage or kale, mashed potatoes, gravy and seasoning.

Heat the fat in a large frying pan (preferably non-stick). Add the mixture and flatten to form a cake. Cook cover a moderate heat for 10 to 15 minutes until the base is brown and crispy.

Turn the cake over and brown the other side or gently mix so that the crispy pieces are evenly distributed through the cake. When piping hot and browned, turn the cake on to a warmed plate and serve.

BEEF IN GUINNESS

SERVES 6

The best beer for drinking is the best beer for cooking. This rich dark casserole will be a winner with all Guinness lovers!

0.9 kg (2 lb) shin beef or lean braising steak
30 g (1 oz) dripping or white fat
110 g (4 oz) rindless streaky bacon, chopped
455 g (1 lb) onions, thinly sliced
230 g (8 oz) carrots, thickly sliced
230 g (8 oz) turnip or swede, peeled and diced
3 tablespoons flour
280 ml (½ pt) Guinness
280 ml (½ pt) good brown stock
A bouquet garni
Salt and pepper

Set the oven at Gas Mark 2, 300°F, 150°C. Cut the beef into 5 cm (2 in) cubes. Heat the fat in a large, heavy flameproof casserole and thoroughly brown the meat, a few pieces at a time. Drain and remove.

Add the chopped bacon and onions to the casserole. Cover and cook very gently until the onions are soft, stirring occasionally. Turn up the heat, add the carrots and turnip or swede and cook for a few minutes, stirring, until lightly browned. Stir in the flour. Cook for a minute then stir in the ale and stock. Bring to the boil, stirring constantly then replace the meat. Add the bouquet garni, a little salt and plenty of pepper. Cover and cook in the oven until the meat is tender – about 2½ to 3 hours.

TO FREEZE: follow the directions for freezing casseroles on page 50.

ROAST VEGETABLE MEDLEY

SERVES 8

An excellent combination of root vegetables – perfect with any roast meats, but especially with the Roast Goose recipe on page 142.

1.35 kg (3 lb) potatoes, peeled
680 g (1½ lb) celeriac, peeled
680 g (1½ lb) parsnips, peeled
Salt
85 g (3 oz) dripping or lard
Freshly chopped parsley,
to garnish (optional)

Cut the potatoes, celeriac and parsnips into evenly-sized pieces. Do not mix the vegetables together. Store in cold water until required.

Cook the vegetables separately in large pans of salted boiling water for 2 to 3 minutes. Drain and refresh under cold water. Drain well, then scrape the surface of the root vegetables with a fork, to make them crispy when roasted.

Set the oven at Gas Mark 6, 400°F, 200°C. Melt the fat in a roasting tin. Add the potatoes and then roast for about 30 minutes. Add the celeriac and the parsnips and roast for a further hour, basting frequently, until they are golden brown and tender. Sprinkle with salt and freshly chopped parsley, if wished, just before serving.

The vegetables may be prepared up to a day in advance and kept immersed in cold water with about a tablespoon of lemon juice.

RED CABBAGE APPLE AND JUNIPER BERRIES

SERVES 8

This colourful vegetable dish is perfect with game, or with goose, duck or pork.

85 g (3 oz) unsalted butter
2 onions, finely chopped
1 tablespoon juniper berries,
coarsely crushed
0.9 kg (2 lb) red cabbage, finely shredded
85 ml (3 fl oz) dry white wine
1 tablespoon soft, light brown sugar
2 tablespoons red wine vinegar
Salt and freshly ground black pepper
455 g (1 lb) Cox's, or other crisp
dessert apple, peeled, cored and
roughly chopped

Melt the butter in a large, flameproof casserole. Add the onions and crushed juniper berries and cook gently until softened but not coloured. Add the red cabbage and cook for about 5 minutes, stirring frequently. Add the wine, sugar, vinegar and seasoning. Mix well and bring to the boil, reduce the heat and simmer for 20 minutes. Add the chopped apple and continue cooking, stirring frequently, for 20 minutes more, or until the apples are softened and the red cabbage is tender. It should be served piping hot, and makes an excellent accompaniment to the Roast Goose recipe on page 142.

This dish can also be made the day before and reheated on top of the cooker for about 15 to 20 minutes. You may need to add a little extra liquid during this time, and stir the dish frequently.

BRAISED CELERY WITH BACON

SERVES 8

Take care not to over-cook the celery – it is delicious when it still has a little texture.

170 g (6 oz) rindless back bacon, chopped
1 tablespoon olive oil
2 carrots, peeled and finely chopped
230 g (8 oz) turnip, peeled and
finely chopped
2 heads of celery, washed and cut into
2.5 cm (1 in) diagonal chunks
280 ml (½ pt) chicken stock
Salt and freshly ground
black pepper
Celery leaves, to garnish

Cook the bacon in its own fat in a heavy-based pan until crisp. Add the oil to the pan and cook the carrot, turnip and celery for about 5 minutes, stirring constantly. Add the chicken stock. Bring to the boil, reduce the heat and cover the pan with a tightly fitting lid. Simmer gently for 30 minutes, stirring occasionally. Using a slotted spoon, transfer the celery to a warmed serving dish and keep warm.

Tip the cooking liquor and remaining vegetables into a small pan and boil rapidly until reduced by half. Season to taste and pour over the celery. Garnish with celery leaves and serve with the Glazed Roast Goose with Prune and Orange Stuffing, recipe on page 142.

145

PEARS IN MULLED WINE

SERVES 8

*This pudding is for those who prefer
something refreshing, fruity and very light
to finish the meal.*

200 g (7 oz) granulated sugar
A cinnamon stick
A strip of lemon rind
170 ml (6 fl oz) red wine,
such as Burgundy
8 Conference pears
2 teaspoons arrowroot

Place the sugar in a heavy-based pan
with the cinnamon stick, lemon rind,
red wine and 170 ml (6 fl oz) water.
Heat gently until the sugar dissolves,
then increase the heat and bring to the
boil. Boil for 5 minutes.

Peel the pears, leaving the stalks
on. Place the pears in the syrup, then
cover the pan and simmer gently for
about 20 to 30 minutes until the pears
are translucent and tender.

Carefully remove the pears and
place on a serving dish. Remove the
cinnamon stick and lemon rind, and
discard. Mix the arrowroot with a little
cold water then add to the sugar syrup.
Bring to the boil and simmer for a few
minutes until the liquid is clear. Pour
over the pears and chill until ready to
serve – up to 6 hours.

ALMOND AND CHOCOLATE CHEESECAKE

*The fairly long, slow baking time is the secret of the luxurious
velvety texture. Although this cake is at its best served hot, it is also good cold, and
can be reheated with care.*

For the base:	140 ml (¼ pt) double cream, lightly
230 g *8 oz) milk chocolate	whipped
digestive biscuits	30 g (1 oz) cocoa, sieved
60 g (2 oz) good quality	45 g (1½ oz) good quality plain chocolate,
plain chocolate	finely chopped
60 g (2 oz) unsalted butter	45 g (1½ oz) ground almonds
For the filling:	2 tablespoons brandy (optional)
2 eggs, size 3, separated	Icing sugar for dusting
85 g (3 oz) golden caster sugar	A 23 cm (9 in) loose-based or
230 g (8 oz) cream cheese	spring-release cake tin

To make the base, crush the biscuits, or process in a blender or food processor. Tip into a mixing bowl. Gently melt the chocolate with the butter, add to the biscuits and mix well. Use to line the base and sides of the tin to a depth of 5 cm (2 in), pressing the mixture down well with the back of a spoon. Chill while preparing the filling for the cheesecake (or for up to 24 hours, covered.)

Set the oven at Gas Mark 3, 325°F, 170°C. Whisk the egg yolks with the sugar until pale and very thick. Beat the cream cheese until smooth and softened, then gently fold in the lightly whipped cream. Carefully stir the cheese mixture into the whisked egg yolks with the cocoa, chopped chocolate, almonds and brandy (if using) and mix gently but thoroughly. Stiffly whisk the egg whites and fold in, in three batches, using a large metal spoon.

Pour the filling into the base and bake for 1½ hours or until set and lightly browned. Leave to cool for 10 to 15 minutes, then carefully remove from the tin, dust with icing sugar and serve while still quite hot, with vanilla ice-cream.

NORTHERN IRELAND

LEFT *Foxgloves.*

BERRY GLORY

SERVES 6

*To crush meringues quickly and neatly,
place in a polythene bag, tie securely and
tap gently with a rolling pin.*

340 g (12 oz) summer fruits – such as
110 g (4 oz) each of raspberries,
strawberries
and blackcurrants
430 ml (15 fl oz) double cream
170 g (6 oz) meringue,
lightly crushed
60 g (2 oz) toasted hazelnuts, chopped
Sprigs of mint, to decorate

Pick over the fruits. Cut up the larger
strawberries. Whip the cream until soft
peaks form. Layer the berries, meringue,
cream and hazelnuts in 6 tall glasses,
finishing with a layer of cream.

Chill before serving to allow the
meringue to soften slightly. Decorate
with sprigs of mint.

*OPPOSITE Tiny Pastel Meringues, and a
selection of summer berries with cream.*

ASSORTED FAIRY CAKES

EACH MIXTURE MAKES 18 TO 20
SMALL CAKES

For chocolate fairy cakes:
110 g (4 oz) unsalted butter, softened
110 g (4 oz) caster sugar
2 eggs, size 3
85 g (3 oz) self-raising flour, sifted
30 g (1 oz) cocoa powder, sifted
1 tablespoon milk
Forty 5.5 cm (2¼ in) paper cake cases
For the chocolate buttercream:
110 g (4 oz) unsalted butter, softened
230 g (8 oz) icing sugar, sifted
110 g (4 oz) plain chocolate
For the coffee and walnut fairy cakes:
110 g (4 oz) unsalted butter, softened
110 g (4 oz) caster sugar
2 teaspoon instant coffee granules
2 eggs, size 3
110 g (4 oz) self-raising flour, sifted
30 g (1 oz) walnuts, roughly chopped

Forty 5.5 cm (2¼ in) paper cake cases
For the coffee glacé icing:
2 teaspoons instant coffee granules
230 g (8 oz) icing sugar, sifted
Walnut halves, to decorate
For the orange fairy cakes:
110 g (4 oz) unsalted butter, softened
110 g (4 oz) caster sugar
2 eggs, size 3
110 g (4 oz) self-raising flour, sifted
2 teaspoons concentrated orange juice
The grated rind of 1 orange
Forty 5.5 cm (2¼ in) paper cake cases
For the orange buttercream:
110 g (4 oz) unsalted butter
230 g (8 oz) icing sugar, sifted
2 tablespoons concentrated orange juice
Candied orange and angelica leaves,
to decorate

To make the chocolate fairy cakes, set the oven at Gas Mark 5, 375°F, 190°C. Cream
the butter and sugar until pale and light. Gradually beat in the eggs, beating well
after each addition. Sift the flour and cocoa powder together. Fold into the creamed
mixture and add a little milk, if necessary, to make a soft, dropping consistency.

Spoon the mixture into double thickness paper cases and bake for 15 to 20 minutes or
until risen and golden brown. Transfer to wire racks and leave to cool completely.

To make the chocolate buttercream, cream the butter until soft, then beat in the
icing sugar. Melt 60 g (2 oz) of the chocolate over a pan of hot water. Add the melted
chocolate to the creamed mixture, beat well and use immediately. Spread the
chocolate buttercream on top of the cooled fairy cakes, then grate the remaining
plain chocolate into the centre of each cake. Remove the outer paper case and store
in an airtight tin for up to 2 days.

To make the coffee and walnut fairy cakes, set the oven at Gas Mark 5, 375°F,
190°C. Dissolve the coffee granules in a tablespoon of hot water. Cream the butter
and sugar until pale and light. Gradually beat in the eggs. Gently fold in the flour
and the dissolved coffee followed by the chopped walnuts. Bake, as before.

To make the coffee glacé icing, dissolve the instant coffee in 2 tablespoons of hot
water. Mix into the sifted icing sugar. Add a little more water, if necessary, to get
the right consistency. Spread on top of the cooled cakes, and decorate with walnut
halves. Remove the outer paper case and store in an airtight tin for up to 2 days.

To make the orange fairy cakes, set the oven at Gas Mark 5, 375°F, 190°C.
Cream the butter and sugar until pale and light. Gradually beat in the eggs, beating
well after each addition. Gently fold in the flour and orange juice. Bake, as before.

To make the orange buttercream, beat the butter until soft. Add the icing sugar
and mix well. Add the orange juice to soften between additions of icing sugar or add
at the end. Chill for a few minutes, then spread on top of the cooled fairy cakes.
Decorate with candied orange and angelica leaves. Remove the outer paper case and
store in an airtight tin for up to 2 days.

TO FREEZE: open-freeze the cakes, without icing, until firm. Pack them into a rigid
plastic container – layered with greaseproof paper – and freeze for up to 2 weeks.

TO USE FROM FROZEN: thaw at room temperature on wire racks, covered with a
clean tea towel, for about 1 to 1½ hours.

BRANDY SNAP BASKETS AND BUTTERSCOTCH SAUCE

MAKES 10 BASKETS

Fill the baskets with vanilla ice-cream and butterscotch sauce and top with raspberries and cream. Use long-life cream to make the butterscotch sauce — it will then keep for considerably longer in the refrigerator.

For the butterscotch sauce:	For the baskets:
60 g (2 oz) butter	60 g (2 oz) butter
60 g (2 oz) caster sugar	60 g (2 oz) caster sugar
85 g (3 oz) soft brown sugar	2 tablespoons golden syrup
140 g (5 oz) golden syrup	60 g (2 oz) plain flour
140 ml (¼ pt) long-life	¼ teaspoon ground ginger
double cream	2 teaspoons brandy
A few drops of	Several baking sheets, greased and lined
vanilla essence	with non-stick baking parchment

To make the butterscotch sauce, place the butter and both sugars in a heavy-based saucepan. Add the golden syrup and heat slowly until all the ingredients have melted and the sugar has dissolved completely. Continue to heat the mixture gently for a further 6 to 7 minutes. Remove the saucepan from the heat and slowly add the cream followed by the vanilla essence. Stir well to make a completely smooth sauce. Store in the refrigerator until required. Serve hot or cold.

To make the baskets, set the oven at Gas Mark 4, 350°F, 180°C.

Melt the butter, sugar and syrup in a saucepan set over a low heat, then stir in the flour, ginger and brandy. Cool slightly. Divide the mixture into 10 portions or spoonfuls. Cook 2 at a time on the prepared trays, spaced well apart. Flatten slightly and bake for 5 minutes or until golden brown.

Allow to cool on the tray for a minute before carefully removing and shaping over a small cup or orange. Continue in this way until all the mixture has been cooked and shaped into baskets.

Store in an airtight container until ready to use – they will keep for up to a week. Fill the brandy snap baskets just before serving.

TINY PASTEL MERINGUES

MAKES ABOUT 15 TO 18

Make these tiny meringues in batches, colouring each half differently. Leave some white and substitute brown sugar for white to give a different flavour.

2 egg whites, size 3
170 g (6 oz) white icing sugar or light brown soft sugar
Food colouring paste in assorted colours – such as red, green and yellow
A piping bag fitted with a large star nozzle

Set the oven at Gas Mark ¼, 225°F, 110°C. Place the egg whites and sugar in a bowl and set it over a saucepan of boiling water for 1 minute. Remove from the heat. Whisk with an electric beater until the mixture is very stiff – this takes about 5 minutes. Remove the bowl from the saucepan and continue to whisk for a further 4 minutes. Divide the mixture into 4, colour each portion with a little food colouring paste and mix in well. Pipe the mixture on to baking trays lined with baking parchment and bake for 1 hour.

Turn off the oven and leave the meringues to cool. When hard right through, store in an airtight container – they will keep for several weeks.

FRESH FRUIT TARTLETS

MAKES ABOUT 10

Choose a selection of prettily shaped tins to make these attractive tiny tartlets.

For the pastry:
230 g (8 oz) plain flour
3 tablespoons icing sugar
1 teaspoon salt
140 g (5 oz) unsalted butter,
softened slightly
1 egg yolk, size 3
10 mini tartlet tins, the same
or assorted shapes
For the pastry cream filling:
140 ml (¼ pt) full cream milk
140 ml (¼ pt) double cream
1 vanilla pod

1 egg, size 3
1 egg yolk, size 3
60 g (2 oz) vanilla sugar
15 g (½ oz) plain flour
15 g (½ oz) cornflour
30 g (1 oz) ground almonds
For the glaze:
3 tablespoons redcurrant jelly
2 tablespoons cassis
1 teaspoon lemon juice
To complete:
455 g (1 lb) fresh fruit, hulled if necessary
Fresh mint leaves, to decorate

Sift the flour, icing sugar and salt on to a clean work surface. Make a well in the centre of the flour and add the butter and egg yolk. Pinch the butter and eggs together lightly with the fingertips of one hand. Start bringing a little flour in from the edges until the mixture is less sticky. Using a palette knife, cut in the remaining flour and blend until crumbly. Form into a smooth ball, wrap in cling film and chill in the refrigerator for about 15 minutes.

Roll out small pieces of dough to a thickness of 3 mm (⅛ in) and line the tartlet tins. Re-roll the trimmings, but avoid adding extra flour, if possible. Arrange the tins on baking trays and chill for 30 minutes.

Meanwhile, set the oven at Gas Mark 6, 400°F, 200°C. Lightly prick the pastry. Line the pastry with greaseproof paper, fill with baking beans and bake 'blind' for about 5 minutes. Remove the baking beans and the greaseproof paper and bake for a further 5-10 minutes. Leave the pastry cases in the oven for 3 minutes, then remove from the tins and place on wire racks to cool. Store in an airtight container in the fridge for up to 2 days, or freeze until required.

To make the pastry cream, place the the milk, cream and vanilla pod in a saucepan and heat until just beginning to boil. Leave to infuse for 10 minutes, then remove the vanilla pod. Whisk the egg, egg yolk and sugar until pale, thick and creamy, then whisk in the flours.

Pour the hot milk mixture over the egg mixture, mix well and return to the rinsed out pan. Stir the mixture over a very low heat, taking care it does not stick to the bottom of the pan. When it thickens, remove from the heat and give it a good whisk. Sift the ground almonds into the mixture and whisk again. Leave to cool. Store in an airtight container in the fridge for up to 6 hours.

To make the glaze, mix all the ingredients in a small pan over a low heat until the jelly has dissolved. Bring to the boil and simmer to form a syrup that will be easy to brush over the fresh fruit.

To assemble, whisk the pastry cream and spoon evenly into the pastry cases. Arrange the fresh fruit on top, brush with a little redcurrant glaze and decorate with mint leaves. The assembled tartlets can be stored for up to 3 hours before serving.

RIGHT *Tangy Lemon Sponge (top)*
with Fresh Fruit Tartlets.

TANGY LEMON
SPONGE

*A light sponge, filled with fresh cream and
lemon, and decorated with a dusting of
icing sugar and crystallised rose petals.
To crystallise the rose petals, dip them in a
little lightly whisked egg white, then into
caster sugar. Let dry, and repeat the
process twice more.*

**4 eggs, size 3
170 g (6 oz) caster sugar
170 g (6 oz) self-raising flour, sifted**
For the filling:
**280 ml (½ pt) double cream
2 teaspoons icing sugar
1 tablespoon lemon juice
170 g (6 oz) lemon curd**
To decorate:
**30 g (1 oz) icing sugar, sifted
A few crystallised rose petals
Two 18 cm (7 in) sandwich tins,
greased and lined**

Set the oven at Gas Mark 4, 350°F,
180°C. Whisk the eggs and caster sugar
together until the mixture is pale and
thick enough to leave a trail for 8 seconds after the whisk is lifted.

Using a large, metal spoon, gently
fold in the flour. Pour the mixture into
the prepared tins and bake for about
25 to 30 minutes. Cover the sponges with
greaseproof paper if they start to brown
too quickly. Transfer to a wire rack and
leave to cool.

To make the filling, whip the double
cream with the icing sugar until soft
peaks form. Add the lemon juice to the
lemon curd and spread over the inner
sides of both sponges. Spread the cream
on the bottom layer, then sandwich the
sponges together. Dust the top of the
cake with icing sugar and decorate with
crystallised rose petals.

TO FREEZE: the unfilled sponge can
be frozen. Open-freeze until firm.
Wrap in clingfilm and freeze for up to
1 month.

TO USE FROM FROZEN: thaw the
sponge on a wire rack, uncovered, for
3 hours before filling.

IRISH PORTER CAKE

Great to have standing by if family or friends are coming to visit.

455 g (1 lb) self-raising flour
1½ teaspoons ground mixed spice
340 g (12 oz) butter, softened
340 g (12 oz) soft, light brown sugar
4 eggs, size 3, beaten
340 g (12 oz) raisins, washed
340 g (12 oz) sultanas, washed
230 g (8 oz) currants, washed
230 g (8 oz) mixed peel, very finely chopped
1 teaspoon bicarbonate of soda
200 ml (7 fl oz) Guinness or porter
A 23 cm (9 in) cake tin, greased and lined with greaseproof paper.

Set the oven at Gas Mark 4, 350°F, 180°C. Sift the flour with the mixed spice and set aside. Cream the butter and sugar together until the mixture is light and fluffy. Gradually beat in the eggs, beating well after each addition. Using a large metal spoon, gently fold in the sifted flour and spice, followed by the thoroughly dried fruit.

Dissolve the bicarbonate of soda in the Guinness or porter and add enough to the mixture to make the cake batter a soft dropping consistency – but do not make the mixture too wet. Spoon into the prepared tin and level the surface.

Bake for about 1 hour, then reduce the oven temperature to Gas Mark 3, 325°F, 170°C and then bake for 1¼ to 1½ hours more, until a skewer inserted into the centre of the cake comes out clean. (If the cake is becoming too brown, cover with greaseproof paper.)

Leave to cool in the tin then wrap in fresh greaseproof paper and foil and store in an airtight tin for a week. Serve sliced, with or without butter.

153

LEFT *The Giant's Causeway.*

PLUM CHUTNEY

MAKES ABOUT
1.8 KG (4 LB)/1.7 L (3 PT)

An attractive, richly coloured chutney with plenty of fruit flavour. Excellent partnered with cold roast meats and pork dishes.

0.9 kg (2 lb) plums, stoned and quartered
230 g (8 oz) cooking apples, peeled, cored and chopped
850 ml (1½ pt) white wine vinegar
15 g (½ oz) fresh root ginger
2 fresh green chillies, quartered
15 g (½ oz) allspice
2 cloves garlic, or to taste, crushed
340 g (12 oz) onions, finely chopped
340 g (12 oz) seedless raisins
680 g (1½ lb) soft, light brown sugar
1 teaspoon salt
Sterilised jars and covers, muslin

Put the prepared plums and cooking apples in a preserving pan with 280 ml (½ pt) of the vinegar and simmer gently for 30 to 40 minutes, or until the fruits have softened.

Bruise the ginger by beating with a meat mallet or rolling pin, then tie the ginger, chillies and allspice in a piece of muslin. Add the garlic and muslin bag to the plum mixture with the remaining ingredients, and stir over a low heat until the sugar is completely dissolved. Simmer, stirring occasionally, for about 45 minutes to 1 hour or until the mixture has thickened. Discard the muslin bag, squeezing well to extract the juices. Pot, seal and label.

PEAR CHUTNEY

MAKES ABOUT 1.6 KG (3½ LB)/1.7 L (3 PT)

Use windfall or slightly hard pears for this super-spicy mixture.

1.35 kg (3 lb) pears, peeled, cored and chopped
455 g (1 lb) onions, finely chopped
570 ml (1 pt) pickling malt vinegar
1 tablespoon yellow mustard seeds
1 teaspoon chilli powder

2 teaspoons salt
The grated rind and juice of 1 lemon
30 g (1 oz) fresh root ginger, peeled and finely chopped
455 g (1 lb) soft, light brown sugar
Sterilised jars and covers

Put the pears and onions in a preserving pan, add 570 ml (1 pt) water and stir well. Bring to the boil, then reduce the heat and simmer for 10 to 15 minutes or until the fruit is softened, stirring frequently. Add half the vinegar, plus the mustard seeds, chilli powder and salt, and simmer for 30 minutes, stirring occasionally. Add the remaining vinegar, lemon rind, juice and chopped ginger. Stir in the sugar over a low heat until fully dissolved, then simmer the chutney for 1 hour or until the mixture has thickened, stirring occasionally. Pot, seal and label.

QUICK SPICED FRUIT CHUTNEY

MAKES ABOUT
2.15 KG (4¾ LB)/2.1 L (3½ PT)
A very simple uncooked chutney. As it uses cooking apples and a dried fruit salad mixture, it can be made at any time of the year.

230 g (8 oz) dried fruit salad mix
430 ml (¾ pt) malt vinegar
230 g (8 oz) large seedless raisins
0.9 kg (2 lb) cooking apples,
peeled and cored
455 g (1 lb) onions, roughly chopped
170 g (6 oz) soft, light brown sugar
2 cloves garlic, or to taste, crushed
½ teaspoon ground cloves
1 teaspoon ground ginger
Sterilised jars and covers

Put the dried fruit salad in a bowl, pour over the vinegar and leave to soak overnight. The next day, process or coarsely mince all the ingredients together in several batches.

Turn into a large bowl and mix thoroughly. Taste the chutney and adjust the seasoning and flavourings as necessary. Pot in cold, sterilised jars, seal and label. Leave to mature for about 3 months before use.

OPPOSITE *Chutneys are excellent accompaniments for cheese, cold meats and pork or game pies.*

BARM BRAC

MAKES ONE 20.5 CM (8 IN)
ROUND LOAF
A cake traditionally made to celebrate Hallowe'en, and the Celtic New Year. Symbolic trinkets are hidden in it, such as rings, predicting a forthcoming marriage, and buttons, indicating bachelorhood.

455 g (1 lb) strong plain flour
A pinch of grated nutmeg
A pinch of salt
60 g (2 oz) butter
1 sachet easy-blend yeast
60 g (2 oz) soft, light
brown sugar
280 ml (½ pt) lukewarm milk
2 eggs, size 3, beaten
230 g (8 oz) raisins
230 g (8 oz) sultanas
110 g (4 oz) mixed peel,
finely chopped
Beaten egg, to glaze
A 20.5 cm (8 in) deep, round
cake tin, greased

Sift together the flour, nutmeg and salt. Rub in the butter, then stir in the yeast and sugar. Beat together the milk and eggs, then beat the liquid into the dry ingredients until the batter is stiff but elastic. Knead in the dried fruit and peel. Knead thoroughly for 10 minutes, until dough is smooth and elastic. Transfer to the prepared tin and cover with a clean cloth. Leave to prove in a warm place until doubled in size – about 1 hour.

Set the oven at Gas Mark 6, 400°F, 200°C. Brush the bread with beaten egg and bake for about 30 minutes. Reduce the oven temperature to Gas Mark 4, 350°F, 180°C and bake for a further 30 minutes until the loaf sounds hollow when tapped underneath. Turn out on to a wire rack and leave to cool.

Serve cold or lightly toasted with butter and marmalade.
TO FREEZE: open-freeze until firm. Wrap in greaseproof paper and foil. Store for up to 3 months.
TO USE FROM FROZEN: thaw, loosely covered, overnight.

SODA BREAD

MAKES ONE 18 CM (7 IN)
ROUND LOAF
We used wholemeal flour to give a nuttier flavour.

625 g (1 lb 6 oz) wholemeal flour
1 teaspoon bicarbonate of soda
1 to 2 tablespoons salt
570 ml (1 pt) milk

Set the oven at Gas Mark 5, 375°F, 190°C. Sift all the dry ingredients together, returning any bran left in the sieve to the bowl. Mix in the milk and knead lightly to form a soft dough. Turn out on to a work surface and shape into an 18 cm (7 in) round, and cut a cross on the top. Place on a greased baking tray and bake for 35 to 40 minutes. Transfer to a wire rack and leave to cool.

Serve the bread warm or cold with butter and marmalade.

REFRESHING LEMONADE

MAKES 2.3 LITRES (4 PTS)
This thirst-quenching drink will disappear fast, so it's well worthwhile making double the quantities!

9 large lemons, preferably unwaxed
280 g (10 oz) caster sugar
To decorate:
Mint leaves
Slices of lemon

Thoroughly wash the lemons and pat dry with absorbent kitchen paper.

Remove the zest from 8 lemons. Cut in half and squeeze out all the juice. Cover and chill. Place the zest in a bowl with the sugar and pour over about 1.7 litres (3 pts) of boiling water. Stir until the sugar dissolves, then leave to cool completely. Add the lemon juice and strain into a clean bowl or jug. Chill and serve decorated with mint leaves and very thin slices of lemon floating on top.

INDEX

INDEX

INDEX

160

NOTES

Both metric and imperial measurements have been given in all recipes. Use one set of measurements only, and not a mixture of both.

Standard level spoon measurements are used in all recipes.
1 tablespoon = one 15ml spoon
1 teaspoon = one 5ml spoon

Milk should be full fat unless otherwise stated.

Pepper should be freshly ground black pepper unless otherwise stated.

Fresh herbs should be used unless otherwise stated. If unavailable use dried herbs as an alternative, but halve the quantities stated

Ovens should be preheated to the specified temperature – if using a fan-assisted oven, follow the manufacturer's instructions for adjusting the time and temperature.

Freezing instructions are included for those recipes which are suitable for freezing. Any recipes which do not have these instructions are not suitable for freezing.